RETURN ON INVESTMENT
IN
MEETINGS AND EVENTS

RETURN ON INVESTMENT IN MEETINGS AND EVENTS

TOOLS AND TECHNIQUES TO MEASURE THE SUCCESS OF ALL TYPES OF MEETINGS AND EVENTS

JACK J. PHILLIPS, PhD
M. THERESA BREINING, CMP, CMM
PATRICIA PULLIAM PHILLIPS, PhD

ELSEVIER

AMSTERDAM • BOSTON • HEIDELBERG • LONDON • NEW YORK • OXFORD
PARIS • SAN DIEGO • SAN FRANCISCO • SINGAPORE • SYDNEY • TOKYO
Butterworth-Heinemann is an imprint of Elsevier

Butterworth-Heinemann is an imprint of Elsevier
Linacre House, Jordan Hill, Oxford OX2 8DP, UK
30 Corporate Drive, Suite 400, Burlington, MA 01803, USA

First edition 2008

Library of Congress Cataloging-in-Publication Data
A catalog record for this book is available from the Library of Congress

British Library Cataloguing in Publication Data
A catalogue record for this book is available from the British Library

ISBN: 978-0-7506-8338-8

For information on all Butterworth-Heinemann publications
visit our web site at books.elsevier.com

Printed and bound in the USA

08 09 10 11   10 9 8 7 6 5 4 3 2 1

Working together to grow
libraries in developing countries

www.elsevier.com | www.bookaid.org | www.sabre.org

ELSEVIER   BOOK AID
             International   Sabre Foundation

Contents

2 The ROI Methodology: A Brief Overview, 23

3 The Alignment: Defining Needs and Objectives, 40

4   Measuring Inputs and Indicators, 73

5 Measuring Reaction and Perceived Value, 83

9   Monetary Benefits, Costs, and ROI, 175

10 Intangible Benefits, 210

11   Reporting Results, 229

Preface

THE NEED

The meetings and events function has experienced a need for increased accountability, from several perspectives. For example, meeting professionals are concerned about the value of meetings and events, and so are the executives within their organizations. The value definitions from the planning staff are much different from those of executives. The planning staff may be comfortable with capturing input (for example, the number of attendees), reaction (overall satisfaction) and learning (the takeaways). However, executives value action, impact, the actual monetary contribution of meetings, and ROI. Today, clients, sponsors, exhibitors, and even participants are asking for more value, including ROI. A range of "values" is needed to meet the needs of different stakeholders.

While this need to show value is important, other measures not converted to money are equally important, if not critical, to most meetings. However, excluding the monetary contribution in a success profile of a key meeting is unacceptable in this age of the "show me" generation. Because so many meetings fail to live up to expectations, a systematic process is needed to uncover barriers and enablers to success and to drive improvements. The challenge is in doing it—developing the measures of value for every meeting, including monetary value, when they are needed and presenting them in a way that stakeholders can use. *Return on Investment in Meetings and Events* offers a guide that addresses this challenge.

WHY THIS APPROACH?

This book presents a methodical approach that can be replicated throughout an organization, enabling comparisons of results from one meeting to another. The process described in this book is the most documented method in the world, and its implementation has been phenomenal, with more than 4,000 individuals participating in a five-day certification program designed for implementation leaders. While other books may delve into accountability in certain types of meetings or data, this book shows a method that works across all types of meetings, ranging from corporate meetings and events to association conferences and exhibitions. With this approach, every meeting is evaluated at some level.

This book is a basic guide for anyone involved in planning and implementing meetings and events. Strategies that will assist in collecting data during and after the meeting are presented. This book addresses a results-based approach to meeting planning, focusing on a variety of measures, categorized into seven data types:

1. Inputs and Indicators
2. Reaction and Perceived Value
3. Learning and Confidence
4. Application and Implementation
5. Impact and Consequences
6. Return on Investment
7. Intangibles

Return on Investment in Meetings and Events helps meeting professionals identify, collect, analyze, and report all seven types of data in a consistent manner that ensures credible results.

CREDIBILITY IS KEY

This book focuses on building a credible process—one that generates value that is believable, realistic, and accurate, particularly from the viewpoint of clients and key stakeholders. More specifically, the methodology presented in this book approaches credibility head-on through the use of:

- Balanced categories of data
- A logical systematic process
- Guiding principles, a conservative set of standards
- A proven methodology based on thousands of applications and uses
- An emphasis on implementing the methodology within an organization so that the process is sustained
- A process accepted by sponsors, clients, and others who fund meetings and events

The book explores the challenges of collecting hard-to-measure data and placing monetary values on the hard-to-value. Building on a tremendous amount of experience, application, practice, and research, the book draws on the work of many individuals and organizations, particularly those who have been reaching the ultimate level of accountability, the ROI. Developed in an easy-to-read format and fortified with examples and tips, this will be an indispensable guide for audiences who seek to understand more about bottom-line accountability.

How This Book is Organized

The book follows the value chain of meetings and events as the measures move through the meeting planning cycle. The first three chapters set the stage for the process. Chapter 1, The Need for ROI in the Meetings and Events Industry, shows the forces that are creating the need for the ROI Methodology, now. From different industry perspectives, the chapter traces why ROI evaluation is necessary and what it can do. Several myths about the ROI Methodology are uncovered. Chapter 2, The ROI Methodology: A Brief Overview, illustrates the challenges and opportunities for evaluating meetings, outlining some of the progress made and challenges faced to bring more accountability to meetings and events. This chapter also introduces the ROI Methodology, detailing the types and levels of data, the systematic step-by-step method, and the standards and principles used throughout the book.

Chapter 3, Business Alignment: Defining Needs and Objectives, describes the beginning point of any meeting evaluation process. The focus of this chapter is identifying the need for the meeting. Here, practical techniques and tips are provided to ensure that the meeting is aligned with organizational needs, particularly the business alignment link. It is at this stage that some meetings go astray. Also, this chapter shows how to develop objectives at different levels, moving beyond the traditional learning objectives to develop application, impact, and even ROI objectives.

Chapter 4, Measuring Inputs and Indicators, discusses the first of the data categories with a focus on inputs. Tracking the inputs to the process is a basic necessity, measuring data such as number of people, number of hours, and number of meetings, as well as costs and efficiencies. This level of data is important, but does not show the value of the meetings.

Chapter 5, Measuring Reaction and Perceived Value, addresses the first level of results based on perceptions. This chapter shows how measurement at this fundamental level has been changed and altered recently to improve its value.

Next, Chapter 6, Measuring Learning and Confidence, focuses on measuring learning, the heart of any evaluation process for meetings and events. It shows how learning measures are being addressed in a methodical and efficient way to ensure that participants leave meetings having acquired the information, knowledge, contacts, or skills necessary to take action in the workplace.

Chapter 7, Measuring Application and Implementation, measures the first level beyond the actual meeting. Essentially, data collected at this level answer a question: What are participants doing differently as a result of the meeting? This chapter presents ways in which this follow-up data can be captured and specific measures that must be monitored.

Chapter 8, Measuring and Isolating the Impact of Meetings and Events, moves to impact and consequences, which are key data that executives want to see. This chapter connects the meeting or event to the business, showing how the data are collected and how the impact of the meeting is isolated from other influences—showing how much of the impact data are actually from other factors.

Chapter 9, Monetary Benefits, Costs, and ROI, shows how the ROI is developed and how the business impact measures are converted to monetary values. It also details how the costs of the meeting are tabulated so that a comparison can be made between the benefits and the costs of the meeting. For some, this is the ultimate level of evaluation.

Chapter 10, Intangible Benefits, addresses the important issue of intangibles. The intangible benefits are those measures that are purposely not converted to monetary values. They must be monitored properly, analyzed appropriately, and reported credibly.

Chapter 11, Reporting Results, focuses on how to report data to a number of target audiences, illustrating some of the most efficient and effective ways to communicate data.

Finally, Chapter 12, Implementing and Sustaining the Evaluation System, provides detail on how to support and sustain this evaluation process. It addresses particular issues of how to overcome the resistance of the meetings and events staff and get the management team more involved in the evaluation process.

About the Authors

Jack J. Phillips, PhD

Jack J. Phillips is a world-renowned expert on accountability, measurement, and evaluation. Dr Phillips provides consulting services for Fortune 500 companies and major global organizations. The author or editor of more than 50 books, Dr Phillips conducts workshops and makes conference presentations throughout the world.

Phillips has received several awards for his books and work. On two occasions, *Meeting News* named Dr Phillips one of the 25 Most Influential People in the Meetings and Events Industry, based on his work on ROI for the industry. The Society for Human Resource Management presented him an award for one of his books and honored a Phillips ROI study with its highest award for creativity. The American Society for Training and Development gave him its highest award, Distinguished Contribution to Workplace Learning and Development, for his work on ROI.

His expertise in measurement and evaluation is based on more than 27 years of corporate experience in the aerospace, textile, metals, construction materials, and banking industries. This background led Dr Phillips to develop the ROI Methodology—a revolutionary process that provides bottom-line figures and accountability for all types of learning, performance improvement, human resources, technology, and public policy programs.

Books most recently authored by Phillips include *Show Me the Money: How to Determine ROI in People, Projects, and Programs* (Berrett-Koehler, 2007); *ROI for Technology Projects: Measuring and Delivering Value* (Elsevier, 2007); and *Proving the Value of Meetings and Events: How and Why to Measure ROI* (ROI and MPI, 2007). He is chairman of the ROI Institute, Inc., and can be reached at (205) 678-8101, or by e-mail at jack@roiinstitute.net.

M. Theresa Breining, CMP, CMM

Theresa Breining, CMP, CMM, is the founder and president of Concepts Worldwide, a meeting management firm headquartered in San Diego County since its inception in 1988. Ms. Breining has been in the meeting planning industry since 1976 and has been responsible for producing meetings around the globe.

Considered by many to be a thought leader, Ms. Breining is an activist working tirelessly for the continuous advancement of the level of professionalism in the meeting industry and has been serving as adjunct faculty for meeting planning programs for universities throughout Southern California for over 20 years. She is a sought after speaker, presenting educational workshops for a variety of business entities.

She has often been recognized professionally, including having her company, Concepts Worldwide, acknowledged as a "Best Company to Work for in San Diego." Within the meeting industry, Ms. Breining was given MPI's highest honor when they recognized her as their International Planner of the Year in 2000, and she has been included on lists of "Most Influential People in the Meeting Industry" by both *Meeting News* and *Smart Meetings Magazine*.

An active member of Meeting Professionals International (MPI) at the local and international level, Ms. Breining served as MPI's Chairwoman of the Board in 2003–04. As of January 2007, she serves as chairwoman of the APEX commission, a national body working to develop and implement standards by which the meeting and event industry functions. Her other volunteer commitments include serving on the Board of Directors of Travelers Aid Society of San Diego, the San Diego Convention and Visitor Bureau, as well as on the Advisory Boards for several convention bureaus, a resort, and an international exhibition producer. Ms. Breining can be reached at TBreining@conceptsworldwide.com.

Patricia Pulliam Phillips, PhD

Patricia Pulliam Phillips is president and CEO of ROI Institute, Inc., the leading source of ROI competency building, implementation support, networking, and research. She helps organizations implement the ROI Methodology in countries around the world—including South Africa, Singapore, Japan, New Zealand, Australia, Italy, Turkey, France, Germany, Canada, and the United States.

After a 13-year career in the electrical utility industry, Dr Phillips took advantage of the opportunity to pursue a career in a growing consulting business where she was introduced to training, human resources, and performance improvement from a new perspective—a perspective that directly reflected her values of accountability and ROI evaluation. Since 1997, she has embraced the ROI methodology by committing herself to ongoing research and practice. Dr Phillips teaches others to implement the ROI Methodology through the ROI certification process, as a facilitator for ASTD's ROI and Measuring and Evaluating Learning Workshops, and as adjunct professor for graduate-level evaluation courses. She speaks on the topic of ROI at conferences such as ASTD's International Conference and Exposition and ISPI's International Conference.

Dr Phillips' academic accomplishments include a PhD in International Development and a master's degree in Public and Private Management. She has authored a number of publications on the subject of accountability and ROI, including *Show Me the Money: How to Determine ROI in People, Projects, and Programs* (Berrett-Koehler, 2007); *The Value of Learning* (Pfeiffer, 2007); and the award-winning *The Bottomline on ROI* (CEP Press, 2002). Her work is published in a variety of journals. She can be reached at patti@roiinstitute.net.

Acknowledgments

Many individuals, groups, and organizations have participated in the development of this book. We owe particular thanks to the hundreds of clients we have had the pleasure to work with. They have helped shape, develop, mold, and refine this methodology. Their contributions are evident in this book.

We are particularly indebted to Elsevier for taking on this project. Sally North, our editor, was very patient with our delivery schedule. Thanks Sally.

From the ROI Institute, we give special thanks to Lori Ditoro, who accomplished the editing of this project under a very hectic schedule and with a demanding workload. Thanks, Lori, for delivering this quality manuscript. Also we thank Michelle Segrest, Publishing Manager, for final editing and coordination.

From Jack:
Thanks to Terri for your support of the ROI Methodology. You are an outstanding leader in this field, and you command respect wherever you go. Your contribution is very significant.

I owe much of my success in this effort to my lovely wife, Patti, who serves as my partner, friend, and colleague in this project. She is an excellent consultant, an outstanding facilitator, a tenacious researcher, and an outstanding writer. Although her name is not on this book, her contribution is immeasurable in this book.

From Terri:
I would like to acknowledge Jack Phillips, who invited me to share author credits with him for this book, which represents another important stride in the evolution and professionalism of those that produce meetings and events. I want to thank my co-workers at Concepts Worldwide, who, through their constant attention to our existing work and clients, enabled me to follow my curiosity and interest in the ROI methodology. Finally, I would like to thank my husband Jack Boyce for his constant support and encouragement as I have pursued the work I love, which regularly keeps me late at the office and frequently takes me away from home.

From Patti:

As always, much love and thanks go to Jack. You invest in others much more than you get in return. Thank you for your inspiration and the fun you bring to my life.

Foreword

My company, iDNA, Inc., is involved in the meetings business in many ways. Some subsidiaries produce meetings. Some use interactive keypads to help meeting participants engage better and to help meeting organizers track progress better. Some of our units create specialized training modules on ethics or compliance, or simply orientation. But every client that is conducting a meeting with one of our companies has the same question: "Is this meeting worth it?"

Over the past several years, the cost of meetings has skyrocketed while the need for accountability has become quite formalized. Ironically, it has become harder to account for the costs of meetings and events, and yet imperative that we do so. When I realized that the only way we could continue to provide real value to our meeting and events clients was to help them measure the real business impact of their programs, I knew there was only one place to go. Our goal was to bring a measurement component to every iDNA client. Our tool would be the ROI Methodology, and our partners would be Jack and Patti Phillips and the ROI Institute.

Every business person and even every business student thinks they know what ROI means. Return on investment. Simple. What was the financial return on the money you spent on something—in this case a meeting or an event? Most often, when you try to figure that out yourself, you'll find more questions than answers. Am I underestimating the cost of this meeting? Should I put participants' salaries in the cost category? How about benefits? This meeting was designed to boost morale, so how do I calculate its financial return?

Jack Phillips has spent a lifetime turning the return on investment concept (loved by all CFOs, in my experience) into a disciplined methodology that allows you to actually calculate the impact that just about anything has on a company's bottom line. The methodology is serious business, but I believe you will see the corporate accountability changing as more and more businesses begin embracing it.

Fortunately, Jack and Patti Phillips are unmatched in their ability to teach their methodology to those like me, who understand why it is needed but who bring a healthy sense of skepticism to the table. Add to this mix, the insight, knowledge and experience of Terri Breining, and you have an unbelievable contribution.

The Phillipses and the ROI Institute have made me a believer—so much so that I had one of our companies develop a keypad system that not only provides the usual audience response services we are known for, but also has ROI Methodology templates and calculations built right into the software. We want to make real accountability easy for every meeting and event planner.

This book is a must read. Jack, Terri, and Patti have developed an outstanding book. And I cannot imagine that after you are finished reading it you will be measuring your meetings and events in the same way as you did before. More important to remember is that the ROI Methodology is a process improvement tool as well as a measurement tool. Your meetings and events get better as you utilize the methodology, because you are measuring what works and what does not work every step of the way.

Spread the word and embrace this methodology. I believe that if you use all the tools and techniques that Jack, Terri, and Patti describe, you will find yourself turning cost centers into profit centers.

I not only believe that . . . I am staking my business on it.

James J. McNamara
Chairman and CEO, iDNA, Inc.
New York, NY

CHAPTER 1

The Need for the ROI Methodology in the Meetings and Events Industry

One of the most important questions in the world of meetings, conferences, conventions, and trade shows is this penetrating issue: How can an event be measured most accurately to prove its importance to business success? The debate over this question is fairly new in the meeting industry, although it is one that other segments of the business community have been asking for decades. However, the meeting industry as a stand alone profession has only existed for a few decades. So the question of ROI within our industry is the next logical step in our evolution. And in response, veterans in the meetings and events field are devoting formidable time and effort to formulating and promoting the solutions that they feel work best.

ROI is a persistent issue that will not go away. As meetings become more visible and are perceived as a more valuable tool in an overall business plan, the search for an ROI methodology that works for meetings has become a priority for many. The good news is that while there are several methods and processes being discussed, there is a methodology for determining ROI that has been proven in other business segments and has been adapted to the meeting industry. This book will show you precisely how that methodology works and enable you to incorporate it into your planning process. This chapter traces some of the issues involved in ROI evaluations and documents some of the progress made. It briefly summarizes the efforts of Meeting Professionals International (MPI) to keep this topic on the minds and on the agenda for professionals in the meetings and events industry. It also describes some of the issues, the benefits, the barriers, the myths, and the best practices for implementing the ROI Methodology. Collectively, this chapter makes a compelling case for any professional involved in this industry to take the ROI Methodology seriously and use it as one of the tools in the planning tool kit.

INDUSTRY EFFORTS
FOR MEETING PROFESSIONALS INTERNATIONAL

No organization has made as much of an impact on introducing the ROI Methodology to an industry than Meeting Professionals International (MPI). This worldwide organization supports the efforts of planners, suppliers, and students in the meeting industry. From international conferences to magazines and Web sites, MPI educates its members (more than 22,000) on many issues, including the use and importance of ROI evaluations. As meeting planners are experiencing increased pressure to measure the value of their meetings and events, MPI has conducted and sponsored many ROI workshops.

MPI has been able to mobilize the senior leadership in this industry to make this a reality. This project has spanned three CEOs at MPI as well as dozens of volunteer leaders, but the mission has always been clear: Help the meeting and events industry show the value of what they do, encourage meeting planners to become more strategic and valuable to those who sponsor, support, and fund meetings, and finally, remove any doubt that this industry is a legitimate, contributing member of the business community.

Through a variety of funding projects from the MPI Foundation, MPI assembled resources to support the use of the ROI Methodology within the industry and help planners succeed using it. The following are some of the major players involved in bringing ROI evaluations to this industry with the support, coordination, and encouragement from MPI leadership.

When sitting with the executive team, meeting professionals become instrumental to strategic decision making and are able to influence change. Organizations are changing. The economy slump brought a new focus to the "bottom line." Technology has increased various meeting opportunities. CEOs want their planners to think in terms of the business of the meeting—NOT the meetings business.

The planner's role will change from an ancillary employee to a more active decision maker. The skills to manage the meeting supply chain are the same skills used to facilitate the communication process within an organization. Meeting professionals bring a unique competency to the table that other executives do not possess. They have the fundamental understanding of human learning and performance and the importance of creating an environment that fosters human growth.

In the meeting profession, this has translated into the need to show value and ROI at two levels. The first level is the challenge to demonstrate how meeting professionals strategically manage "the business of meetings." This is more of a big picture or a macro-level view. Are meeting professionals good managers/guardians of the human and capital investment made by their organizations in their departments? This has led to a great deal of discussion around leveraging such strategies as the consolidation and leveraging of their total spending, supply chain management, partnering with other departments such as procurement, travel and finance, and/or outsourcing.

The second level (and purpose of this book) focuses much more on the micro level or that of the individual meeting or event. This has resulted in the ROI project where a comprehensive model that illustrates from the simplest "I am measured by their satisfaction," and "What is the return on their objectives (ROO)?" to the highest level of justification, which is the ROI.

It is important to understand that just as in other areas of organizations such as sales, marketing, finance or production, not every one uses all the macro-level strategies to run their departments. Nor do they justify a complete ROI impact study at the micro level on every individual project or task that they implement. However, all successful businesses today collect the data, focus on the end objectives and value, and know where and when to evaluate their meetings and events to the ROI level.

Speaking the language of business and focusing on business objectives is critical. ROI is a term that CEOs and CFOs understand. Not ROO, Return on Involvement, Return on Events, Return on Learning, Return on Meetings, etc. Meeting professionals and their teams are in competition for the attention and budgets of all the other departments within their organizations, such as marketing, training, and sales.

In today's world, the ROI will not be calculated for every meeting or event. Nor would that be an appropriate allocation of time and resources. However, an acceptable business model and a process that allows meeting professionals to communicate the value of their efforts, and in the appropriate cases, demonstrate in business terms the ROI of the meetings.

Fundamental to it all is having a common business acceptable model to start measuring the most fundamental task in which we all participate and that is meetings. Today, with the ROI Methodology we have that fundamental starting point. Just as technology and globalism are no longer theory, we have a process that helps us capture and frame all elements of a meeting from satisfaction to ROI.

Gaylord Hotels: Delivering Value is the Key

Much of the funding for the development of an ROI measurement strategy for this industry has been funded by Gaylord Hotels, with the vision of providing quality service to customers who seek meeting, convention, and leisure experiences, Gaylord is not, however, simply a supplier for the meetings and events industry. Gaylord wants to bring leading edge topics and ideas into the industry to promote and support its members in different ways. Here are a few comments provided by Gaylord concerning this ROI effort.

By definition, the word "value" is described as *a fair return or equivalent in goods, services, or money for something exchanged*. In the meetings and events industry, proving this value has been an elusive task. And as the industry becomes more expensive, at almost $150 billion per year in the United States, determining a way to do this has become increasingly important.

The demand for basic ROI measurement systems in our industry became more apparent after 9/11, when meeting and events were among the first massive cutbacks to be made. Although it was widely assumed that meetings and events delivered value when properly designed and conducted, there was no definitive way to prove or measure this. And decision-makers have even been questioning if there is any value to having formal meetings and events. Now, more than ever, it is imperative that there be a method by which planners can demonstrate the value of their efforts.

Faced with this challenge, Gaylord embarked on a mission to find a way to equip this group with a methodology and a set of guidelines by which they could monitor and thereby calculate the value of their meetings and events. Gaylord funded a three-year effort by MPI to locate an ROI measurement strategy, which is fully described in this book. It is a source of cutting-edge information from which professional meeting planners and event organizers can address the critical ROI measurement issue.

Determining increased accountability for meetings and events can be a long and tedious process. Until now, professional planners have not been equipped with this capability. We are very proud to have contributed to this book, which shows how a disciplined, rigorous approach can be applied, yet managed in a way that it does not drain the resources or consume the precious time of the meetings and events staff (Phillips, Myhill, and McDonough, 2007).

ROI Institute, Inc.: Dispelling the Myths is a Critical Issue

ROI Institute, Inc., is a research, benchmarking, and consulting organization that provides workshops, publications, and consulting services on the ROI Methodology. The ROI Institute distributes information and provides support for the ROI evaluation efforts of professionals and organizations around the world. They also conduct several workshops each year exclusively for members of the meetings and events industry.

ROI Institute was contacted by MPI in 2003 to explore the use of the ROI Methodology in this industry. ROI Institute had previous success in implementing a sustainable ROI Methodology in learning and development, human resources, leadership and coaching, technology, quality, and change management. During this time, ROI Institute had trained several meeting planners in the use of the ROI Methodology and had gained some experience in the use of the processes in this industry, including fine-tuning the process to address some of the unique issues in this industry. ROI Institute entered into a partnership with MPI to provide a variety of services including consulting, workshops (including ROI Certification), and developing many tools and materials to help the industry move forward. Great progress has been made in publications, education, understanding, and more important, actual success with the use of the methodology over time. Jack Phillips serves as Chairman of the ROI Institute and Patti Phillips serves as CEO.

One of the most important challenges of ROI Institute faculty is overcoming the myths about the ROI Methodology. While these myths are detailed later in this chapter, it is helpful to discuss a few facts at this point.

1. Planners in general do not have a thorough understanding of how to calculate ROI and the different levels of data which should be gathered. With the ROI Methodology, all meetings can and should be evaluated at Level 0, which describes the inputs and indicators, and at Level 1, which is reaction and perceived value. Some meetings are evaluated at the learning, application, and impact levels, although the number of meetings taken to these subsequent levels tapers off significantly.

2. Planners who wish to grow in their career must be willing to take a sensible approach and evaluate each meeting at some level. At Level 1, the challenge is to focus more on evaluating the content and perceived value of the meeting, moving away from the entertainment perspective of meetings. At Level 2, much effort is needed to measure learning. Only about 10–20% of meetings and events are evaluated at this level. Perhaps the biggest challenge is the follow-up after the meeting, where application and implementation (Level 3) are measured to determine what actions are being taken and the impact and consequences (Level 4) of those actions. These higher-level measurements become more time consuming, but necessary, for some meetings. ROI (Level 5) involves converting data to monetary values, isolating the effects of the meeting on that value, and capturing the meeting's fully loaded costs. Together, these generate the actual ROI.

3. The concept of Return on Objectives (ROO) is not a different process or alternative to the ROI Methodology. Setting objectives is part of the ROI Methodology; objectives are set at each of the six levels, if evaluations are taken to all levels. ROO requires objectives for learning and behavioral change (Levels 2 and 3 in the ROI Methodology).

4. An actual ROI calculation should be limited to those meetings that are strategic, high-profile, and expensive. For most organizations, this may mean that only five to ten percent of the meetings would be evaluated at this level.

5. The ROI Methodology is not easy, but it is also not too complex, time consuming, or expensive. Some shortcuts can reduce the time needed to prove the value of a meeting. Also, the costs can be controlled. When the cost of conducting an ROI study is compared to the actual cost of the meeting, it makes the ROI evaluation costs almost insignificant—usually less than 1%.

The ROI Methodology provides the framework for meeting planners to measure the value of every meeting using different types of value for different types of meetings. This provides a much needed structure of discipline and credibility for the meeting professional.

Concepts Worldwide: The Language of Business

Theresa Breining has assisted in MPI's effort from several perspectives. First, as the former Chair of MPI, she provided leadership during the early phases of the implementation of the ROI Methodology in the meetings and events industry.

Next, as a supplier of the industry, she is concerned about delivering value for the meetings and conferences that her company organizes, so she has a personal interested in accountability. Finally, as one of the members of the first ROI Certification workshop for this industry, Terri embraced this concept quickly and become determined to spread it throughout the industry in different ways. She has become an ROI expert. She is currently the Chair of the APEX (Accepted Practices Exchange) Commission of the Convention Industry Council. She has 30 years of experience in the meetings and events industry. Her comments were recently published in *Successful Meetings* and a few of them are included here.

A critical piece of the evolution of the meeting industry involves our ability to communicate with other business professionals in the language of business—not the language of meeting planners. It is our responsibility to help others understand the significance of meetings as part of an overall business strategy, and then we have to prove their value, using the same standards as other business investments.

The days of holding a meeting just because "we have money in the budget" or because "we have always done it" are disappearing. Implementation of an ROI measurement system gives us the ammunition to make a business case for meetings, and then gives us the information to make good, solid decisions about whether the meeting is working, and where its greatest value exists. We have to go beyond our "smile sheets." Happy attendees are certainly the first measurement of success, but we cannot stop there.

While not an easy task, measuring monetary value of a meeting or event is possible. As a statistician would tell you, "Anything can be measured; it's just a matter of time and money." So, the questions for meeting planners to consider are:

1. How important is this meeting to the organization overall (budget, visibility, etc.)?
2. What are the objectives of the meeting?
3. Are there elements inside the meeting that can or should be measured separately?
4. Is there support in the organization for measurement?

There is no conflict between ROI and ROO, except to say that ROO inherently lives inside of an ROI measurement, but the reverse is not necessarily the case. By design, ROI measurement requires that objectives be identified, and that those objectives become the foundation of determining what is measured and to what degree. For the meetings that do not require a discrete monetary (Level 5) ROI measurement, one can still measure to Level 2 (how much learning took place) or Level 3 (application of the learning). In either case, the objectives have been clearly identified and evaluated.

The Chapter Perspective: Cracking the ROI Code

As part of MPI's ROI Methodology implementation, many MPI chapters organized and sponsored a three-hour ROI workshop. These workshops were presented as part of the platinum series and brought the ROI Methodology to most of the 22,000-plus MPI members. Many chapters became involved in this process and took the lead, organizing workshops and sessions about the ROI Methodology. One such individual is Stacey Krizan (CEO of the WOW factory in Atlanta, Georgia), who has not only served in a leadership role with the MPI Georgia Chapter, but also became involved in ROI Certification. Stacey discussed the role of ROI analysis in the meetings and events industry in a recent article for the Georgia Chapter's newsletter, *BreakOut*. Excerpts of this article are used with permission from the MPI Georgia Chapter.

A CEO of a publicly-traded, Atlanta-based technology company sat around the table with his CCO, CMO, CTO, and vice president of marketing as they were outlining the annual sales meeting agenda, and he said casually, "We spend how much for this meeting?" The CCO answered, "About $800,000 give or take." To which the CEO replied, I guess I should consider measuring the return on investment for this..."

Meanwhile, the American president of a privately held retail flooring cooperative was having dinner with his Canadian counterpart and two of his vice presidents. They were discussing one of their upcoming, semi-annual conventions and what could be improved based on an exit survey of the attendees from the last event. The president had inherited the conventions from his predecessor, and it was generally assumed that the revenue generated by the conventions was worth the $1-million-plus expense it represented to the bottom line. He said to his team, "I would gladly pay an additional $20,000 to measure the ROI that I am actually getting on the convention..."

Yet another case in point arose at the regional headquarters of an international network and telephone company, where the director of marketing had her annual customer conference funding canceled. The company spent approximately $250,000 for an audience of approximately 200 every year. However, the small sales force and even smaller marketing department did not have the manpower or processes in place to track the results that the conference represented. As a last-ditch effort, the director took an ROI analysis plan with her to a company meeting in Europe to try to save the event, but it was too late. Budgets had already been set.

The variations on the ROI theme are as endless as the meetings they represent. Executives want to know how they are doing. For some, it is about growth, for some it is a casual interest, and for some it is the life or death decision about their meeting. Regardless, these very real stories—bring to light how the meetings industry is in an invaluable position to answer a very urgent need that, despite its high level of discussion, is not currently being filled by most meeting planners or suppliers. With executives willing to pay good money for ROI analysis, why are there only a handful of certified ROI experts in the US for the meetings industry?

While ROI has been a hot topic of discussion around meeting circles for a few years now—there are many companies that claim it as a part of their offerings, and many individuals who propose to teach the process at planner conferences and conventions—a general vagueness and confusion still permeate the industry around ROI. On industry blogs, some complain that it is essentially immeasurable and futile. Some companies have added it to their offerings, promising that they "guarantee" a positive ROI on the meetings they produce. Others say that they are measuring ROI and ROO (Return on Objectives) just to add to the acronym soup. Many planners say they are measuring ROI by looking at expenses against profit on events in a budget spreadsheet.

MPI and other sister organizations have worked very hard over the years to professionalize the industry with designations such as CMP, CMM, and CSEP, just to name a few. These designations are driven mostly by standard-ization of learning around meeting and event planning and management. Those that have worked hard to reach the designations have earned the respect of their peers—and although industry outsiders are not always cer-tain what the designations actually mean, they acknowledge that the desig-nation itself carries a certain level of added credibility. It's the same for ROI.

Today, there is actually a standard for ROI measurement and a path to certification—specifically designed for the meeting planner. This certifica-tion is arguably simpler than studying for the CMP or CMM. It involves a five-day course offered by the ROI Institute, an MPI partner. It is taught at regular intervals by Dr. Jack Phillips, a specialist in ROI analysis, and meets the specific needs of the meeting professional. Class schedules can be located on the Institute's Web site at www.roiinstitute.net. They are usually small, allowing for a tremendous one-on-one learning experience, and by the end of the class, the students are presenting their own ROI analysis plans to their peers, just as they would to one of the executives mentioned earlier in this article. By learning about ROI, meeting professionals are earning themselves a seat at the table with the top management of the company they work for, with the credibility of speaking the language executives adore—money and proven value (Krizan, 2007).

The Debate About ROI

The debate about the issue of measuring the return on investment (ROI) in meetings and events is rampant. Rarely does a topic stir up emotions to the degree that the ROI issue does. Some individuals characterize any ROI measurement as seriously flawed and inappropriate for this industry. Others passionately char-acterize ROI as the answer to all accountability concerns. The truth probably lies somewhere in between these extreme viewpoints. The important point is to understand the reasons for ROI and its inherent advantages and weaknesses. Then taking a rational approach to the issue and implementing an appropriate mix of evaluation strategies, including the ROI, are possible. Also, recognizing the benefits of ROI evaluation energizes many to pursue ROI analysis on a proactive basis.

This issue has been debated in all types of media—conferences, magazines, news reports, and blogs. Perhaps the best contributor to the debate has been *Successful Meetings* magazine. They have described and chronicled much of the work in the area and have spirited many of the debates regarding ROI. The magazine recognizes that this process is gaining traction and subsequently provided public recognition of the work that MPI was doing. In 2005, their sister publication, *Meeting News*, recognized Jack Phillips as one of the 25 most influential individuals in the industry based on his work with ROI evaluation. Here are excerpts from two major articles that *Successful Meetings* has published to describe some of the issues surrounding the use of the ROI Methodology within the industry.

The Fifth Element

ROI is not a new concept to the meetings industry, but it is an elusive one. For years, the term has been used so loosely, and in so many contexts, that it's thought to refer to everything from the ergonomics of chairs to the relevance of the keynote address. And while many factors affect ROI, none singularly define it; rather, return on investment measurements must include all the aspects of a meeting to arrive at an explicit and definitive value.

The good news: After years of searching in vain for a reliable method with which to calculate ROI, the meetings industry finally seems poised to adopt an effective methodology that could finally clearly reveal the value of the meeting professional as a strategic member of any organization's executive team.

"The term ROI has been bandied about and misunderstood in this industry for years," says Doug McPhee, national account manager for Experient (formerly Conferon) in San Diego. Although the concept of ROI always carries with it a sense of significance and urgency, it's remained largely ill-defined. As a result, the very mention of this topic frustrates some planners.

Indeed, many efforts to measure ROI in the meetings industry have dealt with what are called "intangibles"—such as whether the attendees and organizers felt the meeting was a success, and whether it improved employee morale, communication, and satisfaction. And while these benefits, far from being exact measurements, are part of a meeting's return on investment—in terms of both time and money—they are only part of a much larger whole.

To promote a more complete understanding of that whole, Meeting Professionals International partnered with the ROI Institute, who initially developed the ROI Methodology for development and training. It quickly grew to include the area of human resources and then migrated into the areas of quality control, technology, organizational development, consulting and most recently, into the meetings industry. The meetings industry is a fairly new application." And while several firms currently offer services to help planners measure ROI, Phillips' Methodology appears to have achieved the most traction in the meetings industry, where he says it enjoys a particular relevance.

"The meeting industry escaped this level of accountability for a long time, and we've seen budgets expand and contract with the economic changes. In good times, there are lots of meetings; in tough times, budgets are cut because executives don't know for sure that they're bringing value. There's been a disconnect between the logistical planners and the content and strategy developers. ROI is a process that bridges that gap.

Phillips' Methodology introduces a concrete, systematic approach to ROI measurement in place of what has, in the meeting industry, traditionally been more of a touchy-feely proposition.

"This takes it to a completely different level than we've been used to," says McPhee. Indeed, Phillips' Methodology enables planners to calculate a precise dollar figure to apply to a meeting's bottom line.

"One of my favorite sayings is that bean-counters need beans to count," says Julia Rutherford Silvers, an author and event planning expert based in Las Vegas. "So when planners talk about having difficulty communicating with their procurement departments, the answer is we've got to show them the beans. We've got to put the numbers before them." And that's exactly what Phillips' Methodology is designed to do. "The idea is to take the analysis all the way through to the end result, which is an actual ROI calculation, and that allows us to speak the language of the CFO (Amer, 2005)."

The Great Debate

In February 2007, *Successful Meetings* devoted a cover story to the debate around ROI measurement and evaluation in the meetings and events industry. Some of the perspectives about the debate were presented earlier in this chapter, and explained MPI's efforts, since some of the contributors were part of the MPI group. Included in this section are a few of the unique inputs that were included in the article.

Sue Tinnish (Principal, SEAL, Inc. and Consultant, International Association of Conference Centers, Arlington Heights, IL) has been in the meetings industry since 1998 and is a past president of MPI's Chicago area Chapter. Here are her comments on the great debate:

Just as beauty is in the eye of the beholder, so is meeting value defined in the eyes of stakeholders. Meeting value looks differently depending upon who is asking, "What's the value?"

The debate over ROO versus ROI masks the real issues in the meetings industry. Our future success in measuring meeting value is tied to three things:

1. *Recognition that measurement and evaluation complete a cycle.* Most planners understand the importance of setting SMART (specific, measurable, attainable, realistic, and timely) outcomes. Ultimately, determining meeting value is dependent upon the advance setting of outcomes. I differentiate between the terms *objectives* and *outcomes*. *Objectives* provide guidance to a process. *Outcomes* define desired results. Most organizations lack a consistent discipline around setting measurable outcomes and creating plans to determine success (and thus value) against those outcomes for meetings. This lack of discipline and consistency is a shared fault across management, stakeholders, and meeting planners—not one shouldered only by that last group.

2. *Use of a consistent and unambiguous vocabulary.* Many of us bandy ROI about as a generic term for meeting value. Generically, using the term ROI to define meeting value is like always referring to photocopies as "Xeroxes". However, ROI has a specific definition and meaning. When planners are asked to demonstrate ROI, we should clarify what stakeholders are looking for. Meeting value can be measured around outcomes that address reaction, learning, application, and execution after a meeting, as well as business impact on the organization. Meeting value is created when meeting participants think differently, act differently, or have new knowledge after a meeting. We should push for specifics when stakeholders demand to know a meeting's ROI.

3. *Moving up the chain of impact when demonstrating value.* The ROI Institute defines the change of impact as moving from the subordinate levels of reaction or satisfaction to learning, application, or business impact. Planners can advance our industry by moving from measuring reaction ("How did you like the speaker, the food, the room temperature?") to measuring intended actions ("What do you intend to do differently?") or learning ("What did you learn?") or application (What are you doing differently?") or business impact ("How have your new thoughts, attitudes, or actions impacted the organization?"). Related to the "vocabulary" problem cited above, but even more pressing, is the need for planners to focus on relevant business metrics.

A push for a more disciplined approach to measuring results that are tied to business issues will garner planners additional respect for the value of the meetings they plan, and for themselves. It puts us all in a position of clearly supporting the business of our organizations rather than simply being in the meetings business.

ROI Will Not Go Away

One thing is certain: ROI is not a fad. It is here to stay. As long as the need for accountability of meetings, events, and trade show expenditures exists and the concept of an investment payoff is desired, ROI will be measured to evaluate major investments in this industry. A fad is a new idea or approach or a new spin on an old approach. The concept of ROI has been used for centuries.

The 75th anniversary issue of *Harvard Business Review* (*HBR*) traced the tools used to measure results in organizations (Sibbet, 1997). In early issues of *HBR*, during the 1920s, ROI was an emerging tool to place a value on the payoff of investments. In recent years, the application of the concept has been expanded to all types of investments including training, change initiatives, technology, quality, and meetings. With increased adoption and use, it appears that ROI is not going away. Today, hundreds of organizations routinely develop ROI calculations for education, training, communication, leadership development, and human resources programs. In the last few years, it has been used to show the value of meetings and events. Is it the only measure of success? Of course not. But it is certainly one of the important tools to determine success.

ROI ISSUES

This debate obviously stirs up many issues. In this section, some of these issues will be clarified. First, the complete definitions of the types and levels of data will be discussed, detailing how the industry must change, with the current status compared to the industry's goal in 5 years. Next, the best practices are presented. Although the use of the ROI Methodology is relatively new to the industry, best practices are beginning to emerge, and 11 best practices are described in this section. Finally, the ROI myths are dispelled. Fifteen myths are presented that inhibit the use of ROI analysis. These are demystified in this section.

The Ultimate Level of Evaluation: ROI

The ROI Methodology collects and processes up to five levels of evaluation results plus another level for inputs and indicators. The concept of different levels of evaluation is both helpful and instructive in understanding how the return on investment is calculated. Table 1-1 shows the six-level framework used in this book. The table also shows the current status and goals for the industry.

At Level 0, Input and Indicators, the inputs of the meeting or event are captured in all meetings now (100%). These include costs, efficiencies, duration (in hours or days), participant profiles, locations, and agendas. This is only input and does not speak to the results.

At Level 1, Reaction and Perceived Value, the reaction from meeting participants is measured along with the perceived value of the meeting. Almost all

Table 1-1
Measurement in the Meetings and Events Field

Level	Measurement Category	Current Status ⬇ Coverage (Now) (%)	Goal in 5 Years ⬇ Coverage (Goal)	Comments About Status
0 ⬇	**Inputs/Indicators** Measures inputs into meetings and events including the number of meetings, attendees, audience, costs, and efficiencies	100	100	This is being accomplished now
1 ⬇	**Reaction and Perceived Value** Measures reaction to, and satisfaction with, the experience, ambiance, contents, and value of meeting	100	100	Need more focus on content and perceived value
2 ⬇	**Learning** Measures what participants learned in the meeting—information, knowledge, skills, and contacts (take-aways from the meeting)	10–20	80–90	Must use simple learning measures
3 ⬇	**Application and Implementation** Measures progress after the meeting–the use of information, knowledge, skills, and contacts	5	15–25	Need more follow-up
4 ⬇	**Impact and Consequences** Measures changes in business impact variables such as output, quality, time, and cost-linked to the meeting	<2	10	This is the connection to business impact
5	**ROI** Compares the monetary benefits of the business impact measures to the costs of the meeting	<1	5	The ultimate level of evaluation

organizations evaluate at Level 1, usually with a generic, end-of-meeting questionnaire. While this level of evaluation is important as a customer satisfaction measure, a favorable reaction does not ensure that participants have learned new skills or knowledge. In some cases, there may be little or no connection between their level of satisfaction and any of the objectives (i.e., they may have loved the venue and the room was the right temperature, but they didn't have a clue about why they were attending).

At Level 2, Learning, measurements focus on what participants learned during the meeting using self assessments, checklists, role plays, simulations, group evaluations, and other assessment tools. A learning check is helpful to ensure that participants have absorbed the meeting material or messages and know how to use or apply them properly. Also, this level measures the number of new professional contacts and the extent to which existing contacts were strengthened. However, a positive learning measure is no guarantee that what was learned or the contacts acquired will actually be used.

At Level 3, Application and Implementation, a variety of follow-up methods are used to determine if participants applied what they learned or explored the contacts acquired. The completion of action items, the use of skills, and the follow up with contacts are important measures at Level 3. While Level 3 evaluations are important to gauge the success of the application after the meeting, they still do not guarantee that a positive impact will occur with the individual or the organization.

At Level 4, Impact and Consequences, the measurement focuses on the actual results achieved by meeting participants as they successfully apply the meeting material, messages, or contacts. Typical Level 4 measures include output, sales, quality, costs, time, and customer satisfaction. Although the meeting may produce a measurable business impact, a concern may still exist that the meeting cost too much.

At Level 5, Return on Investment—the ultimate level of evaluation—the meeting's monetary benefits are compared with the meeting's costs. Although ROI can be expressed in several ways, it is usually presented as a percent or benefit-cost ratio.

Best Practices

With the acceptance of ROI evaluation in many organizations, much of the focus has turned to best practices for ROI Methodology implementation. The following 11 best practices represent the state-of-the-art with those organizations that have successfully implemented the ROI Methodology.

Best Practice 1. The ROI Methodology is implemented as a process improvement tool and not a performance evaluation tool for the meetings and events staff. The meetings and events staff's acceptance is critical for the implementation of this process. No individual or group is willing to create a tool that will ultimately be used to evaluate his or her performance. As a result, many organizations recognize that the ROI Methodology is a process improvement tool and communicate this early.

Best Practice 2.   The ROI Methodology generates a micro-level scorecard with six types of data. These data points reflect six distinct levels, each with a specific measurement focus, as illustrated in Table 1-1. The data represent a scorecard of performance, showing both qualitative and quantitative data, often taken at different timeframes and from different sources.

Best Practice 3.   ROI Methodology data are being integrated to create a macro-level scorecard for the meetings and events function. As more and more studies are conducted, data are rolled up to create a macro-level scorecard, showing the value of the entire function. The individual micro-level scorecard evaluation data are integrated into the overall macro-level scorecard. This approach requires a few similar questions to be asked in each evaluation. These are then integrated, using technology to create the macro-level scorecard for meetings and events.

Best Practice 4.   ROI evaluations are conducted selectively, usually involving 5–10% of all meetings and events. Meetings that are usually targeted for Level 4 and 5 evaluations are those that are strategically focused, expensive, high profile, operationally-based, and reflective of management's interest. This does not mean that other meetings are not evaluated at all. It is recommended that all meetings be evaluated at Levels 0 and 1 and the vast majority at Level 2, but only a few, select meetings are taken to Levels 3, 4, and 5. Most important, meetings selected for a Level 5 evaluation, with an actual ROI calculation, are, as best practice, evaluated across at all six levels, up to and including ROI.

Best Practice 5.   ROI evaluation targets are developed, showing the percentage of meetings and events evaluated at each level. Target levels are developed that reflect the resources available and the feasibility of evaluation at each level. Targets usually begin at 100% of meetings at Levels 0 and 1 and conclude with 5–10% of meetings at Level 5.

Best Practice 6.   A variety of data collection methods are used in ROI analysis. ROI evaluation is not restricted to a particular type of data collection method, such as monitoring of business data. Instead, questionnaires, built-in action plans, focus groups, and observations are used in developing the complete profile of six levels of data in the ROI Methodology.

Best Practice 7.   For an ROI evaluation, the effects of the meeting are isolated from other factors. Although a difficult issue, best practice organizations realize some method must be used to show the direct contribution of the meeting or event to the business improvement. Many best practice organizations currently use a variety of techniques discussed in this book, ranging from control-group analysis to expert estimation, to tackle this issue with each evaluation. Some argue that this is too difficult or impossible. In reality, it must be done for executives to understand the relative contribution of the meeting. Otherwise, there is a temptation to slash the budgets of major meetings because no clear connection between the meeting and the business value is shown.

Best Practice 8.   Business impact data are converted to monetary values. These days, it may not be enough to report outcomes as expressed numbers such as sales increases, quality improvement, cycle time reduction, turnover reduction, or enhancement in customer loyalty or employee engagement. The actual value in monetary terms is absolutely essential in developing ROI because an ROI calculation compares the monetary value with the cost of the meeting. Best practice organizations are using a full array of approaches to develop monetary values.

Best Practice 9.   The ROI Methodology is being implemented for about 3–5% of the meetings and events budget. One of the common fears of implementing the ROI is the excessive cost in both time and direct funds. Best practice firms report that they can implement the ROI Methodology for roughly 3–5% of the total budget, using appropriate evaluation targets recommended in Table 1-1.

When implementing ROI evaluations, many organizations have migrated from a low level of investment (less than 1%) to the 3–5% level by a process of gradual budget enhancements. These enhancements sometimes come directly from the cost savings generated from the use of the ROI Methodology. Cost-savings approaches are also available for resource-constrained environments.

Best Practice 10.   ROI forecasting is being implemented routinely. Senior executives sometimes ask for a forecasted ROI before a meeting begins. Consequently, best practice organizations are routinely using ROI forecasting approaches to enhance the decision-making process. The credibility of the process is greatly increased by the use of conservative adjustments and built-in steps to secure input from the best experts.

Best Practice 11.   The ROI Methodology is used as a tool to enhance and improve meetings and events. A significant payoff for using the ROI process over time is that it transforms the role of meetings and events within an organization. Application of the process increases meeting alignment with business needs; improves the efficiency of design, development, and delivery; and enhances the value of meetings and events. Furthermore, it builds respect, support, and commitment from internal groups, including senior executives and major meeting sponsors.

Collectively, these best practices are evolving as hundreds of organizations conduct ROI evaluations each year. The best practices underscore the progress in the evolution of ROI Methodology application and use.

ROI Myths

Although most meeting professionals recognize calculating the ROI as an important addition to measurement and evaluation, they often struggle with how to address the issue. Many professionals see the ROI Methodology as a ticket to increased funding and influence. They believe that without it, they may be lost in the shuffle, and with it, they may gain the respect they need to continue moving the function forward. Regardless of their motivation for pursuing ROI evaluation, the key question is "Is it a feasible process that can be implemented with reasonable resources, and will it provide the benefits necessary to make it a useful, routine tool?" The answer is "Yes."

The controversy surrounding the ROI Methodology stems from misunderstandings about what the process can and cannot do, and how it can or should be implemented within an organization. In this section, these misunderstandings are summarized as 15 myths about the ROI Methodology. The myths are based on years of experience with ROI analysis and the perceptions discovered during hundreds of consulting projects and workshops. Each myth is presented here, along with an appropriate explanation.

ROI is too complex for most users.   This issue has been a problem because of a few highly complex models that have been presented publicly. Unfortunately, these models have done little to help users and have caused confusion about ROI. The ROI calculation used in the ROI Methodology is a basic financial formula for accountability that is simple and understandable: earnings are divided by investment; earnings equate to net benefits from the meeting, and the investment equals the actual cost of the meeting. Straying from this basic formula can add confusion and create tremendous misunderstanding. The ROI model is simplified with a step-by-step, systematic process. Each step is taken separately and issues are addressed for a particular topic; the decisions are made incrementally all the way through the process. This helps reduce a complex process to more simplified and manageable efforts.

ROI is too expensive.   The ROI Methodology can become expensive if it is not carefully organized, controlled, and properly implemented. While the cost of an external ROI evaluation can be significant, many actions can be taken to keep costs down. Cost savings approaches to ROI are presented later in this book.

If senior management does not require ROI, there is no need to pursue it. This myth captures the most innocent bystanders. It is easy to be lulled into providing evaluation and measurement that simply meets the status quo, believing that no pressure or request means no requirement. The truth is that if senior executives have only seen Level 1 (Reaction) data, they may not be asking for higher-level data because they think that it is not available. In some cases, meeting professionals have convinced top management that meetings cannot be evaluated at the ROI level or that the specific impact of a meeting cannot be determined.

Given these conditions, it comes as no surprise that some top managers are not asking for ROI data.

Another problem with this thinking is that things change—not only within the meetings and events function but within senior management teams as well. Savvy managers are beginning to request this type of data. Changes in corporate leadership sometimes initiate important paradigm shifts. New leadership often requires proof of accountability. The process of integrating the ROI Methodology into an organization takes time—about 12–18 months for many organizations. It is not a quick fix, and when senior executives suddenly ask for this kind of data, they may expect quick results.

Because of this, planners should initiate the ROI process and develop ROI impact studies long before senior management begins asking for ROI data.

ROI is a passing fad.   Unfortunately, this comment does apply to many of the processes being introduced to organizations today. However, accountability for expenditures will always be present, and the ROI provides the ultimate level of accountability. As a tool, the ROI Methodology has been used for years. Previously, ROI has been used to measure the investment of equipment and new plants. Now it is being used in many other areas, including meetings and events. With its rich history, ROI analysis will continue to be used as an important tool in measurement and evaluation.

ROI is only one type of data.   This is a common misunderstanding. The ROI calculation represents one type of data that shows the costs versus the benefits for a meeting. However, seven types of data are generated, representing both qualitative and quantitative data and often involving data from different sources, making the ROI Methodology a rich source for a variety of data, including the intangible benefits gained from a meeting.

ROI is not future-oriented; it only reflects past performance.   Unfortunately, many evaluation processes are past-oriented and reflect only what has happened with a meeting. This is the only way to have an accurate assessment of impact. However, the ROI Methodology can easily be adapted to forecast the ROI.

ROI is rarely used by organizations.   This myth is easily dispelled when the evidence is fully examined. More than 4000 organizations use the ROI Methodology, and more than 200 case studies have been published about the methodology. Leading organizations throughout the world, including organizations of all sizes and sectors, use the ROI Methodology to increase accountability and improve projects, programs, and events. For example, this process is being used by half of the Fortune 500 companies, over 200 governmental units and a dozen professional associations. Molson-Coors, Mayo Clinic, FedEx, British Airways, Wells Fargo, UPS, IBM, GlaxoSmithKline, Cisco Systems, Coca-Cola, Microsoft, Wachovia, Caremark/CVS, Boston Scientific, KPMG, Genentech, BearingPoint and Wal-Mart are just a few of the users. This process is also being used in the nonprofit, educational, and government sectors. It is a new concept in the meeting industry, but there is no doubt that it is a widely used process in other business areas, and its use is growing.

The ROI Methodology cannot be easily replicated. In theory, any process worthy of implementation is one that can be replicated from one evaluation to another. For example, if two different people conducted an ROI evaluation on the same meeting, would they obtain the same results? Fortunately, the ROI Methodology is a systematic process with certain standards and guiding principles. The likelihood of two different evaluators obtaining the same results is high. Because it is a process that involves step-by-step procedures, it can also be replicated from one meeting to another.

The ROI Methodology is too subjective, and therefore not a credible process. This myth has evolved because some ROI studies involving estimates have been publicized and promoted in literature and during conferences. Many ROI evaluations have been conducted without the use of estimates. The issue of using estimates often surfaces when attempting to isolate the effects of the meeting from other factors. Using estimates from the participants is only one of several techniques used to isolate the effects of a meeting. Other well-tested and proven techniques involve analytical approaches such as the use of control groups and trend-line analysis. Sometimes, estimating is used in other steps of the process, such as converting data to monetary values or estimating output in the data collection phase. In each of these situations, other options are often available, but for convenience or economics, estimation is sometimes used. While estimations often represent the worst-case scenario in an ROI analysis, they can be extremely reliable when they are obtained carefully, adjusted for error, and reported appropriately. The accounting, engineering, and technology fields routinely require the use of estimates—often without question or concern.

ROI is not possible for soft issues, only for production and sales. The ROI Methodology is often most effective when used to evaluate meetings involving soft measurements. Soft issues often drive hard data items such as output, quality, cost, or time. Case after case shows the successful application of the ROI Methodology to programs or meetings such as branding, team building, leadership, communications, and empowerment. Additional examples of successful ROI Methodology application can be found in compliance programs such as diversity, sexual harassment prevention, and policy implementation. Any type of meeting or process can be evaluated at the ROI level. The issue surfaces when meetings that should not be evaluated at the ROI level are. The ROI Methodology should be reserved for meetings or events that are expensive, address operational problems and issues related to strategic objectives, or attract the interest of management in terms of increased accountability.

ROI evaluation is for corporate meetings only. Although initial studies appeared in the corporate sector, associations quickly picked up the process as a useful tool. Then it migrated to incentive meetings, golfing events, and familiarization trips.

It is not always possible to isolate the influence of other factors. Isolating the effects of other factors is always achieved when using the ROI Methodology. At least nine ways are available to isolate the influence of other factors, and at least one method will work in any given situation. The challenge is to select an appropriate isolation method for the resources and accuracy needed in each situation. This myth probably stems from an unsuccessful attempt at using a control group arrangement—a classic way of isolating the effect of a process, program, or initiative. In practice, a control group does not work in a majority of situations, causing some researchers to abandon the issue of isolating other factors. In reality, many other techniques provide accurate, reliable, and valid ways to isolate the effects.

Since there is no control over what happens after participants leave a meeting, a process based on measuring on-the-job improvements should not be used. This myth is fading as organizations face the reality of implementing results-based meetings and realize the importance of measuring results. Although the meetings and events team does not have direct control over what happens in the workplace, it can influence on the process. A meeting or event must be considered within the context of the workplace—the meeting is owned by the organization. Many individuals and groups are involved in the meeting, with objectives that push expectations beyond the meeting. Objectives focus on application and impact data used in the ROI analysis. Also, a partnership with key managers produces objectives that drive the meeting. In effect, the meeting or event is a process with partnerships and a common framework to drive results—not just activity during the meeting.

The ROI Methodology is appropriate only for large meetings. While it is true that large meetings with enormous budgets have the greatest need for ROI evaluation, smaller meetings can also be targeted for ROI evaluation, particularly when the process is simplified and built into meetings.

There are no standards for the ROI Methodology. An important problem facing measurement and evaluation is a lack of standardization or consistency. These questions are often asked: "What is a good ROI?" or, "What should be included in the cost so I can compare my data with other data?" or, "When should specific data be included in the ROI calculation instead of as an intangible?" While these questions are not easily answered, some help is on the way. The ROI Methodology has standards, the Guiding Principles, to guide the process. They will be presented later. Also, a database is under development that will share thousands of studies so that best practices, patterns, trends, and standards are readily available. For more information on this two issues, contact the ROI Institute at info@roiinstitute.net.

The Benefits of ROI

The benefits of adopting the ROI Methodology should appear obvious, after reading this chapter. As a summary, there are five key benefits, inherent with almost any type of impact evaluation process, which make the ROI process an attractive challenge for the meetings and events team.

Measure the contribution of an important meeting. The ROI Methodology is the most accurate, credible, and widely used process to show the impact of meetings and events. The meetings and events team will know the specific contributions from a select number of meetings. The ROI Methodology will determine if the benefits of the meeting, expressed in monetary values, have outweighed the costs. It will determine if the meeting made a contribution to the organization and if it was, indeed, a good investment.

Set priorities for meetings. Calculating the ROI in different areas will determine which meetings contribute the most to the organization, allowing priorities to be established for high impact planning. Successful meetings can be expanded into other areas—if the same need is there—ahead of other meetings. Inefficient meetings can be designed and redeployed. Ineffective meetings may be discontinued.

Focus on results. The ROI Methodology is a results-based process that brings a focus on results with all meetings, even those not targeted for an ROI calculation. The process requires that planners, designers, speakers, facilitators, participants, and support groups concentrate on measurable objectives: what the meeting should accomplish. Thus, this process has the added benefit of improving the effectiveness of all meetings and events.

Earn a seat at the table. Developing the ROI Methodology information is one of the best ways to earn the respect of the senior management team and the sponsor (the person who really cares about the meeting). It can help earn a seat at the senior management table. Senior executives have a never-ending desire to see ROI. They will appreciate the effort to connect meetings to business impact and show the actual monetary value. It helps them feel comfortable with the process and makes their decisions easier. Sponsors who often support, approve, or initiate meetings and events see the ROI as a breath of fresh air. They actually see the value of the meetings, building confidence about the initial decision to implement the process.

Alter management perceptions of meetings and the meeting industry. The ROI Methodology, when applied consistently and comprehensively, can convince executives that meetings and events represent an investment and not an expense. Managers will see meetings as adding a viable contribution to their objectives, thus increasing the respect for the function. This is an important step in building a partnership with management and increasing management support for meetings and events.

FINAL THOUGHTS

Convinced? The use of the ROI Methodology is making tremendous strides in the meetings and events industry. From all perspectives—participants, suppliers, professional associations, sponsors—all are concerned about accountability, and all are embracing the ROI Methodology as the ultimate level of evaluation. This level presented some of the historical issues involved in developing the use of ROI analysis for this industry, and the perspectives from many viewpoints. It focused on the basic issues and needs and the progress that is being made. Definitions are offered as well as best practices that have already evolved. Finally, the myths were debunked and the benefits were summarized. The next chapter focuses on the actual process—the ROI process model—and the steps to calculate the ROI.

REFERENCES

Amer, S. "The Fifth Element," *Successful Meetings*. April 2005.
Carey, R. "The Great Debate," *Successful Meetings*. February 2007.
Stacey Krizan. "Planner Solutions," *BreakOut*. MPI Georgia Chapter, Spring 2007.
Sibbet, D. "75 Years of Management Ideas and Practice, 1922–1997." *Harvard Business Review*, Supplement, 1997.
Phillips, J.J., Myhill, M., and McDonough, J. *Proving the Value of Meetings and Events: How and Why to Measure ROI*. Birmingham, AL: ROI Institute and MPI, 2007.

CHAPTER 2

The ROI Methodology: A Brief Overview

With the need for ROI evaluation fully explored in the previous chapter, it is time to focus directly on how the ROI Methodology is used to evaluate meetings and events. This chapter provides an overview of the steps involved in calculating the ROI, a basic process that is dissected in the chapters to come. It is briefly presented here to show the direction of the remainder of the book.

A Paradigm Shift

When it comes to accountability, Chapter 1 clearly illustrated the need for change in this field. This change not only involves measurement issues, such as calculating the ROI, but a change in the approach of organizing meetings. Essentially, this is a paradigm shift in planning, developing, and delivering results-based meetings.

Table 2-1 shows how this dramatic shift has occurred. The left side describes the typical meetings and events process when the focus is on activity. The focal point is producing many meetings, with many participants, and with many activities all at the lowest cost. Very little effort is made to ensure that the meeting is needed, that the right individuals have input, and that it added value to the organization in any way. The reporting at the end of the year is almost entirely dedicated to input issues (i.e., the report would show how many meetings were conducted, how many participants attended, how many hours were spent in meetings, and how much the meetings cost). That is the old way. That can no longer be the mode of operation for meeting professionals. The focus must be on results.

The right side of the Figure shows the approach and process when the meeting is completely focused on results. First a bit of caution: This is not to suggest that every meeting must thoroughly address each of these eight issues. However, if a meeting is important, high profile, significant, expensive, and strategic, then the focus should be on results, not just the activities to produce the meeting.

The meeting starts with the need connected specifically to business results. This is easy for a sales meeting, for example, but would be more difficult for an association's annual conference and exposition. The other steps are very logical. The meeting should address the current performance issues that have caused individuals to perform at an undesired level. For example, if a compliance meeting is organized, the key question is what has caused the employees to be out of compliance.

23

Table 2-1
Paradigm Shift in Meetings and Events

Activity Based – Characterized by:	Results Based – Characterized by:
• No business need for the meeting or event	• Meeting or event linked to specific business needs
• No assessment of performance issues	• Assessment of performance effectiveness
• No specific measurable objectives	• Specific objectives for application and business impact
• No effort to prepare participants to achieve results	• Results and expectations communicated to participants
• No effort to prepare the work environment to support the meeting or event	• Environment prepared to support the meeting or event
• No efforts to build partnerships with key managers	• Partnerships established with key managers and clients
• No measurement of results or benefit-cost analysis	• Measurement of results or benefit-cost analysis (ROI)
• Reporting on meetings and events is input-focused	• Reporting on meetings and events is output-focused

Understanding these behavioral and performance issues can help guide the content of the meeting so that the meeting addresses these performance shortcomings.

Next, specific objectives are developed for application and impact. This step is essential to move the focus of the meeting to the participants' activities beyond the meeting. The application and impact objectives clearly specify what must change and the consequences of those changes. Next, the specific expectations of the participants must be communicated to them. The participants must understand that their role in the meeting has changed. Attending, becoming involved, and reacting favorably are no longer sufficient. The participant must learn something, take it away from the meeting, use it in some productive way, and ultimately add value to the organization through his or her individual work. Participants may be required to provide data beyond their reactions at the meeting. The expectations must be clearly defined for the results-based process to be implemented successfully.

The environment to support the meeting should be examined. Barriers or inhibitors to the use of what is presented during the meeting may be present. If they exist, they should be removed or minimized. Otherwise, the meeting may be a failure. Sometimes, enablers may be needed to help participants with what they are expected to do.

Partnerships may be needed with key executives and managers—individuals who are critical to the implementation of the content in the work environment. They are often the participants' managers. They must be involved in the process and see their roles in achieving success with the meeting. The results-based process also means that meeting professionals must measure beyond what their typical measurements, up to and including an occasional ROI.

Finally, the reporting is more output-focused, showing the contribution of meetings, moving beyond reporting the typical input items of the number of meetings and the costs of meetings. There is a need to show the contributions that these meetings make to the organizations—including ROI, at least for a small number of meetings.

This change will take time, but it has been developing and progressing for decades. The industry is at a point of changing and shifting to focus on results, for all the reasons outlined in Chapter 1.

KEY STEPS AND ISSUES

Instead of examining a particular model or process, identifying some of the key issues, steps, and processes involved in measurement may be helpful. All these must be addressed in some way to have a comprehensive process.

Stakeholders

Many stakeholders are involved in measurement and evaluation. A stakeholder is defined as any individual or group interested or involved in the meeting. Stakeholders may include the functional manager where the meeting is located, the participants, the organizer, the planner, speakers, and key clients, among others. Below are descriptions of these stakeholders, and they will be referred to routinely throughout the book.

Planner. The planners are the individual(s) responsible for the meeting or event. This is the individual who manages the meeting and is interested in showing the value of the meeting before it is implemented, during its implementation, and after it is implemented.

Clients. The individual(s) who fund, initiate, request, or support a particular project or event. Sometimes referred to as the ultimate client, it is the key group—usually at the senior management level—who cares about the meeting's success and is in a position to discontinue or expand the meeting.

Sponsor. These are the people who support the meeting in a variety of ways, usually financially or with in-kind services or support. These sponsors are interested in the meeting's outcome and need to see the value of their sponsorship for the meeting.

Participants. These are the individuals who participate in the meeting. The term "attendee," "delegate," "employee," "associate," "user," or "stakeholder" may represent these individuals. For most meetings, the term "participant" appropriately reflects this group.

Immediate Managers.   These are individuals who are one level above the participant(s) involved in the meeting. For some meetings, this is the team leader for other employees. Often they are middle managers, but most important, these people have supervisory authority over the participants in the meeting.

CEO/Managing Director/Agency Executive.   This person is the top executive in an organization. The top executive could be a marketing manager, division manager, regional executive, administrator, or agency head. The CEO is the top administrator or executive in the organization for whom the meeting is planned.

The Organization.   The organization is the entity within which the meeting or event is evaluated. Organizations may be companies (either privately held or publicly held); government organizations at the local, state, federal, and international levels; associations; non-profit organizations; or non-governmental organizations. They may also include educational institutions, networks, and other loosely organized bodies of individuals.

Planning Team.   The individuals involved in the meeting, helping to analyze and implement it. These are individual team members who may be full- or part-time on the meeting. For larger-scale meetings, these individuals are often assigned full-time, on a temporary basis, or, sometimes, on a permanent basis. For small meetings, these may be part-time duties.

Evaluator.   This individual evaluates the meeting. This person is responsible for measurement and evaluation, following all the processes outlined in this book. If this is a member of the planning team, extreme measures must be taken to ensure this person remains objective. It may also be a person who is completely independent of the meeting planning team. This individual performs these duties full- or part-time.

Exhibitor.   These are the individuals who display their products or services at a meeting. They are concerned about the meeting from their perspective of driving more sales, either directly or indirectly. Is it the best meeting among several for an exhibit? The exhibitor needs to know how that exhibit contributes to the bottom line—its ultimate value.

Finance and Accounting Staff.   These individuals are concerned about the cost and impact of the meeting from a financial perspective. They provide valuable support. Their approval of processes, assumptions, and methodologies is important. Sometimes, they are involved in the meeting evaluation; at other times they review the results. During major meetings, this could include the organization's finance director or chief financial officer.

Analysts.   These individuals collect the data to determine whether the meeting is needed. They are also involved in analyzing different parts of the meeting. Analysts are usually more important in the beginning but may provide helpful data throughout the meeting.

Bystanders.   The bystanders are the individuals who observe, sometimes at a distance, the meeting. They are not actively involved as stakeholders, but are concerned about the outcomes, including the money. These bystanders are important because they can become cheerleaders or critics of the meeting.

Levels and Steps

It may be helpful to examine measurement and evaluation of meetings as a value chain, where data are collected at different times (sometimes from different sources) to provide a process. Figure 2-1 shows this value chain—fundamental to much of the current work in evaluation.

This process shows how value is developed and also provides data from different perspectives. Some stakeholders are interested in knowing about the inputs so that they can be managed and made more efficient; others are interested in reaction; still others are interested in learning. More recently, clients and sponsors have become more interested in actual behavior change (application) and the corresponding business impact, while a few stakeholders are concerned about the actual return on investment.

Chain of Impact

The collected data are arranged as a chain of impact, shown in Figure 2-1. The chain of impact must be evident if the particular meeting or event is adding business value. All stakeholders must be closely involved in the meeting to understand this chain of impact. The sponsor must see this chain as the data are generated throughout the process. Participants must realize that they have a critical role and that their involvement and success are shown through the chain. The planners, developers, and facilitators must understand that the chain of impact is critical. It can be broken, essentially at any stage, and the evaluation data will indicate whether it is broken and where it is broken. Was it broken because of adverse reaction, no learning, no application? Or was there no connection to a business measure? The information described in this book will clearly indicate whether the chain of impact is intact and where it can be strengthened. Also, it will show when it breaks and there is no value.

When the chain of impact is considered throughout the process of evaluation, some interesting characteristics begin to evolve, as shown in Figure 2-2. The evaluation data are collected throughout the chain. The data are more valuable as the process moves from reaction to ROI, at least from the client's perspective.

Level	Measurement Focus	Typical Measures
0. Inputs and Indicators	Measures inputs into meetings and events including the number of meetings, attendees, audience, costs, and efficiencies.	Types of topics, content Number of meetings Number of participants Hours of meetings Costs
1. Reaction and Perceived Value	Measures reaction to, and satisfaction with, the experience, ambiance, contents, and value of meeting.	Relevance Importance Usefulness Appropriateness Intent to use Motivational
2. Learning	Measures what participants learned in the meeting—information, knowledge, skills, and contacts (take-aways from the meeting).	Skills Knowledge Capacity Competencies Confidences Contacts
3. Application and Implementation	Measures progress after the meeting—the use of information, knowledge, skills, and contacts.	Extent of use Task completion Frequency of use Actions completed Success with use Barriers to use Enablers to use
4. Impact and Consequences	Measures changes in business impact variables such as output, quality, time, and costs linked to the meeting.	Productivity Revenue Quality Time Efficiency Customer satisfaction Employee engagement
5. ROI	Compares the monetary benefits of the business impact measures to the costs of the meeting.	Benefit-cost ratio (BCR) ROI (%) Payback period

Figure 2-1. The Types and Levels of Data.

The lower levels of data, for example, reaction and learning, are mostly consumer-oriented data, taken directly from the consumer (i.e., the participant, attendee, or delegate). Reaction data are a consumer satisfaction index. Learning data are often provided to the consumer to build confidence, but impact and ROI data are more client-focused, the type of data that clients want to see from their meetings. However, while the power to show results increases as data move through the chain, evaluating the data becomes more expensive and more difficult. The reverse is true for usage. As expected, a high level of data collection activity occurs at Level 1, but a low level of activity occurs around Level 4 and Level 5. And some good reasons for this exist, as will be described later in the book.

Characteristics of Evaluation Levels

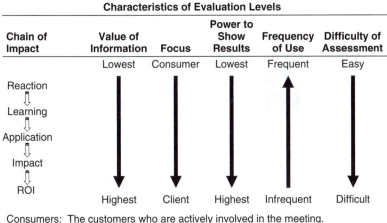

Chain of Impact	Value of Information	Focus	Power to Show Results	Frequency of Use	Difficulty of Assessment
	Lowest	Consumer	Lowest	Frequent	Easy
Reaction ⇕ Learning ⇕ Application ⇕ Impact ⇕ ROI					
	Highest	Client	Highest	Infrequent	Difficult

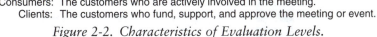

Consumers: The customers who are actively involved in the meeting.
Clients: The customers who fund, support, and approve the meeting or event.

Figure 2-2. Characteristics of Evaluation Levels.

THE ROI PROCESS MODEL

The calculation of the return on investment in meetings, events, trade shows, and sponsorships begins with the basic model shown in Figure 2-3, where a potentially complicated process can be simplified with sequential steps. The ROI process model provides a systematic approach to ROI calculations. A step-by-step approach helps keep the process manageable so users can address one issue at a time. The model also emphasizes that the methodology is a logical, systematic process that flows from one step to another. Applying the model provides consistency from one ROI calculation to another. Each step is briefly described in this chapter.

Objectives

Meeting objectives correspond with the different levels on the value chain. Ideally, the levels of objectives should be in place at all levels up to the highest level desired for evaluation. Essentially, the levels of objectives are:

- Input objectives (Level 0)
- Reaction objectives (Level 1)
- Learning objectives (Level 2)
- Application objectives (Level 3)
- Impact objectives (Level 4)
- ROI objectives (Level 5)

Table 2-2 shows an example of the multiple levels of objectives taken from a business development conference for insurance agents.

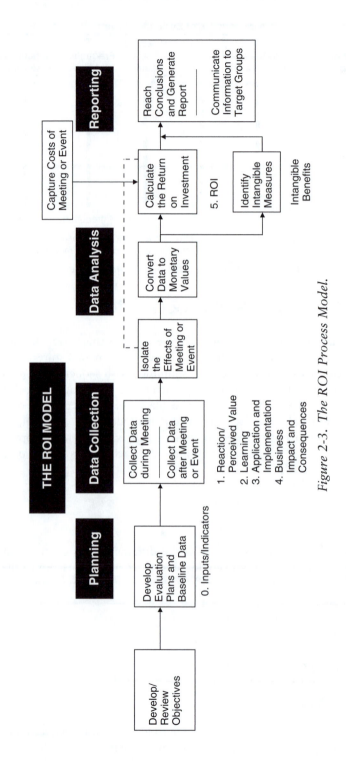

Figure 2-3. The ROI Process Model.

Table 2-2
Examples of Objectives

Reaction Objectives
After attending this conference, attendees will perceive it to be:
- Organized and efficient
- Conducted by effective speakers
- Valuable for business development
- Important to their success
- Motivating
- Challenging
- An excellent use of their time
- Full of new information
- Action-oriented—they intend to use the material

Learning Objectives
At the end of the conference, attendees should be able to:
- Identify the five steps of the business development strategy
- Develop a business development plan
- Select the best community service organization to join for business development
- Explain the changes in three products
- Identify the five most effective ways to turn a contact into a sale
- Identify at least five agents to call for suggestions and advice

Application Objectives
Within six months of the conference, each attendee should:
- Implement a business development plan
- Implement at least two new business development strategies
- Contact at least 10% of the current customer base to offer them the new changes in auto insurance coverage
- Make a random five percent customer service check with current clients
- Follow-up with at least three agents to discuss successes, concerns, or issues
- Join at least one additional community service group targeted for a potential customer base
- Use selling skills to turn a contact into a sale

Impact Objectives
Six months following the conference, the following should occur:
- New policies for automobile insurance should increase 10%
- Revenue of all other products should increase 5%
- New customers should increase by 5%
- Market share should increase
- Customer Satisfaction

ROI Objective
Within one year of the conference, a 20% return on the investment in the conference should be achieved.

Before an evaluation is conducted, these objectives must be identified and developed. Ideally, they should be developed early when the meeting is designed. If they are not readily available, they will have to be included to take the evaluation to the desired level.

Evaluation Planning

The time at which evaluation is considered has changed dramatically in recent years. The traditional meeting design model—analyze, plan, develop, implement, and evaluate—has been replaced with a new model, as illustrated in Figure 2-4. Evaluation must be considered at the conception of the meeting and often throughout the process. If evaluation is not considered early, serious limitations occur in the quality and quantity of data that are collected for evaluation. The old model places evaluation at the end where, unfortunately, meeting professionals waited until after implementation to think about evaluation. That is too late.

Evaluation must be planned—overall and individually—for each meeting. When evaluation is conducted only at reaction levels, not much evaluation planning is involved, but as evaluation moves up the value chain, increased attention and efforts need to be placed on planning. During the typical planning cycle, the purpose of evaluation must be reviewed for specific solutions and to determine where the evaluation will stop on the value chain. The feasibility of evaluating at different levels is explored, and two planning documents are developed when the evaluation migrates to application, impact, and ROI: the data collection plan and the data analysis plan. These documents—explored later—are sometimes used in combination but developed separately.

Data Collection

One important issue is the timing of data collection. In some cases, pre-meeting measurements are taken to compare with post-meeting measures, and in some cases, multiple measures are taken. In other situations, pre-meeting measures are not available and specific follow-ups are still taken after the meeting. The important issue is to determine the timing for the follow-up evaluation.

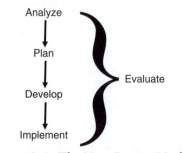

Figure 2-4. The New Design Model.

Another important issue is the data collection method used. Data are collected using the following methods:

- *Surveys* are administered to determine the extent to which participants are satisfied with the meeting, have learned the skills and knowledge, and have used different aspects of the meeting.
- *Questionnaires* are usually more detailed than surveys and can be used to uncover a wide variety of data. Participants provide responses to several types of open-ended and forced-response questions.
- *Tests* are conducted to measure changes in knowledge and skills. Tests come in a wide variety of formal methods (tests, performance tests, simulations, and skill practices) and informal methods (facilitator assessment, self assessment, and team assessment).
- *Interviews* are conducted with participants to determine the extent to which the meeting materials and content have been used on the job.
- *Focus groups* are conducted to determine the degree to which a group of participants has applied the content to job situations.
- *On-the-job observation* captures actual skill application and use. Observations are particularly useful in customer service meeting and are more effective when the observer is either invisible or transparent.
- *Action plans* are developed by participants during the meeting and are implemented on the job after the meeting is completed. Follow-ups provide evidence of the meeting's success.
- *Performance contracts* are developed by the participant, the participant's supervisor, and the facilitator, who all agree on job performance outcomes.
- *Business performance monitoring* is useful when performance records and operational data are examined for improvement.

While this list is rich with variety, most meetings and events are evaluated with surveys and questionnaires.

Analysis

Evaluation requires analysis. Even if the evaluation stops at Level 1, analysis is required, usually involving simple averages and standard deviations. As evaluation moves up the value chain, additional analyses are required. In some cases, not only are the averages and standard deviations used, but simple hypotheses testing and correlations may be required; however, these are very unusual situations. For the most part, analysis is simply tabulating, organizing, and integrating data and then presenting the results in meaningful ways for the audience to understand and appreciate.

Isolation of the Effects of Meetings

An often overlooked issue in some evaluations is the process of isolating the effects of a meeting on outcome data. This step is important because many factors will usually influence performance data after a meeting is conducted. Several techniques are available to determine the amount of performance that is directly related to the meeting. These techniques will pinpoint the amount of improvement that can be attributed to the meeting, resulting in increased accuracy and credibility of the evaluation. The following techniques have been used by organizations to address this important issue:

- *A control group* arrangement is used to isolate a meeting's impact. With this strategy, one group participates in a meeting, while another, similar group does not. The difference in the performance of the two groups is attributed to the meeting. When properly set up and implemented, the control group arrangement is the most effective way to isolate the effects of meetings and events.
- *Trend lines and forecasting* are used to project the values of specific output variables as if the meeting had not been undertaken. The projection is compared to the actual data after the meeting is conducted, and the difference represents the estimate of the impact of the meeting.
- *Participants or managers* estimate the amount of improvement related to the meeting. With this approach, participants or managers are provided with the total amount of improvement that is actually related to the meeting.
- *Other experts,* such as customers, provide estimates of the impact of meetings on the performance variable. Because the estimates are based on previous experience, these experts must be familiar with the type of meeting and the specific situation.

Conversion of Data to Monetary Values

To calculate the return on investment, business impact data collected during the evaluation are converted to monetary values and compared to the meeting costs. This requires that a value be placed on each unit of data connected to the meeting. Several techniques are available to convert data to monetary values. In many cases, standard values are available as organizations have attempted to place values on measures they want to increase and develop costs for measures they want to avoid. When these are not available, the records (or a combination of records) may show the cost or value of the measure. Also, internal experts, external experts, or external databases can be sources of values. Sometimes, participants, supervisors, and other conveniently available team members can provide the values.

This step is necessary for determining the monetary benefits from a meeting. The process is challenging, particularly with soft data, but can be methodically accomplished using one or more of the techniques described above.

The Cost of Meetings

The cost of a meeting is usually developed from one or two perspectives:

1. For budgets, approvals, and general information requests, costs are often reported systematically within the organization, and usually include only the direct costs. Executives and administrators are often interested in the direct costs. In some cases, these reports are changing to include other indirect costs.
2. When the actual ROI is calculated, the costs must be fully loaded to include all direct and indirect costs. In these situations, the cost components should include:
   - Needs assessment, design, and development, possibly prorated over the expected life of the meeting, if it is repeated
   - All materials provided to each participant
   - Speakers/facilitators, including preparation time as well as delivery time
   - Facilities for the meeting
   - Travel, lodging, and meal costs for the participants, if applicable
   - Salaries, plus employee benefits, of the participants of the meeting, for the time attending the meeting
   - Administrative and overhead costs of the meetings and events function, allocated in some convenient way
   - Evaluation, including planning, data collection, analysis, and reporting

The conservative approach is to include all these costs so that the total is fully loaded, and therefore more credible.

The Return on Investment Calculation

Dramatic changes have occurred in the need for data about meetings. Many executives and managers have taken the approach, "Show me the money." Figure 2-5 shows how the "Show Me" request has evolved, leading up to an actual request for ROI. For some professionals, this is an issue that cannot be ignored because of the serious consequences. Executives and managers want this type of data, and it must be delivered. This requires that at least a few major meetings be elevated to the ROI analysis level.

When the ROI is actually developed, it should be calculated systematically, using standard formulas. Two formulas are available. The benefit-cost ratio is the meeting benefits divided by the costs. In formula form, it is:

$$BCR = \frac{\text{Meeting Benefits}}{\text{Meeting Costs}}$$

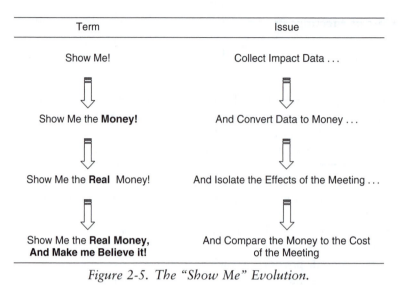

Term	Issue
Show Me!	Collect Impact Data . . .
Show Me the **Money!**	And Convert Data to Money . . .
Show Me the **Real** Money!	And Isolate the Effects of the Meeting . . .
Show Me the **Real Money, And Make me Believe it!**	And Compare the Money to the Cost of the Meeting

Figure 2-5. The "Show Me" Evolution.

The return on investment calculation uses the net meeting benefits divided by the meeting costs. The net benefits are the meeting benefits minus the costs. In formula form, the ROI is:

$$\text{ROI (\%)} = \frac{\text{Net Meeting Benefits}}{\text{Meeting Costs}} \times 100$$

This is the same basic formula used in evaluating other investments for which the ROI is traditionally reported as earnings divided by investment. An example of the benefit/cost ratio and ROI is illustrated below. A meeting is delivered to fifty participants. The first-year meeting benefits (from Level 4 business impact data) are found to be $300,000 from the fifty participants, and the fully loaded costs for these fifty participants are $200,000.

$$\text{BCR} = \frac{\$300,000}{\$200,000} = 1.50{:}1$$

$$\text{ROI (\%)} = \frac{\$100,000}{\$200,000} \times 100 = 50\%$$

The ROI calculation of net benefits ($300,000 minus $200,000) divided by total costs brings an ROI of 50%. This is what is earned after the $200,000 is recovered for the meeting. The ROI calculation accounts for the meeting costs and shows the resulting net gain.

The BCR (benefit-cost ratio) calculation above uses the total benefits in the numerator. Therefore, the expressed BCR of 1.50:1 does not account for replacing the money spent. This is why, when using the same values, the BCR will always be 1 greater than the ROI. The BCR of 1.50:1 in the example means that, for every dollar spent, $1.50 is gained back. One dollar has to pay for the investment, so the net is $0.50 (as expressed in the ROI calculation).

Intangible Benefits

In addition to tangible benefits, most meetings will influence intangible, non-monetary, benefits. Intangible benefits may include:

- Increased job satisfaction
- Increased organizational commitment
- Improved teamwork
- Improved customer service
- Enhanced brand awareness
- Reduced conflicts

During analysis, hard data—such as output, quality, and time—are usually converted to monetary values. The conversion of soft data is attempted. However, if the process used for conversion is too subjective or inaccurate and the resulting values lose credibility during the process, then the data are listed as intangible benefits with an appropriate explanation included. For most meetings, intangible benefits are extremely valuable, often carrying as much influence as hard data items, and when combined with monetary measurement, the intangibles become even more credible and with a greater perceived value.

Data Reporting

This critical step is often not given the proper attention and planning needed to ensure success. This step involves developing appropriate information as impact studies, executive summaries, one-page summaries, and other brief reports. The heart of the step includes the different techniques used to communicate the information to a wide variety of target audiences. In most situations, several audiences are interested in and need to know the information. Careful planning to match the communication method with the audience is essential to ensure that the message is understood and appropriate actions are taken.

OPERATING STANDARDS

To ensure consistency and replication of evaluation studies, operating standards should be developed and applied in the measurement and evaluation process. The results of an evaluation must stand alone and should not vary based on the individual who is conducting the study. The operating standards detail how each step and issue of the process should be addressed. The standards presented in this book are called the Guiding Principles. They are listed below:

1. When conducting a higher-level evaluation, collect data at lower levels.
2. When planning a higher-level evaluation, the previous level of evaluation is not required to be comprehensive.
3. When collecting and analyzing data, use only the most credible sources.
4. When analyzing data, select the most conservative alternative for calculations.
5. Use at least one method to isolate the effects of the meeting.
6. If no improvement data are available for a population or from a specific source, assume that little or no improvement has occurred.
7. Adjust estimates of improvement for potential errors of estimation.
8. Avoid use of extreme data items and unsupported claims when calculating ROI.
9. Use only the first year of annual benefits in ROI analysis of short-term solutions.
10. Fully load all costs of a meeting when analyzing ROI.
11. Intangible measures are defined as measures that are purposely not converted to monetary values.
12. Communicate the results of the ROI Methodology to all key stakeholders.

These specific standards not only serve as a way to consistently address each step, but also provide a much-needed conservative approach to the analysis. Adherence to these standards will build credibility with the target audience.

Implementation Issues

A variety of organizational issues and events will influence the successful implementation of measurement and evaluation. These issues must be addressed early to ensure that evaluation is successful. Specific topics or actions may include:

- A policy statement concerning results-based meetings and events
- Procedures and guidelines for different elements and techniques of the evaluation process
- Meetings and formal sessions to develop the meetings and events team's skills with measurement and evaluation
- Strategies to improve management commitment and support for measurement and evaluation
- Mechanisms to provide technical support for questionnaire design, data analysis, and evaluation strategy
- Specific techniques to place more attention on results

Measurement and evaluation can fail or succeed based on these implementation issues.

FINAL THOUGHTS

More attention must be focused on measurement and evaluation in this indus-try. The use of measurement and evaluation is expanding. The payoff is huge. The process is not difficult. The approaches, strategies, and techniques are not overly complex and can be useful in many settings. The specific model and the steps in the model are outlined in this chapter, showing the overall methodology for developing the actual ROI. This includes not only the details, systematic steps, and process, but also the Guiding Principles, the standards for the process, and the steps involved in implementation. All these issues will be explored in more detail in later chapters.

The combined and persistent efforts of meeting professionals and researchers will continue to refine the techniques and create successful applications. In the next chapter, the first step of the evaluation process, the initial analysis, will be explored.

CHAPTER 3

The Alignment: Defining Needs and Objectives

This chapter presents the first step of a results-based approach to meetings and events: defining the initial needs for the meeting and the corresponding objectives. If needs are not clearly defined early in the process, a less than optimal meeting may be the result, creating inefficiencies and uncertainties. In a worse case scenario, it could be a complete failure. This chapter explores the different levels of needs assessments to ensure that the meeting or event is necessary and is linked to important organizational and individual needs.

This chapter also focuses on the issue of alignment, addressing concerns about the alignment of meetings to specific organizational or business objectives. This chapter explains in detail how this alignment occurs and describes the opportunities to secure alignment. Finally, this chapter focuses on developing objectives. As Chapters 1 and 2 illustrated, objectives are important, even to the point that some people have coined a term *return on objectives* (ROO) to show the importance of having clear, specific objectives. Objectives at multiple levels are inherent in the ROI Methodology, and this chapter details how objectives are developed with structure and discipline and how they are categorized by levels.

THE MEETING PLANNER'S ROLE IN ALIGNMENT

The content of this chapter may be unsettling and frustrating for some meeting professionals. Essentially, this chapter shows how to ensure that a meeting is properly aligned with organizational issues, with the needs clearly defined along different levels, and with specific objectives. When this is achieved, a successful meeting is almost guaranteed, and this is what this industry needs: more alignment and more focus on specific outcomes.

However, some meeting professionals would argue that they do not have the opportunity to do this. Often, meetings or events are assigned to them with the decisions already made, and that they are essentially logistics coordinators who must make sure that the facilities and process are proper and efficient. Others would argue that they are only administrative in their work, following someone else's decisions. This assumption is contrary to the current direction of the meetings and events industry. MPI, Professional Convention Management

Association (PCMA), and other professional organizations suggest that meeting professionals and event organizers must take extra steps to make the change and adjust their roles. This will require the meeting professional to take initiative and do some things in a different way, but this has to be handled delicately, as will be described in this chapter. This action is necessary to become strategic and "Elevate the conversation" as MPI suggests.

If the paradigm shift described in Chapter 2 does not occur, then the meetings and events industry will suffer. Specifically, four outcomes will occur:

1. The meetings will not deliver the desired results. That is almost a given when alignment and focus is not achieved on the front end.
2. The image of the meetings and events function may deteriorate because it does not deliver value, and contribution may come into question.
3. The meeting planning function will be considered administrative or logistical and could be outsourced.
4. Budgets may be cut, particularly in lean times. This industry has a history of moving up and down with the economy, to a much larger degree than other functions within an organization.

From a positive perspective, taking additional steps to ensure alignment and focus, with the needs clearly defined and objectives developed, will provide numerous positive benefits:

1. The planning team's involvement and their contribution to the organization will be highlighted. Every person wants to know that they are making a difference, contributing to the organization, and adding value that is appreciated by important clients.
2. The actual value of specific meetings and events, up to and including ROI, will be developed, at least for some meetings. This quantifiable value takes much of the mystery away from the contribution and value of meetings and events.
3. Budgets can be enhanced, or at least maintained, during down times, and outsourcing will occur only if it makes economic sense. Unfortunately, outsourcing sometimes occurs because executives do not see the value of the function.
4. The industry's image will be enhanced and the field is more professional, more strategic (instead of operational), and more results-based (instead of activity-based).
5. Adjustments and improvements are made along the way to achieve the desired results. With specific, higher level objectives, the direction is set and deviations from the direction can easily lead to important adjustments or changes.

Now, the big question: How can this alignment be obtained in a meeting planning role when the meeting or event is handed off to an individual or a team? Several specific strategies are outlined at the end of this chapter—after the detailed information is presented. It can be accomplished and is an absolute must for the field. Also, this shift represents an important path for those who want to be proactive and make a difference, instead of reacting to a situation and taking orders.

THE FIRST ALIGNMENT OPPORTUNITY: NEEDS ANALYSIS

Meetings and events are sometimes ineffective because of undefined or unclear needs. Also, sometimes there is a lack of alignment between the meeting objectives and specific business needs. Because these issues are so serious, some planners take appropriate steps to ensure alignment, particularly if the proposed meeting is expensive, strategic, or high profile.

When business impact is desired, meetings and events must begin with a clear focus on the outcome. At least for some meetings, the result should be defined in terms of business needs and business measures so that the outcome—the actual improvement in the measures—and the resulting ROI are clear. Knowing the desired outcome provides a necessary focus on the needs through every step in the process. Beginning with the end in mind also involves pinpointing all the details throughout the meeting to ensure that it is properly planned and executed.

Proper analysis requires discipline and determination. A structured, standardized approach that adds credibility and allows for consistent application is necessary. While the process described in this book is comprehensive, not every meeting or event should be subjected to this type of needs analysis. Some needs are obvious and require little analysis other than the planning needed to develop a successful meeting or event. Additional analysis may be required to ensure that the meeting is right for the audience, but the amount of analysis undertaken often depends on the stakes involved.

Linking Need with Evaluation

Before beginning the needs analysis, the relationship presented in Figure 3-1, may be helpful. This shows the link between needs, objectives, and evaluation. This chapter explores the needs at the levels described in the figure, beginning with payoff needs and progressing to input needs. It also explores the objectives derived from these needs which serve as the drivers for the meeting. The right side of the model is essentially the evaluation levels introduced in the previous chapter.

Although it may seem confusing, this figure is helpful for planners. For example, the line between Levels 1 and 2 shows what has traditionally occurred in the industry. In part, most meetings are developed at Levels 0 and 1. The basis for a meeting is often centered on preference and input needs, in terms of attendance, timing, location, budgets, and costs. The objectives focus on a favorable reaction to the meeting, in terms of location, timing, facilities, and the experience. The measurement is often obtained through a questionnaire to capture reactions.

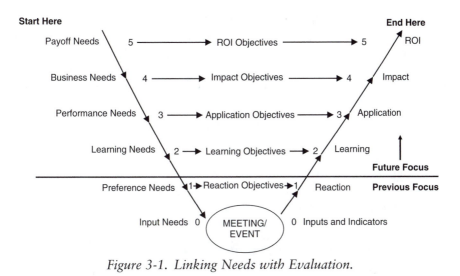

Figure 3-1. Linking Needs with Evaluation.

Little effort has been placed on the other levels—even Level 2. At Level 2, the content is more clearly defined in terms of what participants should know or learn, and specific learning objectives are set—what attendees should take away from the meeting. For many meetings, this may be all that is necessary. However, these days, because of clients and others who demand accountability, moving to higher levels of the evaluation chain is needed, which means that objectives need to be set at higher levels and the needs assessments must include higher levels of analysis.

Business Alignment

Figure 3-1 also shows an opportunity for business alignment at three points. First, during the needs assessment, the alignment occurs when the business need is identified. In this situation, specific business measures are identified which need to be improved by the meeting or event. When the needs assessment is conducted at Level 3 (performance needs) this step indicates the specific behaviors or actions that must change to meet the business need. When these needs are accurately identified, the initial alignment occurs.

The second opportunity for business alignment occurs when the meeting has defined impact objectives. Impact objectives reflect the business measures to be driven by the meeting—for example, to improve sales by 10% or to reduce compliance fines by 5%. These specific objectives, as will be illustrated in this chapter, provide the focus to drive the meeting so that the desired business outcomes are achieved. All the stakeholders can relate directly to those impact measures and will step up to their responsibilities to make them occur.

The third opportunity occurs when the business measure has been changed, as illustrated in the evaluation side of Figure 3-1 at Level 4. When the business measure's improvement has been identified as a quantifiable fact, an extra step is taken to isolate the effects of the meeting on that improvement. Then the conclusion can be made that the meeting was aligned with the business. This last, and perhaps the most important, part of the process shows convincing evidence that the meeting or event made a difference in the business measure.

PAYOFF NEEDS

For meetings and events that address significant problems or possible high-reward opportunities, the potential payoff may be obvious. For lower-profile meetings with a vague purpose, the possible payoff is less apparent. Figure 3-2 shows the potential payoff in monetary terms. A meeting's payoff will essentially be in either profit increases or in cost savings.

Profit increases are generated by meetings that improve sales, increase market share, introduce new products, open new markets, enhance customer service, or increase customer loyalty. These should pay off with increases in sales revenue which are converted to profits. Other revenue-generating measures include: increasing memberships, increasing donations, obtaining grants, and generating tuition from new and returning students—all of which, after subtracting the cost of doing business, leave a profitable benefit.

However, most meetings will payoff with cost savings. Cost savings may be generated through cost reductions or cost avoidances. For example, a meeting that improves quality, reduces cycle time, lowers downtime, decreases complaints, avoids employee turnover, or minimizes delays will generate cost reductions. When the goal is solving a problem, monetary value is often based on cost reduction.

Cost-avoidance payoffs come from meetings implemented to reduce risks, avoid problems, or prevent unwanted events. Some may view cost avoidance as an inappropriate measure for developing monetary benefits and calculating ROI. However, if the assumptions are correct, an avoided cost (e.g., compliance fines) can be more valuable than reducing an actual cost. Preventing a problem is more cost effective than waiting for it to occur and then fixing it.

Determining the potential payoff is the first step in the needs analysis process. This step is closely related to the next step, determining the business need,

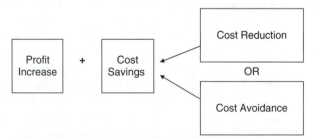

Figure 3-2. The Payoff Opportunity.

since the potential payoff is often based on a consideration of the business measures that need to change. Determining the payoff involves two factors: the potential monetary value derived from the business measure's improvement and the approximate cost of the meeting. Knowing these monetary values in detail can yield a more credible forecast of what can be expected from the meeting. However, this step may be omitted in situations when the issue (business need) must be resolved regardless of the cost or if it is obviously a high-payoff activity.

Probe for Details

The extent of the detail may also hinge on securing funding. If the potential funding source does not see the value of the meeting compared to the potential costs, more detail may be needed to provide a convincing case for funding. Greater detail should be provided under the following circumstances:

- *When the proposed meeting is anticipated to be expensive.* Estimating the potential payoff is important before spending major resources on a meeting or event. Otherwise there is a danger of "throwing money at the solution."
- *When funding is needed for a meeting.* This is particularly true if the funding comes from external resources or when there is serious competition for internal funding sources.
- *When minimal support exists for the proposed meeting.* The payoff analysis can provide an estimated value of the improvement (or avoidance) and the potential contribution to business goals.
- *When a key sponsor wants more analysis before the meeting moves forward.* Although he or she may support it enthusiastically, more analysis may solidify the sponsor's confidence in the proposed meeting and provide the needed information to secure final approval.

Knowledge of the potential payoff is not needed when most individuals involved in the meeting agree that the payoff from the meeting will be high, or if the problem in question must be resolved regardless of the cost. For example, if the problem involves a safety concern, a regulatory compliance issue, or a competitive matter, then a detailed analysis is not needed.

To begin the analysis, several questions should be answered. Table 3-1 shows some appropriate questions to ask about the proposed meeting. The answers to these questions may make the case for proceeding without analysis or indicate that additional analysis is needed. They may also show that the meeting is not needed. Understanding the implications of whether to move forward can show the legitimacy of the proposed meeting. For many potential meetings, answers to these questions may be readily available. The need may have already been realized and the consequences might be validated.

Table 3-1
Key Questions to Ask for Potential Payoffs

- What is the business case for this meeting or event?
- Why is this an issue?
- Is there a potential payoff (positive ROI)?
- Is this issue critical?
- Is this a problem?
- Is it possible to correct the problem?
- Is it feasible to improve it?
- How much will the meeting cost?
- Are there some important intangibles involved?
- Is a forecast needed?
- What happens if we do nothing?
- Is this issue linked to strategy?
- How much does the problem cost?
- Who will support the meeting or event?
- Who will not support the meeting or event?
- How can we fund the meeting or event?

Obvious versus not so Obvious

The potential payoff is obvious for some meetings but not so obvious for others. Table 3-2 lists some opportunities with obvious payoffs. Each item is a serious problem that needs to be addressed by executives, administrators, or politicians. For these situations, moving to the business needs level would be safe. After the solution is developed at Level 3, a forecast may be appropriate.

In other meetings, the issues might be unclear and arise from political motives or biases. Table 3-3 shows some opportunities where the payoff may not be as obvious. The not-so-obvious opportunities need more detail. Some requests are common as executives and administrators suggest a different meetings and processes to change a dysfunctional process or to achieve vague or non-specific goals. The opportunities listed are common requests that can deliver value, but only if they are focused and clearly defined at the start. Some of the more open-ended and vague opportunities can pay off tremendously. However, many of

Table 3-2
Obvious Payoff Opportunities

- Sales growth is the lowest in the industry
- Excessive turnover of critical talent: 35% above benchmark data
- Inadequate customer service: 3.89 on a 10 point customer satisfaction scale
- Safety record is among the worst in the industry
- This year's out-of-compliance fines total $1.2 million, up 82% from last year
- Excessive product returns: 30% higher than previous year
- Excessive absenteeism in call centers: 12.3% compared to 5.4% industry average
- Sexual harassment complaints per 1,000 employees are the highest in the industry
- Very low market share in a market with few players
- Grievances are up 38% from last year

Table 3-3
Not-so-Obvious Payoff Opportunities

- Organize a business development conference
- Improve leadership competencies for all managers
- Become a technology leader
- Create a great place to work
- Establish a project management office
- Improve branding
- Become a green company
- Implement crucial conversations organization-wide
- Make employers aware of sexual harassment issues
- Develop an "open-book" company
- Implement the same work out process that GE has used
- Implement a transformation program involving all employees
- Implement a career advancement program
- Create a wellness and fitness center
- Build capability for future growth
- Create an empowered workforce

---

these examples may turn into valuable meetings. Because of this, overlooking a vague request may be an injustice, because the meeting may be a valuable contribution if it is clearly defined, approved, and focused to secure the desired result.

The Reasons for Meetings and Events

From the ROI perspective, the main reasons that meetings and events fail to deliver monetary value and a positive ROI are:

- They are not needed.
- They are not focused on results.
- They are not connected closely enough to a business issue to overcome the cost of the meeting.

A lack of initial business alignment brings into question the reasons for new meetings or events. Table 3-4 shows some of the main reasons that new meetings are implemented. Some of these appear to be legitimate reasons to move forward. If analysis supports a reason and it is credible, then it is probably needed. If a regulation requires it, then it must be implemented. These other reasons for a new meeting may mean that the meeting is necessary, but it is necessary only if it is implemented efficiently. For example, if a meeting supports new policies

Table 3-4
The Reasons for Meetings and Events

1. An analysis was conducted to determine need.
2. A regulation requires it.
3. It appears to be addressing serious problem.
4. Management requests it.
5. It focuses on a change that is needed.
6. Other organizations in industry have conducted similar meetings.
7. The topic is a trend.
8. It supports new policies and practices.
9. The meetings and events management thought it was needed.
10. It supports new equipment, procedures, or technology.
11. It supports other processes such as Six Sigma, transformation, continuous process improvement, etc.
12. A best selling book has been written about the topic.

and practices; new equipment, procedures or technology; or existing processes, it appears to be a legitimate request, but only if support for implementation exists.

Other reasons for a new meeting become suspect, and some are often misguided. For example, if other organizations have implemented a meeting or if it is based on a trend or touted in a bestselling book, it is suspect from the beginning. These are the types of meetings that often do not contribute adequate value and create concerns about chasing a fad. Unfortunately, executives often pursue these meetings in their never-ending desire to find the right solutions or to chase any new idea.

Determining Costs of the Problem

Problems are expensive and, once resolved, can have a tremendous impact. To determine the cost of the problem, the potential consequences of the problem must be examined and converted to monetary values. Table 3-5 shows a list of potential problems. Some can easily be converted to money, and some already are. Those that cannot be converted are left as intangibles. Inventory shortages often result in the direct cost of the inventory as well as the cost of carrying the inventory. Time can easily be translated into money by calculating the fully loaded cost of the individual's time spent on unproductive tasks. Calculating time for completing a project, task, or cycle involves measures that can be converted to money. Errors, mistakes, waste, delays, and bottlenecks can often be converted to money through their consequences. Productivity problems and inefficiencies, equipment damage, and equipment under use are other examples of easy conversions.

When examining costs, considering *all* the costs and their implications is critical. For example, the full costs of accidents include not only the cost of lost workdays and medical expenses, but their effect on insurance premiums, the time

Table 3-5
Potentially Costly Problems

• Inventory shortages	• Incidents
• Time Savings	• Excessive fines
• Errors/mistakes	• Excessive employee turnover
• Waste	• Employee withdrawal
• Delays	• Accidents
• Bottlenecks	• Excessive staffing
• Productivity problems	• Employee dissatisfaction
• Inefficiencies	• Customer dissatisfaction
• Excessive direct costs	• Excessive conflicts
• Equipment damage	• Tarnished image
• Equipment underused	• Lack of coordination
• Excessive project time	• Excessive stress

required for investigations, damages to equipment, and the time of all employees who work with the accident. The cost of a customer complaint includes the cost of the time in resolving the complaint, as well as the value of the item or service that is adjusted because of the complaint. The most important item is the cost of lost future business and goodwill from the complaining customer and potential customers who learn of the issue.

The Value of Opportunity

Just as the cost of a problem can be tabulated in most situations, the value of an opportunity can also be determined. Examples of opportunities include:

- Implementing a new process or procedure
- Installing new technology
- Preparing for a more competitive environment
- Preventing Compliance Issues

In these situations, a problem may not exist, but a tremendous opportunity to get ahead of the competition by taking immediate action may be available. Properly placing a value on this opportunity requires considering what may happen if the meeting is not pursued or taking into account the windfall that might be realized if the opportunity is seized. The monetary value is derived by following the different scenarios to convert specific business impact measures to money. The difficulty in this situation is ensuring a credible analysis. Forecasting the value of an opportunity takes into account many assumptions; whereas, calculating the value of a known outcome is often grounded in a more credible analysis.

To Forecast or not to Forecast

Seeking and placing value on a meeting opportunity leads to an important decision: to forecast or not to forecast ROI. If the stakes are high and the support for the meeting is not in place, a detailed forecast may be the only way to gain needed support and funding for the meeting. When a forecast is pursued, how thorough the analysis should be becomes an issue. In some cases, an informal forecast is provided, giving certain assumptions about alternative outcome scenarios. In others, a detailed forecast is needed and may involve collecting data from a variety of experts, using previous studies from another meeting, or perhaps more sophisticated analysis.

BUSINESS NEEDS

Determining specific business needs is linked to the previous step in the needs analysis, developing the potential payoff. When determining the business needs, specific measures are pinpointed so that the business situation can be clearly assessed. The term "business" is used in governments, non-profit organizations, non-government organizations, and educational institutions, as well as in private sector firms. Meetings and events in all types of organizations and associations can show the money by improving productivity, quality, and efficiency, and by saving time and reducing costs.

A business need is represented by a business measure. Any process, item, or perception can be measured, and this measurement is critical to this level of analysis. If the meeting focuses on solving a problem—something clearly in the mind of the client—the measures are often obvious. If the meeting prevents a problem, the measures may also be obvious. If it takes advantage of a potential opportunity, the measures are usually still there. Otherwise, how will the opportunity be described? The important point is that measures are usually in the system, where the meeting participant resides, ready to be captured for this level of analysis. The challenge is to define the measures and find them economically and swiftly.

Define the Measure—Hard Data

To help focus on the desired measures, clarification between hard data and soft data is needed. Hard data are primary measures of improvement presented in rational, undisputed facts that are usually accumulated. They are the most desired type of data because they are easy to measure and quantify and are relatively easy to convert to monetary values. The ultimate criteria for measuring the effectiveness of an organization rests on hard data items—such as sales, productivity, profitability, cost control, and quality assurance.

Hard data are objectively based and represent very common and credible measures of an organization's performance. Hard data can usually be grouped into four major categories, as shown in Table 3-6. These categories—output, quality, cost, and time—are typical performance measures in every organization.

Table 3-6
Examples of Hard Data

Output	Time
Sales	Cycle time
Units produced	Equipment downtime
Tons manufactured	Overtime
Items assembled	On time shipments
Money collected	Time to project completion
New accounts generated	Processing time
Forms processed	Supervisory time
Loans approved	Time to proficiency
Inventory turnover	Learning time
Patients visited	Meeting schedules
Applications processed	Repair time
Students graduated	Efficiency
Tasks completed	Work stoppages
Output per hour	Order response
Productivity	Late reporting
Work backlog	Lost time days
Incentive bonus	
Shipments	Quality
	Scrap
Costs	Waste
Unit costs	Rejects
Costs by account	Error rates
Variable costs	Failure rates
Shelter costs	Dropout rates
Treatment costs	Rework
Budget variances	Shortages
Fixed costs	Product defects
Overhead cost	Deviation from standard
Operating costs	Product failures
Project cost savings	Inventory adjustments
Accident costs	Timecard corrections
Meetings costs	Incidents
Sales expense	Compliance discrepancies
Participant costs	Agency fines

Output. The visible hard-data results from a particular meeting or event involve improvements in the output of individuals, the work unit, section, department, division, or entire organization. Every organization, regardless of type, must have basic measurements of output, whether they are the sales generated, rooms rented, patients treated, students graduated, tons produced, packages shipped, or other production or sales figures. Since these factors are monitored by organizations, changes can easily be measured by comparing before and after outputs. When meetings are anticipated to drive an output measure, estimates of output changes can usually be made by those who are knowledgeable about the situation.

Quality. One of the most significant hard-data measure categories is quality. If quality is a major concern for the organization, processes are most likely in place to measure and monitor quality. Thanks in part to the rising popularity of quality-improvement processes (such as total-quality management, continuous quality improvement, and Six Sigma), tremendous success has been attained in pinpointing the correct quality measures—and in many cases, with placing a monetary value on them. For meetings and events designed to improve quality, the results can be documented using the standard cost of quality as a value.

Cost. Another important hard-data category is an improvement in cost. Many meetings and events are designed to lower, control, or eliminate the cost of a process or activity. Achieving these cost targets contributes immediately to the bottom line. Some organizations have an extreme focus on cost reduction. Consider Wal-Mart, whose tagline is "Always low prices. Always." The entire organization focuses on lowering costs on all processes and products and passing the savings along to customers. When direct cost savings are used, no efforts are necessary to convert data to monetary value. There can be as many cost items as there are accounts in a cost accounting system. In addition, costs can be combined in any number of ways to develop the costs needed for a particular meeting or project.

Time. Time, which is becoming a critical measure in organizations, is also a hard-data category. Some organizations gauge their performance almost exclusively on time. For example, consider FedEx, whose tagline is "The World on Time." When asked what business FedEx is in, the company's top executives say, "We engineer time." For FedEx, time is so critical that it defines success or failure. Time savings may mean that a meeting is completed faster than originally planned, a product was introduced earlier, or the time to restore a network was reduced. These savings can translate into lower costs. In many organizations, it is an important measure, with meetings and events aimed directly at time savings.

Define the Business Need—Soft Data

Hard data may lag behind changes and conditions in the human organization by many months. Therefore, supplementing hard data with soft data—such as attitude, motivation, and satisfaction—may be useful. Often more difficult to collect and analyze, soft data are used when hard data are not available or to supplement hard data. Soft data are also more difficult to convert to monetary

Table 3-7
Examples of Soft Data

Work Habits	*Customer Service*
Tardiness	Customer complaints
Visits to the dispensary	Customer satisfaction
Violations of safety rules	Customer dissatisfaction
Communication break-downs	Customer impressions
Excessive breaks	Customer loyalty
	Customer retention
Work Climate/Satisfaction	Customer value
Grievances	Lost customers
Discrimination charges	
Employee complaints	*Employee Development/*
Job satisfaction	*Advancement*
Organization commitment	Promotions
Employee engagement	Capability
Employee loyalty	Intellectual capital
Intent to leave	Programs completed
Stress	Requests for transfer
	Performance appraisal ratings
Initiative/Innovation	Readiness
Creativity	Networking
Innovation	
New ideas	*Image*
Suggestions	Brand awareness
New products and services	Reputation
Trademarks	Leadership
Copyrights and patents	Social responsibility
Process improvements	Environmental friendliness
Partnerships	Social consciousness
Alliances	Diversity
	External awards

values and are often subjective. They are less credible as a performance measurement and are often behavior oriented. Table 3-7 shows common examples and types of soft data.

Work Habits. Employee work habits are important to the success of work groups. Dysfunctional habits can lead to an unproductive and ineffective work group, while productive work habits can boost the group's output and morale. Some examples of work habits that may be difficult to measure or convert to monetary values are shown in Table 3-7. The outcome of some work habits— including employee turnover, absenteeism, and accidents—are in the hard-data category because they are easy to convert to monetary values.

Work Climate/Satisfaction. When employees are dissatisfied or the work climate is unfavorable, several measures can show the employees' discontent or dissatisfaction. Complaints and grievances are sometimes in the hard-data category because of their ease of conversion to money. However, most of the items are considered soft-data items. Job satisfaction, organizational commitment, and employee engagement show how attitudes shape the organization. Stress is often a by-product of a fast-past work climate. These issues are becoming increasingly important.

Customer Service. Because increased global competition fosters a greater need to serve and satisfy customers, more organizations are putting into place customer service measures that show the levels of customer satisfaction, loyalty, and retention. Few measures are as important as those linked to customers.

Employee Development/Advancement. Employees are routinely developed, assigned new jobs, and promoted throughout organizations. Building capability, creating intellectual capital, enhancing readiness, and fostering networks are important processes. Many soft-data measures are available to indicate the consequences of those activities and processes.

Initiative/Innovation. Creativity and innovation are critical processes within successful organizations. A variety of measures can be developed to show the creative spirit of employees and the related outcomes—such as ideas, suggestions, copyrights, patents, and products and services. While the collective creative spirit of employees may be a soft-data item, the outcomes of creativity and innovation may be placed in the hard-data category. Still, many executives consider innovation a soft-data item.

Image. Perhaps some of the softest measures are in the image category. Executives are attempting to increase brand awareness, particularly with sales and marketing programs or projects. Reputation is another key area, as more organizations seek to improve their standing as a good employer, a good citizen, and a good steward of investors' money. Leadership is probably the most sought-after measure and is influenced by projects and meetings designed to build leadership within the organization. Image, social responsibility, environmental friendliness, and social consciousness are key outputs of a variety of programs and projects aimed at making the organization well-rounded. Diversity is important for many organizations. Many meetings are aimed at increasing diversity of ideas, products, people, and programs. Finally, external awards are the outcomes of many activities and programs, often reflecting the external variation of an organization.

Tangible versus Intangible—A Better Approach

The important issue with soft-data categories is the difficulty of converting them to monetary values. While some of the measures listed in Table 3-7 could be converted to money, considering most of them soft-data items is more realistic and practical. The definition of an intangible measure (based on the standards of the ROI Methodology) is a measure that cannot be converted. If a soft-data measure can be converted to money, it becomes tangible and is reported as a monetary value or placed in an ROI calculation. If a data item cannot be converted to money credibly with minimum resources, it is listed as an intangible measure; these are usually referred to as the very soft categories. To avoid debates over what should be considered soft or hard data, the terms *tangible* and *intangible* will be used more often in this book. This is the best approach to meeting evaluation because the data classification is specific to the organizational setting. Each organization determines if a measure is tangible or intangible. For example, in most sales organizations, a measure for customer satisfaction is easily available and costs little to obtain. Therefore, the measure is tangible because it can easily be converted to money. However, in other organizations where sales is not necessarily the focus, the measure is intangible.

Data Sources

The sources of impact data, whether hard or soft, are plentiful. They come from routine reporting systems in the organization and individual work units. In many situations, these items have led to the need for the meeting or event. Table 3-8 shows a vast array of possible documents, systems, databases, and reports can be used to select the specific measure or measures to monitor throughout the meeting.

Some planners and participants believe that data sources are scarce because the data are not readily available to them near their workplace or within easy reach through database systems. With a little determination and searching, the data can usually be identified. In our experience, more than 90% of the measures that matter to a specific meeting or event have already been developed and are readily available in databases or systems. Rarely do new data-collection systems or processes need to be developed.

Table 3-8
Sources of Data

Department records	Safety and health reports
Work unit reports	Benchmarking data
Human capital databases	Industry/trade association data
Payroll records	R&D status reports
Quality reports	Suggestion system data
Design documents	Customer satisfaction data
Manufacturing reports	Project management data
Test data	Cost data statements
Compliance reports	Financial records
Marketing data	Scorecards
Sales records	Dashboards
Service records	Productivity records
Annual reports	Employee engagement data

Identifying all the Measures

When searching for the proper measures to connect to the meeting and pinpoint business needs, considering all the possible measures that could be influenced is helpful. Sometimes, collateral measures move in harmony with the meeting. For example, efforts to improve safety may also improve productivity and increase job satisfaction. Thinking about the adverse impact on certain measures may also help. For example, when cycle times are reduced, quality may suffer; or when sales increase, customer satisfaction may deteriorate. Finally, the planning team needs to prepare for unintended consequences and capture them as other data items that might be connected to or influenced by the meeting.

Performance Needs

The next step in the needs analysis is understanding what caused the business measure to miss its mark and not be where it is desired. This step determines the specific performance of the participant that is not in place. It answers this question: What is the participant doing or not doing to inhibit the business measure (e.g., sales associates do not show the features and benefits of a product; managers do not use project management tools; engineers do not use the latest technology)?

If the proposed meeting addresses a problem, this step focuses on the cause of the problem, from an individual perspective. If the meeting takes advantage of an opportunity, this step focuses on what inhibits the organization from taking advantage of that opportunity.

This step may require using a variety of analytical techniques to uncover the causes of the problem or inhibitors to success. Table 3-9 shows a brief listing of the many techniques used to uncover what can inhibit business measures. It is important to relate the issue to the organizational setting, to the behavior of the individuals involved, and to the functioning of various systems. These

Table 3-9
Diagnosis Tools

Diagnostic instruments	Statistical process control
Focus groups	Brainstorming
Probing interviews	Problem analysis
Job satisfaction surveys	Cause and effect diagram
Engagement surveys	Force field analysis
Exit interviews	Mind mapping
Exit surveys	Affinity diagrams
Nominal group technique	Simulations

analytical techniques often use tools from problem solving, quality assurance, and performance improvement fields to search for these causes. Searching for multiple solutions is also important, since measures are often inhibited for several reasons. However, multiple solutions must be considered in terms of implementation—deciding if they should be explored in total or tackled in priority order. The detailed approaches of all the techniques are contained in many references (Langdon et al., 1999).

Considering the resources needed to examine records, research databases, and observe situations and individuals is important. Analysis takes time. The use of expert input, both internally and externally, can add to the cost and time of the evaluation. The needs at this level can vary considerably and may include:

- Ineffective behavior
- Dysfunctional work climate
- Inadequate systems
- Disconnected process flow
- Improper procedures
- Unsupportive culture
- Insufficient technology
- Unsupportive environment

These needs have to be uncovered using many of the methods listed in Table 3-9. When needs vary and techniques are abundant, an opportunity exists for over-analysis and excessive costs. Consequently, a sensible approach must be taken.

LEARNING NEEDS

The performance needs uncovered in the previous step often require a learning component to address them—such as when participants must learn how to perform a task differently, to use a process or a system, or to seek new ideas. Learning needs address the take-aways from the meeting and define the content and topics discussed. For many meetings, defining learning often involves simply understanding the process, procedure, policy, or new contacts. For example, when implementing a new ethics policy at a meeting, the learning component requires understanding how the policy works and the participant's role in policy implementation. In some cases, learning is the principal goal, as in competency development, major technology changes, capability development, and system installations. In these situations, the learning becomes the solution.

A variety of approaches are available to measure specific learning needs. Often, multiple tasks and multiple jobs are involved in any meeting, and each should be addressed separately. Sometimes, the least useful way to find out what skills and knowledge are needed is to ask the meeting attendees. They may not be sure of what is needed or may not know enough to provide adequate input.

Subject Matter Experts

One of the most important approaches to determine learning needs is to ask the individuals who understand the process. They can best determine what skills and knowledge are necessary to address the performance issues defined earlier. Then it may be appropriate to understand how much of the knowledge and skills already exist.

Job and Task Analysis

A job and task analysis is effective when a new job is created or when an existing job description changes significantly. As jobs are redesigned and the tasks must be identified, this technique offers a systematic way of detailing the job and task. Essentially, a job analysis collects and evaluates work-related information. A task analysis determines specific knowledge, skills, tools, and conditions necessary to perform a particular job. The primary objective of a job and task analysis is to gather information about the scope, responsibilities, and tasks related to a particular job or new responsibilities. In the context of developing learning needs, this information is useful because it helps in preparing job profiles and job descriptions. These descriptions, in turn, serve as a platform for linking job requirements to specific information or training needs.

Performing a job and task analysis not only helps the individuals who will use the meeting content develop a clear picture of their responsibilities, but will also indicate what is expected of them. The amount of time needed to complete a job and task analysis can vary from a few days to several months, depending on the complexity of the need. It involves identifying high performers, preparing a job analysis questionnaire, and developing other materials as necessary to collect information. Conducting a complete job analysis is usually beyond the scope of a planner.

Observations

Current practices and procedures in an organization may have to be observed to understand the situation as the meeting is implemented. This often indicates the level of capability as well as the correct procedures. Observing is an established and respected data-collection method. Observations can be used to examine workflow and interpersonal interactions, including those between management and team members. Sometimes, the observer is unknown to those being observed (placed in the environment specifically to observe the current processes). At other times, the observer is someone previously in the work environment but now in a different role. Another possibility is that the observer is invisible to those being observed. Examples include retail mystery shoppers, electronic observation, or individuals who have joined a group temporarily but have been there long enough to be considered part of the team. Here, it is important to remember that observation can be a tool used to uncover what individuals need to do as a result of the meeting.

Demonstrations

In some situations, having employees demonstrate their abilities to perform a certain task, process, or procedure is important. The demonstration can be as simple as a skill practice or role play, or as complex as an extensive mechanical or electronic simulation. The issue is to use this as a way of determining if employees know how to perform a task or procedure. From that, specific learning needs can evolve.

Tests

Testing as a needs assessment process is not used as frequently as other methods, but can be very useful. Employees are tested to find out what they know about a situation. This information helps guide learning issues. For example, in one hospital chain, management was concerned that employees were not aware of the company's policy on sexual harassment, or what actions constitute sexual harassment. In the early stages of the analysis, a group of supervisors and managers, the target audience for the meeting, were given a 20-item test about their knowledge of the sexual harassment policy (10 items) and knowledge about sexual harassment actions (10 items). The test scores revealed where insufficient knowledge existed and formed the basis of a meeting to reduce the number sexual harassment complaints.

Management Assessment

When conducting meetings in organizations where there is an existing manager or team leader, input from the management team may be used to assess the current situation and the knowledge and skills required by the new situation. This input can be collected through surveys, interviews, or focus groups. It can be a rich source of information about what the meeting participants will need to know to make it a success.

Where the learning component is minor, as in most meetings and events, learning needs are simple. Determining the specific learning needs can be very time consuming for major meetings and events where new procedures, technologies, and processes are developed. As in the previous step, it is important not to spend excessive time analyzing at this early stage in the process but to collect as much data as possible with minimum resources.

PREFERENCE NEEDS

The final level of needs analysis is based on preferences, which drive meeting requirements and specifications. Essentially, participants prefer certain locations, schedules, or activities for the structure of the meeting or event. Preferences define how, where, and when a meeting will be conducted. Table 3-10 shows the

Table 3-10
Typical Preference Needs

We need this meeting to be:	Parameter
At a convenient time	Timing
At the appropriate time of year	Timing
Within the budget	Costs
Not too expensive	Costs
At a great location	Location
At a convenient place	Location
At a beautiful facility	Facility
At a comfortable place	Facility
Relevant to the job	Content
Important to success	Content
Valuable	Value
A good investment of time	Value
Conducted by motivating speakers	Speakers/facilitators
Presented by effective facilitators	Speakers/facilitators
Organized	Logistics/service
Coordinated	Logistics/service

typical preference needs. These represent statements that define the parameters of the meeting in terms of timing, costs, location, facility, content, value, speakers, and logistics. Because everyone involved will have certain needs or preferences for the meeting, input of several stakeholders is needed rather than that of one individual. For example, participants involved in the meeting (those who attend), may have a particular preference, but their preference could exceed time and budget requirements. The immediate manager's input may help drive the content. The funds that can be allocated are also a constraining resource. The urgency for a meeting may create a constraint in the preferences. Those who support or own the meeting offer preferences about the meeting in terms of cost and content. Because this is a Level 1 need, the structure and solution will directly relate to the reaction objectives and to the initial reaction to the meeting.

INPUT NEEDS

The inputs to the meeting are often defined at the same time that the preference needs are. The inputs are the constraints or resources available to the meeting. They form the requirements and specifications for the meeting to a certain degree.

Table 3-11 shows the input needs. These represent statements that define the parameters of the meeting in terms of duration, timing, budget, audiences,

Table 3-11
Typical Input Needs

This meeting must be:	Parameter
Completed in two days	Duration
Completed by September 1	Timing
Within 3% of the estimated budget	Budget
For the R&D staff only	Audience
Supported by managers	Support
Planned with the current staff only	Resources
Convenient for travel	Location
In a multimedia format	Technology
Relevant to goals	Content
Implemented without work disruption	Disruption

resources, support, location, technology, content, and disruption. As with the preference needs, everyone involved will have certain inputs for the meeting, so the input of several stakeholders must be considered. For example, the client will have inputs about budget and timing. The immediate manager's input may help decrease work disruption and maximize resources. The funds that can be allocated are also a constraining resource. The necessity of the implementation may create an important input. Those who support or own the meeting often provide input about the meeting in terms of timing, budget, and the location. Because this is an input, the structure and solution will directly relate to the input objectives.

DEVELOPING OBJECTIVES FOR MEETINGS AND EVENTS

Meetings and events are driven by objectives. In some situations, the meeting is aimed at creating a positive reaction to the experience, and that may be all that is needed. At some meetings, a need to define objectives about what must be learned or acquired at the meeting exists, requiring learning objectives. For other meetings, there is a need to understand more precisely what individual participants will do or should do as a result of the meeting. Therefore, application and implementation objectives are needed. In still other situations, understanding the impact that the meeting had on the individual or the organization is necessary. In these cases, specific impact objectives must define the ultimate consequences. Finally, in a few circumstances, a comparison of the costs to the monetary benefits is needed and ROI objectives are necessary.

Regardless of the type of meeting or event, multiple levels of objectives are desired. These levels of objectives, ranging from qualitative to quantitative, define more precisely what will occur as a meeting or event is implemented. Table 3-12 shows the different levels of objectives briefly discussed in this chapter.

Table 3-12
Multiple Levels of Objectives

Levels of Objectives	Focus of Objectives
Level 0 Inputs and Indicators	Defines the inputs in terms of duration, timing, budget, and location.
Level 1 Reaction and Perceived Value	Defines a specific, desired level of reaction to the meeting or event as it is revealed and communicated to stakeholders
Level 2 Learning	Defines specific skills, knowledge, information, and contacts that will be acquired during the meeting
Level 3 Application and Implementation	Defines the successful application of the meeting's content
Level 4 Impact and Consequences	Defines the specific business measures that will change or improve as a result of the meeting or event
Level 5 ROI	Defines the acceptable return on investment from the meeting or event, comparing the meeting's monetary benefits to the meeting's costs

These objectives are so critical that they need special attention in their development and use.

Input Objectives

Every meeting will have requirements and specifications—the inputs into a successful meeting. Ideally, several stakeholders should provide input. This creates a win-win relationship for all stakeholders. Table 3-13 shows some of the typical areas for specific input objectives. This information must be obtained before the meeting planning begins.

Developing input objectives is straightforward and relatively easy. The objectives reflect immediate success with specifications and requirements. Table 3-14 provides some key issues about developing input objectives.

Table 3-13
Typical Areas for Input Objectives

• Duration of the meeting	• Meeting location
• Use of resources	• Cost of the meeting
• Use of technology	• Project time line
• Perceived support for the meeting	• Audience coverage
• Amount of disruption	• Timing of the meeting

Table 3-14
Developing Input Objectives

The best input objectives:
- Identify issues that are important and measurable
- Are clearly worded and specific
- Specify what is required to make the meeting successful
- Provide the beginning point for the meeting
- Define the parameters for the meeting
- Pinpoint the costs for the meeting

Key questions are:
- Who should attend?
- What are the resources?
- What is the budget?
- When is it needed?
- What is the content?
- What are the time issues?

Reaction Objectives

For any meeting or event to be successful, stakeholders must react favorably—or at least not negatively—to the event. Ideally, the participants should be satisfied with the meeting and see its value. This creates a win-win relationship. This information must be obtained routinely during and at the end of the meeting so that feedback can be used to make adjustments and perhaps even redesign certain parts. Typical reaction objectives are presented in Table 3-15.

Developing reaction objectives should be simple and uncomplicated. The objectives reflect immediate and long-term satisfaction with issues important to a meeting's success. They also form the basis for evaluating the chain of impact and emphasizing planned action, when feasible and useful. (Table 3.16)

Learning Objectives

Every meeting or event involves at least one learning objective and usually more. With major events, the learning component is incredibly important. In other situations, such as the implementation of a new policy, the learning component is minor but necessary. To ensure that participants learn what they need to know to make the meeting successful, learning objectives are developed. Table 3-17 shows typical learning objectives.

Learning objectives are important because they define the desired information, knowledge, or skills necessary for meeting success. Learning objectives provide a

Table 3-15
Typical Reaction Objectives

After this meeting, participants should have positive ratings on the following issues:

- Relevance of the meeting to my work
- Importance of the meeting to my success
- Effectiveness of speakers
- Appropriateness of meeting topics
- Amount of new information
- Motivational aspect of the meeting
- Planned use of the concepts/advice
- Recommend the meeting to others
- Value of the meeting to me
- Location of the meeting
- Facilities
- Service of the staff

Table 3-16
Developing Reaction Objectives

The best Reaction Objectives:
- Identify issues that are important and measurable
- Are attitude-based, clearly worded, and specific
- Specify the participant's reaction to the content
- Underscore the link between attitude and the success of the meeting
- Represent a satisfaction index from key stakeholders
- Can predict meeting success

Key questions are:
- How relevant is the meeting?
- How important is the meeting?
- Will you use the content?

---

focus for participants, indicating what they must know and learn to do. Developing learning objectives is straightforward as shown in Table 3-18.

Application and Implementation Objectives

As the meeting is conducted, application and implementation objectives clearly define what is expected and sometimes to what level of performance. Application

Table 3-17
Typical Learning Objectives

After completing the meeting, participants will be able to:
- Identify five new technology trends explained at the conference
- Name at least three new technology trends in this field
- Name the six pillars of the division's new strategy
- Identify the six features of the new ethics policy
- Describe at least five products or services from the exhibit hall
- Demonstrate the use of each software routine in the standard time
- Use problem solving skills when faced with a problem
- Know if they are eligible for the early retirement program
- Score 75 or better on the new-product quiz
- Demonstrate success with all five customer interaction skills
- Explain the value of diversity in a work group
- Document and submit suggestions for award consideration
- Score at least 9 out of 10 on a sexual harassment policy quiz

Table 3-18
Developing Learning Objectives

Learning objectives are critical to measuring learning because they:
- Communicate expected outcomes from learning
- Describe competent performance that should be the result of learning
- Focus on learning for participants

The best learning objectives:
- Describe behaviors that are observable and measurable
- Are outcome-based, clearly worded, and specific
- Specify what the participant must do as a result of the meeting
- May have three components:
  - Performance—what the participant will be able to do during the meeting
  - Condition—circumstances under which the participant will perform the task
  - Criteria—degree or level of proficiency that is necessary to perform the job

Three types of learning objectives are:
- Awareness—familiarity with terms, concepts, and processes
- Knowledge—general understanding of concepts and processes
- Performance—ability to demonstrate a skill, at least at a basic level

levels are similar to learning objectives but reflect actual use in the participant's work or life situation. They also involve specific milestones, indicating when part or all of the process is implemented. Table 3-19 shows typical application objectives.

Table 3-19
Typical Application Objectives

When the meeting content is implemented:

- 50% of conference attendees follow up with at least one contact from the conference
- Pharmaceutical sales representatives have communicated adverse effects of a specific prescription drug to all physicians in their territories
- Sales and customer service representatives use all five interaction skills with at least half the customers
- At least 99.1% of software users will follow the correct sequences after three weeks of use
- Within one year, ten percent of employees will submit documented suggestions for saving costs
- The average 360-degree leadership assessment score will improve from 3.4 to 4.1 on a five-point scale
- 95% of high-potential employees will complete individual development plans within two years
- Employees will routinely use problem-solving skills
- Sexual harassment activity will cease within three months after the zero-tolerance policy is implemented
- 80% of employees will use one or more of the three cost-containment features of the health-care plan

Application objectives are important because they describe the expected outcomes in the intermediate area—the time between the learning and the impact that the learning will deliver. Application and implementation objectives describe how things should change or the state of the workplace after the content is implemented. They provide a basis for the evaluation of on-the-job changes and individual performance. Table 3-20 shows the key issues involved in developing application objectives.

Impact Objectives

Meetings and events should drive one or more business impact measures. Impact objectives represent key business measures that should be improved as the application and implementation objectives are achieved. Impact objectives are critical to measuring business performance because they define the ultimate expected outcomes of the meeting. They describe business-unit performance that should be connected to it. Above all, impact objectives emphasize achieving bottom-line results that key client groups expect and demand. Table 3-21 shows typical impact objectives.

Impact objectives may be based on measures such as sales, output, quality, cost, time, customer service, work climate, and job satisfaction. Table 3-22 shows the key issues when developing impact objectives.

Table 3-20
Developing Application Objectives

The best application objectives

- Identify behaviors, tasks, and actions that are observable and measurable
- Are outcome-based, clearly worded, and specific
- Specify what the participant will change as a result of the meeting
- May have three components:
  - Performance—what the participant has changed or accomplished at a specified follow-up time
  - Condition—circumstances under which the participant performed the task, procedures, or action
  - Criteria—degree or level of proficiency under which the task or job was performed

Key questions are:

- What new or improved *knowledge* was used on the job?
- What new or improved *skill* was applied on the job?
- What is the *frequency of skill* application?
- What new *tasks* will be performed?
- What new *steps* will be implemented?
- What *follow-ups* will be required?
- What new *action items* will be implemented?
- What new *procedures* will be implemented or changed?
- What new *guidelines* will be implemented or changed?
- What new *processes* will be implemented or changed?

ROI Objectives

The fifth level of objectives for meetings and events is the acceptable return on investment (ROI)—the financial impact. These objectives define the expected payoff from the meeting, and compare the cost of the meeting to the monetary benefits. An ROI objective is typically expressed as an acceptable return on investment percentage that compares the annual monetary benefits minus the cost, divided by the actual cost, and is multiplied by one hundred. A 0% ROI indicates a break-even meeting. A 50% ROI indicates that the cost of the meeting is recaptured, and an additional 50% "earnings" (50 cents for every dollar invested) is achieved.

The Importance of Specific Objectives

Developing specific objectives at different levels for meetings and events provides important benefits. First, they provide direction to the participants involved in making the meeting successful—to help keep them on track. Objectives define

Table 3-21
Typical Impact Objectives

After completion of actions from the meeting, the following conditions should be met:

- Personal productivity will increase by 5%.
- Pharmaceuticals, Inc., brand awareness should increase ten percent among physicians during the next two years.
- The average number of new accounts opened at Great Western Bank should increase from 300 to 350 per month.
- Tardiness at the Newbury foundry should decrease by 20% within the next calendar year.
- An across-the-board reduction in overtime should occur for front-of-house managers at Tasty Time restaurants in the third quarter of this year.
- Sales will increase overall by 12% in six months.
- Employee complaints should be reduced from an average of three per month to an average of one per month at Guarantee Insurance.
- The company-wide job satisfaction index should rise by two percentage points during the next calendar year.
- Sales expenses for all titles at Proof Publishing Company should decrease by 10% in the fourth quarter.

Table 3-22
Developing Impact Objectives

The best impact objectives:

- Must contain measures that are linked to the skills and knowledge gained as a result of the meeting
- Describe measures that are easily collected
- Are results-based, clearly worded, and specific
- Specify what the participant has accomplished in the business or work unit as a result of the meeting

Four types of impact objectives involving hard data are:

- Output-focused
- Quality-focused
- Cost-focused
- Time-focused

Three common types of impact objectives involving soft data are:

- Customer-service focused
- Work-climate focused
- Job-satisfaction focused

exactly what is expected at different timeframes and show the anticipated outcomes of the meeting. Objectives provide guidance for the speakers so that they
understand the goals and intended impact of the meeting. They also provide
information and motivation for the planners and developers as they see the
implementation and impact outcomes. In most meetings, multiple stakeholders
are involved and will influence the results. Specific objectives provide goals and
motivation for the stakeholders so that they see the gains that should be achieved.
Objectives provide important information to help the key sponsor groups clearly
understand how the landscape will look when the meeting is successful. Finally,
from an evaluation perspective, objectives provide a basis for measuring the
success of the meeting.

Case Study

The process described in this chapter can be overwhelming, particularly when
most of the tasks needed are not within the meeting professional's current duties.
However, the process does not have to be so burdensome, and there may be
others in the organization that can help with some of the initial analysis. The
key is to take steps, raise questions, to clearly understand why the meeting is
being conducted and what is desired from it. The following case study shows
how the corporate meetings and events staff worked with the human resources
function to present a series of sexual harassment prevention meetings involving
7,500 employees. This part of the case study reveals the upfront analysis that
was achieved.

Background

Faith Hospitals (FH) is a regional provider of a variety of healthcare services
through hospitals, HMOs, and clinics in a large metro area. FH has grown
steadily in the last few years and has earned a reputation as a progressive and
financially sound company. The non-supervisory employment level is at 6,844.
First- and second-level managers number 655, while the senior management team
numbers 41.

In the U.S., sexual harassment continues to grow as an important employee
relation's issue. Sexual harassment claims throughout the U.S. and in the health
care industry continue to grow, sparked in part by increased public awareness
of the issue and the willingness of the victims to register harassment complaints.
FH has experienced an increasing number of sexual harassment complaints, with
some of them converting to charges and lawsuits. The complaint record was
considered excessive by executives and represented a persistent and irritating
problem. In addition, FH was experiencing an unusually high level of turnover,
which appeared to be linked to sexual harassment.

Senior management, concerned about the stigma of continued sexual harassment complaints and the increasing cost of defending the company against claims,

instructed the Human Resources (HR) Vice President to take corrective and preventive action to reduce complaints and ultimately rid the workplace of any signs of harassment. The HR Vice President asked the corporate meeting and events department to schedule and conduct a series of meetings with all employees, but only if there is a lack of understanding and knowledge of the issue.

Initial Needs Assessment

In response to the request, the meeting planning staff conducted interviews with the EEO and Affirmative Action staff during which the magnitude of the problem and the potential causes were explored. Most of the staff indicated there appeared to be a significant lack of understanding of the company's policy on sexual harassment and what actually constitutes inappropriate or illegal behavior.

In addition to interviews, the complaints for the last year were examined by the EEO/AA representatives for issues and patterns. From an analysis of complaints, the typical person accused of sexual harassment was a supervisor and usually male. The typical victim of harassment was a non-supervisory and female. The analysis also revealed that the type of sexual harassment typically experienced at FH was defined by the EEOC as "an individual making unwelcome sexual advances or other verbal or physical conduct of a sexual nature with the purpose of, or that creates the effect of, unreasonably interfering with an individual's work performance or creating an intimidating, hostile, or offensive working environment." This type of harassment should be minimized by developing a clear understanding of FH's policy regarding harassment, and by teaching managers to identify illegal and inappropriate activity.

Exit interviews of terminating employees for the last year were reviewed by the HR staff to see if there was a link to sexual harassment. Approximately 11% of those departing employees identified sexual harassment as a factor in their decision to leave FH. Exit interview data were computerized and readily available. Because of the request to proceed with this project, the HR staff did not conduct a full-scale needs assessment. Instead, they augmented the input from the EEO/AA staff and exit interviews with ten randomly selected interviews with first-level supervisors to explore the level of understanding of the policy, inappropriate and illegal behavior, and the perceived causes of the increased complaint activity.

The Meeting

Armed with input from ten supervisor interviews, detailed input from the EEO/AA staff, and information from company records, the major causes of the problem were identified. There was an apparent lack of understanding of (1) the company's sexual harassment policy and (2) what constitutes inappropriate and illegal behavior. In addition, there was an apparent insensitivity to the issue. As a result, a half-day meeting was designed for all employees and managers, in separate sessions. The objectives of the meetings were to enable participants to:

- Understand and administer the company's policy on sexual harassment
- Identify inappropriate and illegal behavior related to sexual harassment
- Ensure that the workplace is free from sexual harassment
- Reduce the number of sexual harassment complaints

Because of the implications of this issue, it was important for the information to be discussed with all employees so that there would be no misunderstanding about the policy or inappropriate behavior. The meeting design was typical, using a combination of purchased and internally developed materials. The half-day meetings were conducted over a 45-day period with seventeen sessions, involving all employees. Managers attended a separate meeting, with two of the seventeen sessions devoted to them. HR managers and coordinators served as meeting facilitators.

HOW TO MAKE THE TRANSITION

Early in this chapter, the challenges involved with having the meeting aligned with the organization and individual needs were clearly defined. This approach represents a tremendous shift for meeting professionals. As an ending point in this chapter, some practical advice is needed on how this change can be accomplished within the resources and responsibilities of the meeting professional. When a meeting or event is requested or suggested that may appear to be unclear, unnecessary, or out of alignment with the organization, taking these steps might be helpful to change the request so that it is more aligned with organizational goals:

1. Raise issues about the business case for the meeting and other questions that were addressed in this chapter. These questions should not be threatening, demanding, or annoying, but merely raising issues to point toward a more successful meeting.
2. Entice the requester with higher levels of evaluation than is customarily offered. Using Figure 3-1 from this chapter, the requester can be shown that it is possible to measure meetings credibly beyond the current levels of measurement. Most sponsors have not seen evaluations beyond reaction measures that are collected at the end of a meeting. This enticement often leads sponsors and clients (those who pay for the meeting) to ask for at least an impact evaluation (connected to the business measures) or occasionally an ROI. If this is desired, then the logical next question is: What are the impact objectives and the business needs? Figure 3-1 may encourage the client to think through the process in more detail.
3. Show them that the evaluation can be done at multiple levels with case studies, comments, processes, tips, and the experience of others. Essentially, the meeting professional must educate the requester about what is being done and can be done to show the contribution of meetings.

4. Consider having short briefings about measurement and evaluation, including ROI. Show the requester that the system is there and has been adopted by MPI to move the industry toward results-based processes.

5. Above all, do what is within the current responsibilities of a meeting professional. Most professionals do not need to get permission to do a better job at Levels 0, 1, and 2. This is all part of planning an effective meeting. When this is more clearly presented, it lays a foundation for higher levels of analysis.

6. Be prepared to take baby steps with this process. This is a significant change in the way that the industry conducts business, and this change will take time. One person can make a difference, even at the lowest level in the meetings and events chain.

The challenge for meeting professionals is to do some things in a different way. An entire industry can be changed when individuals take actions one at a time. It is up to each planner.

FINAL THOUGHTS

This chapter outlines the beginning point in the ROI Methodology. It shows how meetings and events can be structured from the beginning, with detailed needs identified, ultimately leading to developing meeting objectives at six levels. This kind of detail ensures that the meeting is aligned with individual and business needs and is results-based throughout the process. Without this analysis, the meeting runs the risk of failing to deliver the value that it should, or not aligning with one or more business objectives. These steps take time but are essential for success. They are systematic and structured. When followed in a disciplined and determined way, they can make a meeting highly successful.

REFERENCE

Langdon, D., Whiteside, K., and McKenna, M. (Eds). *Intervention Resource Guide: 50 Performance Improvement Tools*. San Francisco, CA: Jossey-Bass Pfeiffer, 1999.

CHAPTER 4

Measuring Inputs and Indicators

The first of the different types of data presented in this book, briefly described in Chapter 2, is presented in this chapter. Inputs and indicators are the first step in capturing data for meetings and events evaluations. For some meeting and event planners, this is the principal source of data collected. For example, reports published by various magazines and associations in the industry, including MPI and PCMA, are dominated with this type of data. This chapter highlights some of the more common measures, including monitoring the types of events held and the number of meetings, events, exhibitors, people, hours, topics, and requests. It also explores the importance of tracking the costs in a variety of ways and presents how meetings and events have been managed.

THE IMPORTANCE OF MEASURING INPUTS AND INDICATORS

While debate exists regarding the importance of this level of data, few would suggest that it is not needed. Inputs and indicators are an important first step in the analysis, and these data show insight, commitment, support, and the scope for the meeting or event. This is particularly helpful for companies, organizations, and associations where the commitment is low. Often, executives in these organizations boast about the amount of commitment to meetings, indicating statistics—such as the total number of participants, the number of days or hours, and the cost per participant—to show the amount of resources allocated to this effort.

This level of data represents the most common benchmarking data—they are easy to count. In some organizations and associations, they must be counted because they are part of the budget and cost-control processes. Tracking inputs provides an opportunity to show who participates by location, organization, occupation, area, topic, and a variety of other areas. This helps clients understand who attends, identify gaps, and make adjustments as needed.

Another consideration is the way that investments in meetings and events are managed and used. A variety of efficiencies can be captured, indicating the extent to which processes are streamlined, deadlines and cycle times are met, and the planning function is operated on a lean basis, with a constant focus on improving efficiencies and effectiveness. This responsiveness to clients is often an important measure of customer service.

Planners and organizers must know how much money is spent on meetings and events. Many organizations calculate this expenditure and make comparisons with those of other organizations, although comparisons may be difficult due to the different basis for cost calculations. The cost per participant for one meeting could be compared with the cost per participant for a similar meeting. Huge differences may signal a problem. Also, costs associated with marketing or registration could be compared with those of other meetings to develop cost standards.

Input Categories

Several major input categories are needed to show the costs and efficiencies of meetings. Some overlap with the different categories may occur, but for the most part, they stand alone.

Tracking Meetings and Events—Topics and Themes

One of the most basic measures is tracking the number of meetings and events that have been organized—often by types. Different topics and themes can be tracked—for example, business development conferences, compliance meetings, and management retreats. Tracking can also be maintained with categories for business types, such as corporate or association meetings, professional or educational conferences. Tracking in this way shows the full scope of what types of meetings and events meeting professionals are conducting using logical categories.

Tracking People

The most obvious place to start with input is tracking the people involved in meetings and events. Several measures may be important to show the variety of the audience. The first measure, total number attending, is the actual number of people participating in a meeting or event. This can also be expressed as a percent of some target group or potential audience. The number of people can be divided into different categories, as well. For example, showing participants involved in meetings and events by job, industry, age, gender, race, and other categories may be helpful in marketing and coverage issues.

Mike Johnson advocates reporting activities and efforts in this area along six categories.

- Twinkies (still at college and under 20)
- Point 'n Clickers (20 to 25)
- Generation X (25 to 35)
- Middle-aged and Manic (35 to 45)

- Growing old Frantically (45 to 55)
- Grey Tops (55 and over).

While this may be a bit overboard for some, it underscores the importance of presenting data by key groups. Some of these groups represent important challenges for the meetings and events industry. The Point 'n Clickers and Generation X will need different types of learning approaches than the older generations. Some will prefer on site activity while others will prefer online learning (Johnson, 2002).

Another way to count people is to divide them by gender. Some organizations and associations want to ensure that upward mobility exists for all employees, particularly females. The glass ceiling is still alive and well in many organizations and to prepare females for opportunities will require not only appropriate meetings and events but an appropriate number of female participants. Extending beyond gender and providing the numbers of participants in meetings and events by diversity categories (e.g. race, national origin) are important considerations.

Tracking Duration

Consistent with tracking people would be the hours or days involved in meetings and events, a common measure for benchmarking. Breaking down the number of hours into job, job groups, and even functional areas may be more meaningful. Still others track the number of hours involved in the meeting or event by group, including age, gender, and race. Some organizations may track the total hours of meetings and events to create an impressive figure of how much time is consumed by participants' involvement in these activities.

Still other organizations make a commitment for an average number of hours per person. In some situations this is necessary, but in others it may create more activity than change. For example, if the employees in an organization must spend a certain number of hours in compliance meetings, then these data are helpful as it shows the extent to which the organization is in compliance. An association sometimes offers continuing education units (CEU) for its meetings, and this causes the number of meeting hours to be an important issue. The participants then can use the CEUs to continue or achieve a certification or recognition.

On the other extreme, requiring a certain number of hours in meetings for the sake of having the involvement may create more activity than actual change or results. In this situation, participants may be required to attend a meeting that they would prefer not to attend or that they do not need to attend just to reach some goal for the number of hours per person. Fortunately, this is not a common practice for most corporate meetings and events function.

Tracking Coverage

Another important way to track people and hours is to track the coverage by jobs, job groups, functional areas, or types of customers. For example, tracking

Table 4-1
Company Data by Job Category

Job Category	Percent of Meetings and Events spent on ... (%)
Executives	10
Managers (Exempt)	31
Professionals (Exempt)	43
Non-Exempt	16

coverage may involve tracking the numbers and hours spent in the meeting or event by individuals who are in the critical job categories. Still another way is to show the breakdown of coverage by people and hours according to the different functions of the organization, beginning with research and development and continuing through sales, marketing, and customer support. Association planners may track attendance by type of member.

Another way to express coverage is by specific job levels. For example, Table 4-1 shows some data taken from a large technology company. This shows the meetings and events by four general groups: executives, managers, professional, and non-exempt employees. Further detail can be provided on an individual basis to show where the budget goes. Many organizations are concerned about particular job groups, for example the sales and marketing staff. If an individual job category is critical to an organization, perhaps this important group should receive most of the budget.

Since meetings are often aligned with strategic objectives, coverage can focus on them. The total number of hours spent on and the number of people attending the meeting can show current alignment with strategy. When certain strategic objectives have little or no coverage, immediate action must occur to devote resources to them.

Finally, another way to show coverage by people and hours is to focus on particular operational problems. For example, one organization experienced serious customer service problems. Several meetings were held, with a focus on improving customer service. The number of people and the number of hours involved in the meetings were presented as a measure of commitment to customer satisfaction.

Tracking Requests

An often overlooked tracking issue is to indicate the percent of the meetings that are requested for various reasons. As discussed in Chapter 3, some meetings are implemented for the wrong reasons, or at least questionable ones. By coding each project based on how it originated, some insight can be gained about why meetings are conducted.

Table 4-2 shows the tracking of reasons for meetings and events at a major oil company. What is revealing in this example is that over fifty percent of the

Table 4-2
Tracking the Reasons for Meetings and Events

1. A needs analysis was conducted to determine need.	3%
2. Required: compliance or regulation.	19%
3. A serious problem is tackled.	13%
4. Management requests it.	31%
5. The meeting is based on a trend, hot topic, or book.	16%
7. The meeting supports new policies, practices, and procedures.	3%
8. Meetings and events management thought it was needed.	5%
9. Supports new equipment or technology.	7%
10. Supports improvement processes such as Six Sigma, transformation, continuous process improvement, etc.	3%
Total	100%

meetings were implemented for questionable reasons. (i.e., reasons 4, 5, and 8). This is not to suggest that management requests are inappropriate, but as the material in Chapter 3 clearly indicated, sometimes, the analysis is incomplete and the meeting may not be needed or as clearly focused as it should be. Obviously, implementing a meeting based on a trend or hot topic or because the meetings and events staff think it should be offered are questionable reasons for a meeting. Unfortunately in this example, a very small number of meetings were implemented after an analysis of the situation that led to a need for a meeting.

With this tracking over time, the meetings and events staff and executives can see this critical input information and how it is changing or should change in the future.

Tracking Technology Use

Another area that should be tracked is the extent to which the internet and technology are used in the meetings and events industry. One of the most interesting and mysterious processes is the extent to which virtual meetings are being used. Although significant progress is being made in transforming from traditional, face-to-face meetings to more technology-based delivery, progress has been slower than most experts forecasted. For an organization attempting to make dramatic shifts in delivery, this becomes an important area to monitor. Figure 4-1 shows how meetings have evolved over time, as reported by a large pharmaceutical company.

A virtual meeting takes place completely over the Internet, and the participants do not leave their workplace. Ground-based is where they go to a facility for a face-to-face meeting. Blended is a combination of both—an onsite meeting and other participants attend via the Internet or a portion of the meeting occurs over the Internet or the speakers present over the Internet. For meeting professionals

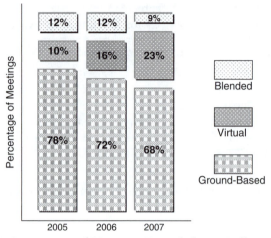

Figure 4-1. Percentage of Meetings Provided Via Different Methods.

attempting to make dramatic shifts in delivery, this becomes an important area to monitor. If the forecasts are correct, a much larger percent of meetings will fall in the virtual category in the future, although ground-based meetings will never disappear. For meeting professionals attempting to make dramatic shifts in delivery, this becomes an important area to monitor.

Tracking Costs

The cost of conducting meetings and events is increasing—creating more pressure to know how and why money is spent. The total cost is sometimes required, which means that the cost profile goes beyond the direct costs, including all indirect costs. Fully loaded cost information is used to manage resources, develop standards, measure efficiencies, and examine alternative delivery methods.

Tabulating meeting costs is an essential step in developing the ROI calculation, and these costs are used as the denominator in the ROI formula. Focusing on costs is just as important as focusing on benefits. In practice, however, costs are often more easily captured than benefits.

There are two key issues when tracking costs. First is the basic issue of understanding the amount of direct costs connected to meetings and events. In larger organizations, so many meetings and events are organized in the different areas that it becomes difficult to understand the total costs of this function. As a result, the first step for many organizations is to clearly understand the total costs of meetings and events, and this amount is staggering. For example, in one organization, the meetings and events budget was a little over $2 million. However, executives knew that other meetings and events were being organized by other regions and divisions. After a detailed tabulation, the total costs were over $10 million. This situation may not be unusual. Therefore, the first step is to understand the total direct costs.

Next, the indirect costs must be considered. Today, increased pressure to report all costs exists, or what is referred to as fully loaded costs. This takes the cost profile beyond direct costs and includes the time that participants are involved in meetings, including their benefits and other overhead. For years, management has realized that many indirect costs of meetings and events are accumulated. Now, for some meetings, management wants these costs included.

Communicating the costs without presenting the benefits is dangerous. Unfortunately, many meeting professionals have fallen into this trap for years. Costs are presented to management in many ingenious ways, such as the cost of the meeting, cost per participant, and cost per hour of meeting time. While these may be helpful for efficiency comparisons, presenting them without the benefits (or at least some plan to capture them) can cause problems. When most executives review meeting and event costs, a logical question comes to mind: What benefit was received from the meeting? This is a typical management reaction, particularly when costs are perceived to be too excessive. Because of this, some planners have developed a policy of not communicating cost data for a specific meeting unless the benefits can be captured and presented along with the costs, even if the benefit data are subjective and intangible. This helps maintain a balance between the two.

The sources of costs must be considered. The three major categories of sources are illustrated in Table 4-3. The meetings and events staff expenses usually represent a small percent of the costs and are sometimes transferred directly to the client or meeting sponsor. The second major cost category is the participant expenses, both direct and indirect. These costs are not identified in many budgets of meetings, but, nevertheless, reflect a significant amount. The third cost source is the payments made to external organizations. These include payments directly to hotels and conference centers, destination management companies, suppliers, and services used for the meeting. As Table 4-3 shows, some of these cost categories are often understated. The finance and accounting records should be able to track and reflect the costs from these three different sources. The process presented in a later chapter helps track these costs, as well.

The most important task is to define which specific costs are included in a tabulation of the meeting costs. Table 4-4 shows a complete list of costs for

Table 4-3
Sources of Costs

Source of Costs	Cost Reporting Issues
1. Staff expenses	A. Costs are usually accurate. B. Variable expenses may be underestimated.
2. Participant expenses (direct and indirect)	A. Direct expenses are usually not fully-loaded. B. Indirect expenses are rarely included in the costs.
3. External expenses (equipment and services)	A. Sometimes understated. B. May lack accountability.

Table 4-4
Recommended Cost Categories

Cost Item	Prorated*	Expensed
Needs Assessment		✓
Design, Development, and Production	✓	
Acquisition Costs	✓	
Administration Expenses		✓
Marketing/Promotion		✓
Legal Fees		✓
Insurance		✓
Registration Expenses		✓
Meeting Delivery:		
• Salaries/Benefits and/or Honoraria/Fees – Facilitators, Presenters, Entertainers, Meetings Staff, Production Staff, etc.		✓
• Meeting Materials (handouts, signage, decoration, etc.)		✓
• Travel (staff, meeting participants, facilitators, presenters, etc.)		✓
• Housing/Sleeping Rooms		✓
• Food & Beverage		✓
• Facility Rentals(s)		✓
• Audio Visual Rental and Services		✓
• Transportation		✓
• Translation and Interpretation		✓
• Exhibitions		✓
• Tips and Gratuities		✓
• Participant and Staff Salaries/Benefits – Contact Time		✓
• Participant and Staff Travel Time		✓
• Participant Preparation Time		✓
• Evaluation		✓
• Overhead	✓	

* In some situations, major expenditures may be prorated if they can be used in other meetings.

meetings and events. The final list involves decisions by the meetings and events staff and is usually approved by management. If appropriate, the finance and accounting staff may need to approve the list. More will be discussed on this topic in Chapter 9.

Tracking Efficiencies

Efficiency is an extremely important issue for meetings and events, particularly the larger ones. Efficiency is measured in different ways and from different viewpoints. One of the first measures is the efficiency of using the meetings and events staff, such as the number of meetings per planner. These data can also be misleading because outsourcing could make a big difference. The use of part-time planners changes the number as well, but it still represents a gross efficiency measure at the function level. While the goal is to have the number of meetings per planner as large as possible, a smaller number sometimes demonstrates a commitment to quality.

Efficiency data include the meeting hours provided per staff member. The hours provided is a reflection of how much content per staff is presented. The average cost per hour provided or the cost per participant shows the efficient use of funds. Several time measures are appropriate. The average time to conduct the initial analysis and assessment, the average time to design an hour of content, the average time to plan the meeting, and the total time from a request to a launch of a new meeting are possibilities.

Tracking Outsourcing

More companies and associations are moving to outsourcing part of, if not all their meetings and events functions. If that is the goal, tracking the extent to which outsourcing is used is helpful. The percent of the total meetings or events outsourced to external contractors compared to the percent conducted by the internal staff is one way to measure outsourcing. The percentage of meetings organized internally and externally is monitored to see if the goals are being met. These percentages vary significantly based on the philosophy of the organization and the success achieved in outsourcing.

Key Issues

It is fitting to end this chapter with several key issues that have been briefly discussed. Input and indicator data are the largest data set, but the least valuable to executives. Input data do not represent results. They only show what goes into the process and do not reflect outcomes.

Except for cost data, executives care little about this level of data. In a broad sense, they are curious about certain measures that represent volumes and efficiencies, but essentially, they want to see data that represent application, impact, and ROI. Therefore, the challenge is to select data sets that attract management attention, or those that emphasize key areas that are under consideration or need attention. In terms of the space and time used to present it, this data set should be minimized in reports to executives.

The most important value for this level of data is from the operational management perspective. These data represent costs, inputs, efficiencies, and other issues that are necessary to plan, organize, and manage the process. Ideally, these data are used by the operations part of the meetings and events team and used in a way that drives maximum effectiveness and efficiency.

Because of the sheer volume of this data, they must be automated as they are captured, integrated, and reported. Fortunately, many systems provide mechanisms for capturing most of the data sets described in this chapter. Because these data sets represent the greatest amount of data but represent the least value to executives, they must be captured in the most efficient way, thus, automation is critical.

Final Thoughts

This chapter is the first of seven that describe the different levels of data. At Level 0, inputs and indicators describe what goes into the process of conducting a meeting or event. An abundant amount of information is available that can be captured, analyzed, and reported to key stakeholders. These include data about the number of meetings, events, people, days, audiences, topics, and requests. In addition, tracking costs, efficiencies, and outsourcing are also important, as they help the meetings and events staff manage their resources carefully, consistently, and efficiently. The next chapter focuses on measuring reaction and perceived value.

Reference

Johnson, M. *Talent Magnet: Getting Talented People to Work For You.* (New York, NY: Prentice Hall, 2002).

CHAPTER 5

Measuring Reaction and Perceived Value

The next four chapters present ways to measure results data when evaluating meetings and events. This chapter focuses on measuring reaction and perceived value. Collecting this level of data at the end of the meeting is the first operational phase of the ROI Methodology. Participant feedback may represent powerful data to use when making adjustments and measuring success. Although several methods may be used to capture reaction and perceived value data—at the beginning and during the meeting—this chapter outlines the most common approaches for data collection and explores ways to use the information for maximum value.

IMPORTANCE OF MEASURING REACTION AND PERCEIVED VALUE

It would be difficult to imagine a meeting being conducted without collecting feedback from those involved in it. Collecting this type of data involves several key issues and audiences, making this one of the most important data collection steps in the process.

Customer Service

With the constant focus on customer service, measuring customer satisfaction with each meeting is important. Without continuous feedback from customers and favorable reactions, meetings and events will not succeed. The different customers groups involved in meetings and events are sources of input. The individuals who have the most direct role in the meeting, the participants, are very important customers. Ultimately, they are key stakeholders who must change processes, procedures, or thinking. In addition, they must learn new information, contacts skills, tasks, or behaviors to make the meeting successful. A negative reaction will inhibit these learning and application issues. Participant feedback is critical to making adjustments and changes in the meeting as it is implemented or for the next meeting.

The next key customer group is the speakers, the individuals who also play an important role in making the meeting successful. They facilitate the meeting processes and influence the participants, and feedback from them will be helpful to make adjustments.

Exhibitors, who display their products or services at a meeting are another key client group. They are concerned about meeting success from their perspective. The exhibitor needs to know how that exhibit contributes to the bottom line—its ultimate value.

The fourth group of key customers is perhaps the most important. It is the client who funds all or part of the meeting. This individual, or group of individuals, requested the meeting, supports the meeting, approves budgets, allocates resources, and ultimately lives with the meeting's success or failure. This important individual or group must be completely satisfied with the meeting—with his/her level of satisfaction being determined early, often, and at the end of the meeting and perhaps in a follow up.

The fifth group of key customers is the individuals on the sidelines and not directly involved, but they have an interest in the meeting. Sometimes called the supporters, they are concerned about the meeting and are usually supporting or assisting it in some way. Their perception of the meeting's success or potential success is important feedback because this group will be in a position to influence the meeting's continuation and development.

In short, customer satisfaction is critical to the meeting's success and must be collected and used. Sometimes, a new meeting is planned for several repeat presentations. Early feedback is necessary so that adjustments can be made. Doing this helps avoid misunderstandings, miscommunications, and more important, misappropriations. There must be an important link between obtaining feedback, making changes, and reporting changes to the groups who provide the information. This survey-feedback-action loop is critical for any meeting.

Forecasting Capability

A recent application of reaction data is using them to predict the future success of a meeting using analytical techniques. This involves asking the participants of a meeting to estimate the application and, in some cases, the impact of that application. The reaction data become a forecast. Countless studies have been conducted to validate the correlation between reaction measures and application data. In this analysis, the reaction measures are taken as the meeting is conducted, and the success of the implementation is later judged using the same scales (e.g., a one to five rating). When positive, significant correlations are developed, reaction measures can have predictive capability.

For Some, This Is the Most Important Data

Because feedback data are important to a meeting's success, they should be collected for every meeting. They have become some of the most important data collected. Unfortunately, for most meetings, success is only measured by reaction data.

While reaction data are and should be an important measure, they should be included with other measures in the value chain. As this book clearly shows, feedback data are only one of the seven types of data (including costs).

Compare Data with Other Meetings

Some organizations collect reaction data using standard questions, and the data are then compared with data from other meetings so that norms and standards can be developed. This is particularly helpful in the early stages of a new meeting that will be repeated. Reaction data are collected and compared. Some firms even base part of the planning team's success on the level of participant satisfaction, making reaction data important to the success of every meeting.

Macro-Level Scorecards

One of the important reasons for collecting data at each level is to create a scorecard for the success of all meetings. While the evaluation of one meeting is a micro-level scorecard of performance, a macro-level scorecard shows the performance of all meetings and events organized by the meetings and events function. An important and necessary part of the scorecard is reaction data. Unfortunately, all the reaction data collected should not be included in the macro-level scorecard but only small parts of it, as will be described later.

DATA COLLECTION ISSUES

Several important issues can affect data collection and are discussed here. These issues represent the fundamentals and concerns that must be addressed along the way.

Sources of Data

When considering possible data sources for feedback on the success of a meeting, several categories can be used in all meetings as described earlier:

1. *Participants* are key stakeholders who must attend and be involved. Feedback is critical to making adjustments and changes in the future.
2. *Exhibitors* are an important source when exhibits are involved.
3. *Speakers and facilitators* also play a role in a successful meeting and their input is helpful.

4. *Sponsors* are because of their contribution to the success of the meeting and the meeting's continuation.
5. The *client*, who funds or approves the meeting, must be completely satisfied with it.
6. Other supporters (or stakeholders) of the meeting may provide input (for example, top executives or the participants' managers).

Content versus Non-Content

Capturing reaction data about the content of the meeting is an important consideration. Too often, feedback data reflect aesthetic issues and may not include much information about the substance of the meeting. For example, a planner needed to show the value of a marketing meeting, for relationship managers, who have direct contact with customers. This meeting was designed to discuss product development, marketing, and business development strategies. Table 5-1 shows the comparison of content vs. non-content issues that can be explored on a reaction questionnaire.

The traditional way to evaluate these activities is to focus on non-content issues. As the table shows, the column to the left indicates areas important to activity surrounding the meeting, but few measures reflect the value achieved from it. The column on the right shows a focus on content with only minor input on non-content issues, such as the facilities and service provided. This does not imply that the quality of the service, the atmosphere of the event, and the location of the meeting are not important. These issues will be taken care of and

Table 5-1
Comparison of Content versus Non-Content

Focus on Non-Content Issues	Focus on Content Issues
Demographics	Facilities
Location	Service
Transportation	Timing of meeting
Registration	Relevance of materials
Logistics	Importance of content to my success
Hotel service	Appropriate use of time
Media	Amount of new information
Food	Quality of speakers
Breaks and refreshments	Perceived value of meeting
Cocktail reception	Contacts made
Speakers	Planned use of material
Materials/topics	Forecast of impact
Overall satisfaction	Overall satisfaction

addressed appropriately. A more important data set tracks information about the perceived value of the meeting, the importance of the content, and the planned use of material—all indicators of a successful meeting. This example underscores the tremendous shift occurring in the meetings and events industry: a move from measuring entertainment to measuring reaction; learning; and sometimes, application, impact, and ROI.

The Deceptive Feedback Cycle

Sometimes, too much reliance is placed on overall reaction data, particularly when they are used as the principal tool for evaluating planners. It is easy to manipulate the overall satisfaction rating, which is often referred to as a "smile" or "enjoyment" rating. Superb lunches, lavish cocktail parties, and a great golf event will almost guarantee high ratings. The objective is for the participants to enjoy the meeting, and the planner is the centerpiece of that enjoyment. As shown in Figure 5-1, if the participants enjoy the meeting, the overall satisfaction ratings are often high. Therefore, planners are primarily rewarded on those ratings. When this is the case, they naturally focus their actions on enjoyment—making the meetings they plan enjoyable experiences. Certainly, nothing is wrong with enjoying the meeting. The problem lies in the excessive use of this measure, "Overall, how satisfied are you with the meeting?" Satisfaction data do not correlate with important outcome measures. A certain level of enjoyment and satisfaction is an absolute must. However, planners risk focusing on entertainment only and short-changing the content. As some professional planners say, "We quickly migrate to the business of entertaining instead of the business of learning, change management, or business alignment."

To avoid this, planner effectiveness should also be evaluated on learning measures and, occasionally, application and impact measures. This keeps a balanced perspective and prevents an over-reliance on reaction data. More evaluations should focus on content-related issues. The value of overall reaction data has

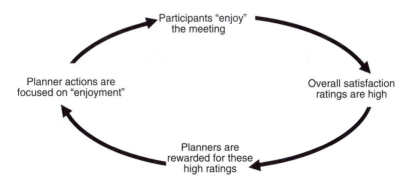

Figure 5-1. The Deceptive Feedback Cycle.

to be constantly put into perspective. For the content developer, speakers, and participants, reaction data are important, but from the point of view of the client and sponsor, these data may not be very valuable.

Key Areas for Feedback

Many topics are targets for feedback because so many issues and processes are involved in a typical meeting. Feedback is needed for almost every major issue, step, or process to make sure outcomes are successful. Table 5-2 shows the typical areas of feedback for most meetings.

Table 5-2
Detailed Reaction Data

Data Category	Rationale for Collecting	Specific Data Item
Participant demographics	Audience served versus needs Trends in attendance Future planning Diversity	Job/role/occupation Department/division Education Experience Tenure Age/gender Reason for participation
Logistics and service	Facility changes Customer satisfaction	Location Room Comfort Communication Access to food and refreshments
Readiness	Appropriate participant Proper timing Ready to learn	Appropriate experience level Prerequisites Motivation to learn Opportunity to use the concepts Timing of meeting
Objectives	Proper objectives Progress with objectives	Clarity of objectives Appropriateness of objectives Success with objectives
Meeting materials	Appropriate content Design changes Stimulate interest	Usefulness of materials Appearance of materials Amount of new information
Speakers	Speaker performance data Complaints with speakers	Experience level Knowledge and expertise Presentation Responsiveness to participants Involvement of participants Pacing of presentation
Delivery/media	Comparison of types of media Effectiveness of media	Delivery effectiveness Media effectiveness Activities/exercises

Table 5-2
(Continued)

Data Category	Rationale for Collecting	Specific Data Item
Value of content	Alignment with business Adjustments to content Design changes	Business alignment Why meeting was selected Relevance of content to job Importance to job success Motivational aspect Connection to strategies Satisfaction with content
Networking	Networking success	Number of contacts Quality of contact Level of interaction
Special events	Effectiveness	Success of activity Importance to meeting content
Social activities	Effectiveness	Applicability to meeting content
Value of meeting	Marketing Pricing Commitment Support	Good investment in me Good investment of my time Fair price for the meeting Overall satisfaction the meeting
Planned use	Follow-up potential Adjust expectation Transfer of learning Support of meetings	Planned actions Intent to use Barriers to use Enablers of use Recommend to others Willingness to provide data
Marketing and registration	Source of enrollment Decision-making process Pricing Ease of registration	Source of enrollment Decision-making process Pricing Registration process
Future needs	Planning meetings	Additional needs Other meetings
Open comments	Opportunity to identify unknown issues	Other comments Suggestions for improvement

For the most part, this table is self explanatory. It shows the typical data categories for collecting reaction data from meetings. Collecting data on all the categories would be too much because the survey or questionnaire would be too long. A few important areas are discussed in this section.

Meeting Content. Content includes the principles, steps, facts, ideas, and situations presented in the meeting. The content is critical and participant input is necessary.

Amount of New Information.   In too many situations, meetings simply rehash old material. Sorting out what is considered new information and what is old information can be helpful.

Meeting Materials.   The handouts, workbooks, job aids, books, and other materials should be evaluated regarding their applicability, usefulness, and relevance to the meeting. This is helpful in deciding if adjustments should be made or if materials should be added or deleted from the meeting.

Activities and Exercises.   Often, exercises are provided for participants—some before, some during, and others after the meeting. An assessment of the effectiveness of these assignments and how they relate to meeting objectives is important.

Presentation and Delivery.   Because many different ways are available for delivery, participants should provide insight into the appropriateness and effectiveness of the delivery method. Whether the delivery is by lectures, case studies, discussions, exercises, or simulations, understanding the effectiveness of the process from the perspective of the consumer is important.

Facilities and Environment.   Sometimes, the environment is not conducive to learning, and feedback can identify issues that may need attention. This type of data includes the actual meeting space, the comfort level, the learning environment, and several other environmental issues, such as temperature, lighting, and noise. A word of caution: if nothing can be done about the meeting environment, then data should not be collected about it.

Speaker Evaluation.   Perhaps one of the most common uses of reaction data is to evaluate the speaker. If properly implemented, helpful feedback data can be provided so that adjustments can be made to increase effectiveness in the future. The issues usually involve experience, presentation, level of involvement, and pacing of the process. Some cautions need to be taken since speaker evaluations can sometimes be biased—either positively or negatively—and other evidence may be necessary to provide an overall assessment of performance.

Relevance.   Participants want to explore information, knowledge, and skills that are relevant to their work. Because of this, assessing the relevance of the material to the participants' current work or future responsibilities is helpful. This type of data focuses on a critical issue, helping ensure that the information, skills, and knowledge will be used later. If they are relevant, more than likely, they will be used.

Importance.   Participants need to see that the content is important to their job success. This provides a little of "What's in it for me?"

Intent to Use Material. Asking participants about their intentions to use the material can be helpful. The extent of planned use can be captured along with the expected frequency of use and the anticipated level of effectiveness when using the information, skills, and knowledge. Intent to use usually correlates to actual use and is important for enhancing the transfer of learning to work or life use.

Planned Improvements. Sometimes, collecting specific, detailed information about how participants will use what they have learned is helpful. This input is often provided on a supplementary form and contains a sequence of questions about the intended use and the consequence of use. Supplementary questions are not appropriate for every meeting, but they could be helpful in many settings when the participants are in sales, professional, supervisory, managerial, or technical positions. When completed, the responses provide an opportunity to show the anticipated value of the meeting.

Overall Evaluation. Almost all organizations capture an overall satisfaction rating, which reflects the participant's overall satisfaction with the meeting. While this may have very little value in terms of understanding the real issues and the meeting's relationship to future success, comparing one meeting to another and with meetings over time may be helpful. Because the data can be easily misinterpreted and misused, the other areas may provide a better understanding of needed adjustments or improvements.

Data Collection Timing

The timing of data collection revolves around events connected to the meeting. Any event or activity is an appropriate time to collect data, beginning with pre-meeting data collection and progressing to end-of-meeting collection.

Sometimes, collecting pre-assessment data is helpful. Although this may not be common, it is a way to solicit attitudes and perceptions about topics or issues that will be discussed during the meeting. Also, pre-assessments may involve learning assessments that can be used to understand the degree to which participants currently understand the content. Therefore, pre-assessments may contain reaction and learning questions.

Data collection timing during meetings that occur over multiple days is important. For example, if a meeting lasts three days, waiting until the end of the third day to collect feedback data may be inappropriate. By then, participants may not be able to judge some of the issues, events, and processes that occurred earlier. Capturing daily feedback is better. At the end of each day, feedback is collected about the material covered on that day, including the pace and flow of the session, the degree of involvement of the participants, and the content's value.

Another approach is to collect data immediately after each session, giving the participants an opportunity to judge key issues while the material is fresh in their minds. Still another approach is evaluating different events separately. For example, if a tour is connected to the meeting, the tour may need to be evaluated separately. Perhaps participants attend a separate networking event in the evening and are given an opportunity to provide quick feedback at the beginning of the next day. Even with daily or event-based feedback, capturing the end-of- meeting data is still important to evaluate the entire meeting experience.

QUESTIONNAIRES AND SURVEYS

Questionnaires and surveys are the most common data collection methods for measuring reaction. Questionnaires and surveys come in all sizes, ranging from short reaction forms to detailed, multi-paged instruments. They can be used to obtain subjective data about participants' reactions as well as to document data for future use in an ROI analysis. With their versatility and popularity, properly designing questionnaires and surveys is critical.

Several basic types of questions are available. Depending on the purpose of the evaluation, the questionnaire or survey may contain any or all of the types of questions shown in Figure 5-2.

The key is to select the question or statement that is most appropriate for the information needed. A dichotomous question (yes/no) and the numerical scale (1–5) are typical reaction measurement types. Essentially, the individual indicates the extent of agreement with a particular statement, providing an opinion of a varying degree. Still, open-ended questions can be used, particularly when asking about specific problem or opportunity areas. Checklists, multiple-choice questions, and ranking scales are more appropriate for measuring learning and application, which are described in later chapters.

Surveys are a type of questionnaire but focus on participant's attitudes. Surveys have many applications for measuring reaction in meetings designed to improve work, policies, procedures, the organization, or even the team. Measuring reaction is a complex task in which attitudes are crucial. Measuring an attitude precisely is impossible, since information gathered may not represent a participant's true feelings. Also, the behavior, beliefs, and feelings of an individual will not always correlate. Over time, attitudes tend to change, and several factors can affect an individual's attitude. Recognizing these shortcomings, getting a reasonable assessment of an individual's attitude about a meeting is possible.

Designing Questionnaires/Surveys

Survey and questionnaire design is a simple and logical process. Poorly designed questionnaires/surveys are confusing, frustrating, and potentially embarrassing. The following steps will help ensure that a valid, reliable, and effective instrument is developed:

1. *Determine the information needed.* The first step of any instrument design is to itemize the topics, issues, and success factors. Questions are developed later. Developing this information in outline form is helpful in grouping related questions.

1. Open-Ended Questions:

What problems will you encounter when attempting to use the knowledge or information in this meeting?

2. Checklist:

For the following list, check all the business measures that may be influenced by this meeting.

☐ Revenue	☐ Cost Control
☐ Productivity	☐ Cycle Time
☐ Quality	☐ Customer Satisfaction
☐ Efficiency	☐ Job Satisfaction

3. Dichotomous Question (Yes/No Responses)

As a result of this meeting, I have a better understanding of my responsibilities for customer service.

Yes ☐   No ☐

4. Numerical Scale

	Strongly Disagree	1	2	3	4	5	Strongly Agree
A. This meeting is relevant to my work.		☐	☐	☐	☐	☐	
B. This meeting is important to my success.		☐	☐	☐	☐	☐	

5. Multiple Choice Question:

Which of the following describes the networking in this meeting?

a. Too little
b. Too much
c. Just right

6. Ranking Scales:

The following list contains six important factors that will influence the ultimate success of this meeting. Place a one (1) by the item that is most influential, a two (2) by the item that is second most influential, and so on. The item ranked six (6) will be the least influential item on the list.

Proper tools	_____	Technology	_____
My teams' culture	_____	Management support	_____
Communications	_____	Technical support	_____

Figure 5-2. Types of Questions or Statements.

2. *Select the type(s) of questions/statements.* Determine whether open-ended questions, checklists, dichotomous questions, multiple-choice questions, or a ranking scale is most appropriate for the purpose of the questions. Take into consideration the planned data analysis and variety of data to be collected.

3. *Develop the questions.* The next step is to develop the questions based on the types of questions planned and the information needed. The questions should be simple and straightforward enough to avoid confusion or lead the participant to a desired response. Terms or expressions unfamiliar to the participant should be avoided.
4. *Keep survey statements as simple as possible.* Participants need to understand the meaning of a statement or question. There should be little room for differing interpretations.
5. *Test the questions.* After the questions are developed, they should be tested for understanding. Ideally, the questions should be tested on a small sample of participants who will attend the meeting. If this is not feasible, the questions should be tested with individuals at approximately the same level of experience and education as the participants. Collect as much input and critique as possible, and revise the questions as necessary.
6. *Ensure that participant responses are anonymous.* Participants must feel free to respond openly to statements or questions. The confidentiality of their responses is of the utmost importance. If data are collected that can identify a respondent, then a neutral third party should collect and process the data.
7. *Design for easy tabulation.* In an attitude survey, yes/no or varying degrees of agreement and disagreement are the usual responses.
8. *Prepare a data summary.* A data summary sheet should be developed so data can be tabulated quickly for summary and interpretation. This step will help ensure that the data can be analyzed quickly and presented in a meaningful way.
9. *Develop the completed questionnaire or survey.* The questions should be finalized in a professional manner with proper instructions. After completing these steps, the questionnaire is ready to be administered.
10. *Communicate the purpose of the survey.* Participants tend to cooperate in an activity when they understand its purpose. When a survey is administered, participants should be given an explanation of its purpose and told what will be done with the information that they provide. Also, they should be encouraged to give correct and proper statements or answers.
11. *Identify comparisons.* Reactions by themselves are meaningless. They need to be compared to objectives or expectations, to data before or after the meeting, or compared to another group or meeting. Data may be compared to all employees, a division, a department, or previous meetings. For standard surveys, information may be available for similar meetings. In any case, specific comparisons should be planned before administering the survey.

Uniform responses make tabulation and comparisons easier. On a scale of strongly agree to strongly disagree, numbers are usually assigned to reflect the responses. For example, a one (1) may represent strongly disagree and a five (5) strongly agree. If only 15% rated a four or five on a pre-meeting survey followed by a post-meeting response of 85% for a four or five, a significant change in attitude is indicated. Some argue that a 5-point scale merely permits the respondent to select the midpoint and not to be forced to make a choice. If this is a concern, an even-numbered scale should be used.

Some organizations use existing surveys designed by external suppliers. This approach can save time in development and pilot testing. Most of the reputable companies producing and marketing surveys have designed them to be reliable and valid for their intended purposes. Also, outside surveys allow for results comparisons with other organizations within the same industry or in similar industries. For example, KnowledgeAdvisors (www.knowledgeadvisors.com), Guidestar Research (www.guidestarco.com), and IDNA Systems (www.idnausa.com) offer subscribers the opportunity to measure reaction data using a standard questionnaire. By administering a standard questionnaire, an organization can compare its results to over a million other data points generated by other organizations using the system.

Intensities

Because different meetings require different types of questions and questionnaires, thinking of three levels of reaction feedback instruments can be helpful. The first is a low intensity questionnaire and usually consists of five to eight questions, simply worded, requesting simple feedback. These are for meetings that are short in duration, ranging from a half day to one day, in which a need to get quick feedback exists. Using a scale that is suitable for automated analysis and avoiding written comments is essential for efficient scoring.

The second intensity is a moderate intensity questionnaire and would cover most of the reaction feedback. This is made up of ten to twenty questions and covers many of the issues described in Table 5-2. The questions are designed for easy tabulation—either using a 5-point Likert Scale, true/false questions, or multiple-choice questions. Few open-ended questions are included.

The third category is high intensity and is used to collect detailed feedback. This is designed for pilot meetings, where quality, in-depth feedback is needed. Sometimes, a detailed questionnaire of up to forty or fifty questions may be necessary. In-depth interviews or focus groups could also be used. The purpose is to secure high-quality, high-content feedback, requiring one hour or less of participant time. Because of its expense, this type of questionnaire is reserved for situations when this kind of feedback is critical to the meeting. Key introductions or the initial offerings to the first group of a pilot meeting would be a typical application of this type of data collection.

Samples Surveys

The design of the reaction surveys can vary considerable, as this chapter has shown. To show some appropriate questions for Level 1 (Reaction) evaluation, we have a sample of a low-intensity and a moderate-intensity reaction sheet.

Instructions: Circle the appropriate response to each statement below and add any comments you have about the meeting.

Question	Not at all	Somewhat	Definitely
1. Are the objectives of the meeting clear to you?	1	2	3
2. Did the facilitators know the materials?	1	2	3
3. Did you find the interaction and hands-on participation helpful?	1	2	3
4. Can you apply what you are learning to your current job?	1	2	3
5. Overall, did the meeting meet your expectations?	1	2	3

Comments:

Figure 5-3. Low-Intensity Reaction Survey at General Mills.

Figure 5-3 shows the low-intensity feedback and focuses on five issues in a meeting at General Mills (Phillips, Myhill, and McDonough 2007). Again, this is for use in short meetings and would have to be tailored to specific meetings, but for the most part would cover the issues across all content areas.

Figure 5-4 shows a moderate-intensity reaction survey and would be the dominant form of most meetings. It would be appropriate for one-day to one-week meetings. The more detailed the meeting, the more this survey may need to be adjusted.

Securing High Response Rates

For most reaction evaluations, questionnaires and surveys will be used. When an evaluation is planned, exploring a wide range of issues and details is tempting. However, asking for too much detail in the reaction questionnaire can negatively impact the response rate. The challenge, therefore, is to approach questionnaire and survey design and administration to attain maximum response rates. The following actions can be taken to ensure a successful response rate. Although the term questionnaire is used, the following also apply to surveys:

- Early in the process, let participants know that they will need to complete a questionnaire.
- Indicate how the data will be used and perhaps how it has been used in the past.
- Design for a quick response, usually not to exceed five to ten minutes.
- Make responding to the questionnaire easy, using forced-choice questions.
- Communicate the estimated amount of time required to complete the questionnaire.
- Ask participants if they would like to see a copy of the summary.
- Make it look professional.
- Collect the data anonymously.

More information on improving response rates will be discussed in Chapter 7.

Please circle the appropriate response to each statement, and add comments in the appropriate places.

Logistics and Service	Strongly Disagree				Strongly Agree
1. The meeting environment was appropriate.	1	2	3	4	5
2. The food and refreshments were satisfactory.	1	2	3	4	5
3. The registration and enrollment process was satisfactory.	1	2	3	4	5
4. The facility was appropriate.	1	2	3	4	5
Objectives and Readiness					
5. This meeting met the objectives	1	2	3	4	5
6. I will have an opportunity to use the information	1	2	3	4	5
Speaker					
7. The speaker was knowledgeable	1	2	3	4	5
8. The speaker was responsive to participants.	1	2	3	4	5
Value of Delivery					
9. Method of delivery was satisfactory.	1	2	3	4	5
Value of Content					
10. The content was relevant to my work.	1	2	3	4	5
11. The content is important to my success.	1	2	3	4	5
Value of Meeting					
12. This was a good investment in me.	1	2	3	4	5
13. This was a good investment of my time.	1	2	3	4	5
Planned Use					
14. I intend to use the information.	1	2	3	4	5
15. I can minimize the barriers to application.	1	2	3	4	5
16. I will recommend this meeting to others.	1	2	3	4	5

Comments

_____

_____

_____

_____

Figure 5-4. Moderate-Intensity Reaction Survey.

INTERVIEWS AND FOCUS GROUPS

Another data collection method is the interview, which is not used as frequently as questionnaires to capture reaction data. Interviews may be conducted by the planner or a third party. While more expensive than questionnaires, they are more versatile. They are more focused, allow for clarification, and provide an opportunity for probing.

The focus group may also be helpful when in-depth feedback is required. A focus group involves a small group discussion, including participants, and is facilitated by a person experienced with focus groups.

Interviews and focus groups should be used only when in-depth feedback about reaction is required (high intensity). They are only appropriate when significant consequences could result due to this feedback. For example, they would be used when a meeting is conducted on a pilot basis and serious adjustments may be needed to implement the process. Additional information on interviews and focus groups will be discussed in Chapter 7.

IMPROVING REACTION EVALUATION

There is no doubt that the value and use of reaction evaluation is in question. There is much debate on its usefulness, even to the point where some question if it should be collected at all (Boehle, 2006). The fact is that it is needed to complete the value chain and it does provide very valuable information as this chapter has shown.

In addition to the questionnaire design principles, several helpful guidelines can improve the effectiveness of reaction data.

Keep Responses Anonymous

Anonymous feedback is highly recommended. It allows the participants to be open with their comments, which can be helpful and constructive. Otherwise, the input can be biased and perhaps stifled because of concerns about the direct reaction from the speaker or facilitator.

Have a Neutral Person Collect the Feedback

In addition to anonymous responses, having a neutral person collect the feedback questionnaires may be helpful. For some meetings a representative of the sponsor will conduct the evaluation at the end, independent of the planner or speaker. This action increases the objectivity of the input.

Provide a Copy in Advance

For lengthy evaluation forms covering a lengthy meeting that spans several days, distributing the feedback questionnaire early in the meeting is helpful. This way, participants can familiarize themselves with the questions and statements. Participants can also address topics as they are covered and have more time to think through the issues. They should be cautioned, however, not to reach a final conclusion on general issues until the end of the meeting.

Explain the Purpose of the Feedback and How it Will be Used

Although this is sometimes understood, repeating where the information goes and how it is used within the organization is always a good idea. Some mystery still surrounds the use of feedback data. Restating the process in terms of the flow of data and the use of data can clarify this issue. Providing an example of how the data have been used to improve other meetings is also effective.

Explore an Ongoing Evaluation

For lengthy meetings, an end-of-the-meeting evaluation may leave participants unable to remember what was covered at what time. As described earlier, an ongoing evaluation can be used to improve this situation. One approach is for the evaluation forms to be distributed at the beginning of the meeting, and participants are instructed when and how to supply the information. After each topic is presented, participants are asked to evaluate it and the speaker. The participants can easily recall the information, and the feedback is more useful to evaluators. Another approach is to use a daily feedback form to collect input on pacing, degree of involvement, unclear items, etc.

Consider Quantifying Ratings

Some organizations attempt to solicit feedback in terms of numerical ratings. Although subjective, overall ratings can be used to monitor performance and make comparisons. With a large number of meetings repeated several times, these ratings can be useful for comparisons. In some cases, targets or norms are established to compare ratings. When using a norm scale, a rating that is usually considered good may prove to be quite low when compared to the norm of the factor being rated. Another caution is needed since these are subjective ratings. Comparing numerical values may create an impression that the data are objective. This point should be underscored in evaluation communications.

Collect Information Related to Improvement

Although obtaining realistic input on a feedback form related to profits, cost reductions, or cost avoidance is difficult, it may be worth the effort. The response may be surprising. Just a simple question may cause participants to concentrate on how they influence monetary values. A possible statement might be:

> Please estimate the monetary values that will be realized (i.e., increased sales, enhanced productivity, improved methods, reduced costs, cost avoidance, etc.), as a result of this meeting, over a period of one year. Please explain the basis of your estimate.

> _____

> _____

> Express as a per cent the confidence you place on your estimate. (0% = no confidence, 100% = certainty)._____

Additional detail on this concept will be provided in other works (Phillips and Phillips, 2007). This type of forecasting is included in technology design to support this methodology (www.idnausa.com).

Allow Ample Time for Completing the Form

A time crunch can cause problems when participants are asked to complete a feedback survey at the end of a meeting, particularly if they are in a hurry to leave. As a result, participants may not provide complete information and may be cut short in an effort to finish and leave. A possible alternative is to allow ample time for evaluation as a scheduled session before the end of the meeting. This evaluation session could be followed by a wrap-up of the meeting and the last speaker. A 10- to 15-minute session will provide an opportunity to enhance the quality and quantity of information.

Delayed Evaluation

An increasingly common approach is to delay the feedback evaluation until a later point. This avoids the pressure to provide part of the feedback during the meeting and reduces the influence of the excitement that participants' feel at the end of a meeting. After participants have returned to work, their evaluations may be more objective. However, a downside may be that the response rate might not be as high. To overcome this, some of the techniques described in this chapter can help create the desire to send more information. Also, the methods to improve response rates described in later chapters may be helpful as well. Realistically, a one hundred percent response rate is not necessary. A 70% response rate on a post-meeting collection is appropriate. Another risk with delaying Level 1 data collection is that, if too much time passes, the data may not be as useful in making immediate changes to the content, design, or facilitation.

Ask for Honest Feedback

Too often, planners and speakers do not explain the value of participant feedback. The facilitators must explain that they need honest feedback and that this feedback will be used to make things better. Participants should know that the information they provide is used to determine when something should be improved or changed. Their feedback will be used for adjustments and fine-tuning the meeting. When they are stressed to be open, honest, and candid with their feedback, this may make a difference in their response rates.

USING DATA

Unfortunately, reaction data are often collected and immediately disregarded. Too often, speakers and planners use the information to feed their egos and then let it quietly disappear into their files, forgetting the original purpose behind its collection. For successful evaluation, the information collected must be used to make adjustments or validate early success; otherwise, the exercise is a waste of time. A few of the common uses for collecting reaction and satisfaction data are summarized below.

Monitor Customer Satisfaction

Because this input is the principal measure taken from participants, it provides an indication of their reaction to, and satisfaction with, the meeting. Therefore, planners, developers, speakers, and sponsors will know the participants' level of satisfaction. Data should be reported to these key stakeholders.

Identify Strengths and Weaknesses

Feedback is extremely helpful in identifying weaknesses as well as strengths of a meeting. Participant feedback on weaknesses often leads to adjustments and changes in future meetings. Identifying strengths helps in future designs so that the strengths can be replicated. This may be the most important use of reaction data.

Evaluate Speakers

A common use of reaction data is to evaluate the speaker. If properly constructed and collected, helpful feedback data can be provided to speakers so that adjustments can be made to increase their effectiveness. Some caution needs to be taken, though, since participant evaluations can sometimes be biased. Other evidence is needed for an overall assessment of team performance.

Determine Participant Needs

An often overlooked reason to collect feedback is determining additional needs or future needs of participants. Often a particular meeting sparks interest or perhaps has shortcomings. Participation in the meeting may provide participants with the knowledge and experience to indicate additional needs or future needs for continuing their development. This feedback can drive other meetings or help enhance current meetings and may be some of the most legitimate analysis of participant needs.

Evaluate Planned Improvements

Feedback data from a questionnaire can provide a profile of planned actions and improvements. This can be compared with actions resulting from the meeting. This initial input provides a rich data source in terms of what participants may be changing or implementing because of their reactions to the meeting.

Develop Norms and Standards

Because reaction evaluation data can be automated and are collected in nearly all meetings, developing norms and standards becomes easy. Target ratings can be set for expectations; particular results are then compared to those norms and standards.

Link with Follow-up Data

In many cases, planned actions are often inhibited in some way through on-the-job barriers. When a follow-up evaluation is planned, linking reaction data with follow-up data may be helpful to see if planned improvements became reality. This validates the predictive relationship between reaction and application data.

Marketing Future Meetings

For some organizations, feedback data provide help for marketing future meetings. Quotes and reactions provide information that may be convincing to potential sponsors. Marketing brochures for meetings often contain quotes and summaries of feedback data.

Building the Macro-Level Scorecard

As described in Chapter 4, a macro-level scorecard, showing the combined contribution of all meetings, is recommended. This involves collecting data at each level to be included in the overall scorecard. Because up to thirty or forty items can be selected, the challenge is to select only those measures that have value to the senior management team. Therefore, the following measures are recommended:

- This is relevant to my work at the present time.
- This is important to me and my success.
- This information is new.
- I intend to use the information from this meeting.
- This is a good investment in me.

FINAL THOUGHTS

This chapter discusses the second set of measures of data reported in the ROI Methodology. Measuring reaction should be included in every meeting evaluation and is a critical part of success. Although data can be used in many ways, two important ones stand out. The first is making adjustments and changes. The second is reporting the level of satisfaction with the meetings and including this as one of the key types of data. Reaction data can be collected with questionnaires, surveys, interviews, and focus groups. By far, the questionnaire or survey is the most common instrument. Sometimes, a simple, one-page reaction questionnaire is appropriate. Whatever method is used, collecting data, reacting quickly, making adjustments, and summarizing the data for reporting to stakeholders is critical to a successful meeting. Using the data in constructive ways brings new life to the most common evaluation data.

REFERENCES

Boehle, S. "Are You too Nice to Train?" *Training*. August 2006, p. 16.

Phillips, J.J., M. Myhill, and J. McDonough. *Proving the Value of Meetings and Events: How and Why to Measure ROI*. Birmingham, AL: ROI Institute and MPI, 2007.

Phillips, P.P. and Phillips, J.J. *Show Me the Money: How to Determine ROI in People, Projects, and Programs*. San Francisco: Berrett-Koehler, 2007.

CHAPTER 6

Measuring Learning and Confidence

Learning is an important measure when evaluating meetings and events. Understanding how much learning has occurred is critical, particularly for meetings in which significant amounts of information, knowledge, and skills must be processed and put into action. In this case, measuring learning may be one of the greatest determinants of meeting success. This chapter focuses on simple, inexpensive techniques for learning measurement, often included with the reaction feedback.

THE IMPORTANCE OF MEASURING LEARNING

Several issues illustrate why learning is an important measure for successful meetings and events. Individually, each can justify the need to measure learning. Collectively, they provide motivation for taking a more rigorous approach to measuring the amount of information, knowledge, change, or skills learned during a meeting.

Learning versus Entertaining

The first reason for measuring learning focuses on the purpose of meetings and events. When meeting planners and event organizers are asked about the nature of their business or field, some interesting responses are provided. A recent article in Successful Meetings highlighted this issue (Welch, 2007). When pressed for the distinction of whether meetings and events represent entertainment or learning, planners quickly indicated that the business has to be learning and networking. If there is no learning, then the event was nothing but entertainment. This is an important issue because the measurement processes in place for the vast majority of meetings and events have focused on the entertainment perspective—creating an enjoyable atmosphere and experience. While these issues are important, they do not connect to the more vital issue of learning. The learning measure must be at the forefront of the meeting agenda. In reality, however, the learning measure tends to be overlooked in the majority of meeting evaluations.

The Learning Organization

In the last two decades, organizations have experienced rapid transformation in competitive global markets and economic changes. Organizations must learn new ways to serve customers and use innovations and technology as they attempt to be efficient, restructure, reorganize, and execute globally. To meet this change in strategy, the concept of a learning organization has evolved. This requires organizations to use learning proactively in an integrated way and to support and enhance growth for individuals, teams, and entire organizations. Peter Senge popularized the learning organization phenomena (Senge, 1990). A learning organization must capture, share, and use knowledge so that its members can work together to change the way the organization responds to challenges. Managers must question old social constructs and create new ways of thinking.

Learning must take place in teams and larger groups in which individuals can work together to create new knowledge. The process is continuous, focusing on creating learning organizations in which countless activities and processes are in place to promote, encourage, and support continuous learning. As a result, meetings and events become an important learning tool, perhaps the most important tool.

The Compliance Issue

Organizations face an increasing number of regulations with which they must routinely comply. These regulations involve all aspects of business and government and are considered necessary to protect customers, citizens, investors, and the environment. Sometimes, meetings are implemented to ensure that the organization is in compliance. When compliance is based on knowledge of regulations, measuring learning becomes the most critical measure to ensure compliance.

The Development and Use of Competencies

The use of competencies and competency models has dramatically increased in recent years. In a struggle to have a competitive advantage, many organizations have focused on people as the key to success. Competency models ensure that employees are doing the right things. They clarify and articulate what is required for effective performance. A competency model describes a particular combination of knowledge, skills, and characteristics needed to perform a role consistent with the strategic direction of the organization. In some definitions, the concept of a competency includes innate and acquired abilities. Definitions include behavior, skills, and knowledge as well as aptitude and personal characteristics.

With this increased focus on competencies, the need to measure learning surfaces. Behaviors are learned or knowledge is acquired directly from formal and informal processes. In some situations, meetings and events are implemented to explain, develop, or enhance competencies.

The Role of Learning in Meetings and Events

When new equipment, processes, policies, procedures, and technology are implemented, the human factor is critical to success. Whether there is restructuring or the addition of new systems, employees must learn how to function in the new environment; this requires the acquisition of new information, knowledge, or skills. Simple tasks and procedures are not always built into work or automated within processes. Instead, complex environments, complex processes, and complicated tools must be used in an intelligent way to reap the desired benefits for the organization. Employees must learn in different ways, not just in a formal classroom environment, but through meetings and events.

The Chain of Impact

At times, participants do not fully understand what they must learn to make a meeting successful. The chain of impact, described in Chapters 1 and 2, can be broken at any part of the chain. One place for the break is at Level 2 (Learning and Confidence). Participants just do not know what to do or how to do it properly. Learning measurement is needed to understand why employees are, or are not, performing the way they should be. When the performance does not occur, the first problem to examine is what went wrong: Where was the chain broken? What areas need to be adjusted? What needs to be altered? When learning data are obtained, planners can determine whether a lack of learning is the cause of the breakdown. In most cases, they may be able to eliminate the learning deficiency if one is the problem.

Consequences of an Unprepared Workforce

Perhaps the most important reason for the focus on learning measurement is to ensure that the workforce is prepared. There are many stories, some of them sad and disappointing, detailing how employees are not capable of doing what they need to do to perform their jobs and deliver excellent customer service. This has caused management teams to implement solutions to ensure that the workforce is prepared. In some situations, meetings and events are used to prepare these participants. The only way to make sure that employees have the knowledge and skills to perform their jobs successfully is to measure learning with credible processes.

MEASUREMENT ISSUES

Several factors can challenge or inhibit learning measurement. Determining how to measure and when to measure is critical. Also, addressing several issues is necessary to help clarify which measures must be collected and analyzed.

The Challenges of Measuring Learning

Measuring learning is not without its major challenges, which may inhibit a comprehensive approach to this issue. Measuring learning is sometimes equated with testing, which some organizations—and people—fear. For example, a quiz may be administered at a product launch event to measure how well participants understood the information presented at the event. Few people enjoy taking tests. The challenge is to make testing (or learning measurement) less threatening.

Another challenge is that learning measurement questions the professional autonomy of many individuals. Often, meetings will involve engineers, scientists, accountants, physicians, lawyers, or other professional groups. These individuals often feel that, because they have satisfied professional credential requirements, they have the knowledge and expertise required for whatever issues that may arise in their professional roles. A learning measure may make them feel that their professional competence is in question and, therefore, may be resisted.

When tests are used, another challenge is the ethical and legal considerations. When test scores affect participants' job status, a test must be formally checked for validity and reliability. This issue is not common for most meetings. The challenge is to take a reasonable approach, allocating resources to check for validity or reliability when necessary. This rare issue is beyond the scope of this book. Other books cover it in more detail (Phillips and Phillips, 2008).

A final challenge for measuring learning is the resources required. Budgets are often tight and spending excessive amounts of resources on learning measurement may not be desired or necessary. There is always a trade-off of additional resources versus the accuracy desired. Keeping the resource allocation reasonable is important. This often leads to some informal measures, combined with reaction questionnaires.

Objectives

As mentioned earlier, the starting point in any measurement system is the objectives. As with other levels of measurement, the measurement of learning builds on the learning objectives. Meeting professionals must improve the skills to create learning objectives following the process described in Chapter 3. The first step in the learning value chain is to ensure that objectives are in place. When they are in place, they are the basis for learning measurement. Typically, the objectives are broad and only indicate specific major knowledge or skills areas that should be achieved as the meeting is conducted.

Typical Measures

Measuring learning focuses on information, knowledge, skills, and perceptions. Sometimes, these are expanded to different categories. Table 6-1 shows some typical measures collected at this level.

Table 6-1
Typical Learning Measurement Categories

Skills	Attitudes
• Knowledge	• Capability
• Awareness	• Capacity
• Understanding	• Readiness
• Information	• Confidence
• Perceptions	• Contacts

Knowledge is general and includes the assimilation of facts, figures, and concepts. Instead of knowledge, the terms awareness, understanding, or information may be specific categories. Sometimes, perceptions or attitudes may change based on what a participant has learned. For example, in a diversity meeting, the participants' attitudes about having a diverse work group are altered. In other situations, the issue is developing a reservoir of knowledge and skills and referring to it when developing capability, capacity, or readiness. When individuals are capable, they are often described as being ready for the job. When participants use skills, an appropriate measure might be the confidence the participant has to use those skills in a job setting. This becomes critical in job situations where skills must be performed accurately and within a certain standard, as in customer service skills. Networking is often part of a meeting. When this is the situation, developing contacts is important whether within, or external to, an organization.

Timing

The timing of learning measurement can vary. In some situations, a pre-measure is taken, creating a pre-test to determine the extent to which participants understand or know the specific topics and content in the meeting. A pre-measure can be important to assess the current level of information, knowledge, and skills so that learning additional information can be planned efficiently. This may prevent participants from repeating sessions that they already know thereby reducing meeting costs by limiting participants to those who lack the knowledge. When the pre-measure shows that knowledge is lacking, a post-measure can show whether knowledge has been acquired. The post-measure can be administered during or after the meeting.

Assuming that no pre-measure is taken, measuring learning can occur at different times. In most formal meetings, the measure of learning is taken at the end of specific sessions for a lengthy meeting. For shorter meetings, the learning measure is taken at the end of the meeting, usually on the reaction questionnaire.

DATA COLLECTION METHODS

One of the most important considerations with regard to measuring learning is the specific way in which data are collected. For some meetings, collecting data at Level 2 involves what most consider testing, whether testing is objective or subjective. However, a variety of methods are available.

Table 6-2 presents the types of data collection for measuring learning, including tests. Sometimes, classification is difficult because of the overlap in methodologies. However, these are well-known approaches. Each major category is discussed next.

Questionnaires and Surveys

Different questionnaires and surveys were described in Chapter 5, with the focus on measuring reaction. The types of questionnaires and surveys include the two-way or true-false tests, where the participants are provided with statements and must either agree or disagree. These are easy to write and score. Rating scales are common in surveys and were described previously. The typical scale is a 5-point scale, although 3, 4, 7, and 10-point scales are used. Multiple-choice is the most common objective test and has the advantage of easy scoring. Matching exercises are also useful. They are easy to write and can be scored quickly. Fill-in-the-blank items are open-ended and easy to write, but more difficult to score, and short-answer questions can be easy to develop, but also difficult to score. Essay questions are less likely to be used because they are difficult to score and less reliable due to the subjective opinion of the scorer. The good news about using questionnaires is that the questions can be included on the reaction feedback questionnaire.

Objective Tests

Objective tests require precise responses. Answers to questions are either right or wrong. Multiple-choice is the most common objective test, where the

Table 6-2
The Many Ways to Measure Learning

- Questionnaires/Surveys
- Objective Tests
- Performance Tests
- Technology and Task Simulations
- Case Studies
- Role Playing/Skill Practice
- Assessment Center Method
- Exercises/Activities
- Informal Assessments

participants are provided a statement (the stem) and are asked to choose from a series of alternative answers (the detracters). This type of test has the advantage of easy scoring and is relatively unbiased. Two-way or true-false questions are often used. They are simple to develop and leave little room for interpretation, either by the respondent or the scorer.

Matching exercises, where participants match items on a choice basis, are also useful. They are easy to write and can be scored quickly. Fill-in-the-blank items are open-ended and easy to write, but more difficult to score. Short-answer questions can be easy to develop, but are also challenging to score. They often ask for responses or provide a place for a few sentences. Essay questions are less likely to be used because they are difficult to score and rely on a high degree of subjectivity by the scorer instead of the participant's actual knowledge.

Collectively, two-way, multiple-choice, matching, fill-in-the-blank, short-answer, and essay tests are the types of objective tests used to measure learning. Table 6-3 shows the basic guidelines for developing the different types of tests (Schrock and Coscarelli, 2000). Test development is a fairly simple and straightforward process and is covered adequately in many other resources (Phillips and Phillips, 2008).

Performance Tests

Performance testing allows the participants to exhibit a skill (and occasionally knowledge or attitudes) that have been learned during a meeting. The skill can be manual, verbal, or analytical, or a combination of the three. Performance testing is used frequently in task-related meetings for which the participants are allowed to demonstrate what they have learned and show how they would use the skill on the job (for example, participants are asked to demonstrate that they can use the software).

For a performance test to be effective, the following steps are recommended in the design and administration of the test:

- The test should be a representative sample of the work/tasks related to the meeting content. The test should allow the participant to demonstrate as many of the skills presented during the meeting as possible. This increases the validity of the test and makes it more meaningful to the participant.
- Every phase of the performance test should be planned—the timing, the participant's preparation, the collection of necessary materials, and the evaluation of the results.
- Thorough and consistent instructions are necessary. Variations in the instructions can influence the outcome of a performance test.
- Procedures should be developed for objective evaluation, and acceptable standards must be developed for a performance test.

With these general guidelines, performance tests can be effective evaluation tools. Although more costly than written tests, performance tests are essential for

Table 6-3
Guidelines for Developing Tests

True/False

❑ Use true/false items in situations in which there are only two likely alternative answers.
❑ Include only one major idea in each item.
❑ Make sure that the statement can be judged reasonably true or false.
❑ Keep statements as short and as simple as possible.
❑ Avoid negatives, especially double negatives.
❑ Randomly distribute both true and false statements.
❑ Avoid "always" and "never" statements.

Multiple-Choice

Guidelines for Writing the Stem

❑ Write the stem using simple and clear language.
❑ Place as much wording as possible in the stem, rather than in the alternative answers.
❑ If possible, state the stem in a positive form.
❑ Highlight negative words if they are essential.

Guidelines for Writing the Distracters

❑ Provide four or five alternative answers, including the correct response.
❑ Make certain you can defend the intended correct answer as clearly the best alternative.
❑ Make all alternatives grammatically consistent with the stem of the item.
❑ Vary randomly the position of the correct answer.
❑ Vary the relative length of the correct answer.
❑ Avoid all, always, and never.
❑ Use familiar looking or verbatim statements that are incorrect answers to the question.
❑ Use true statements that do not answer the question.
❑ Anticipate the options that will appeal to the unprepared test-taker.
❑ Avoid the use of "All of the above."
❑ Use "None of the above" with caution.
❑ Avoid alternatives of the type "both a and b are correct."
❑ If there is a logical order to options, use it in listing them; for example, if the options are numbers, list them in ascending or descending order.

Matching

❑ Include only homogeneous, closely related content in the lists to be matched.
❑ Keep the lists of responses short—five to 15 entries.
❑ Arrange the response list in some logical order—chronologically or alphabetically.
❑ Clearly indicate in the directions the basis on which entries are to be matched.
❑ Indicate in the directions how often a response can be used; responses should be used more than once to reduce cueing due to the process of elimination.
❑ Use a larger number of responses than entries to be matched to reduce process-of-elimination cueing.

(Continued)

Table 6-3
(Continued)

Fill-in-the-Blanks

❑ State the item so that only a single, brief answer is likely.
❑ Use direct questions as much as possible, rather than incomplete statements, as a format.
❑ If you must use incomplete statements, place the blank at the end of the statement, if possible.
❑ Provide adequate space for the test taker to write the correct answer.
❑ Keep all blank lines of equal length to avoid cues to the correct answers.
❑ For numerical answers, indicate the degree of precision required (e.g., "to the nearest tenth") and the units in which the answer is to be recorded (e.g., "in pounds").

Short-Answer

❑ State the question as clearly and succinctly as possible.
❑ Be sure that the question can be answered in only a few sentences.
❑ Provide guidance regarding the length of response anticipated (e.g., less than 75 words).
❑ Provide adequate space for the test taker to write the response.

Essay

❑ State the question as clearly and succinctly as possible; present a well-focused task to the test taker.
❑ Provide guidance regarding the length of response anticipated (e.g., "in three to five pages...")
❑ Provide estimates of the approximate time to be devoted to each essay question.
❑ Provide adequate space for the test taker to write the response.
❑ Indicate whether spelling, punctuation, grammar, and organization will be considered in scoring the response.

Adapted from Schrock and Coscarelli (2000).

situations in which a high degree of similarity is required between work and test conditions.

Technology and Task Simulations

Another technique for measuring learning is simulations. This method involves the construction and application of a procedure or task that simulates or models the content of the meeting. The simulation is designed to represent, as closely as possible, the actual job situation. Participants try out their performance in the simulated activity and are evaluated based on how well they accomplish the task. Simulations offer several advantages. They permit a job or part of a job to be reproduced in a manner almost identical to the real setting. Through careful planning and design, the simulation can have all the central characteristics of the real situation. Even complex jobs, such as that of a manager, can be simulated adequately.

Although initial development can be expensive, simulations can be cost-effective in the long run, particularly for large meetings or situations in which a meeting may be repeated. Another advantage of using simulations is safety. The safety component of many jobs requires participants to be trained in simulated conditions. For example, emergency medical technicians risk injury and even death if they do not learn emergency medical techniques prior to encountering a real-life situation.

Two of the most common techniques for delivering simulations are *technology* and *task*. A technology simulation uses a combination of electronics and mechanical devices to simulate real-life situations. They are used in conjunction with meetings to develop operational and diagnostic skills. Expensive examples of these types include simulated "patients" or a simulator for a plant operator. Other less-expensive types of simulators have been developed to simulate equipment operation. Task simulations replicate specific tasks or steps in which a participant must demonstrate that he or she knows how to do them. An example is demonstrating CPR on a dummy.

Case Studies

A perhaps less-effective but still-popular technique of measuring learning in meetings and events is the use of case studies. A case study is as much a teaching tool as it is an evaluation method. A case study represents a detailed description of a problem and usually contains a list of several questions posed to the participant. The participant is asked to analyze the case and determine the best course of action. The problem should reflect conditions in the real world and the content of the meeting.

The most common categories of case studies include:

- *Exercise case studies* provide an opportunity for participants to practice the application of specific procedures.
- *Situational case studies* give participants the opportunity to analyze information and make decisions surrounding their situations.
- *Complex case studies* are extensions of situational case studies, where the participant is required to process a large amount of data and information, some of which may be irrelevant.
- *Decision case studies* require the participant to go a step further than the previous categories and present plans for solving a particular problem.
- *Critical-incident case studies* provide the participant with a certain amount of information and withhold other information until it is requested by the participant.
- *Action-maze case studies* present a large case in a series of smaller units, and the participant is required to predict at each stage what will happen next.

The difficulty in a case study lies in objectively evaluating the participant's performance. Frequently, many possible courses of action are available, some equally as effective as others. This makes obtaining an objective, measurable performance rating for the analysis and interpretation of the case difficult. A self assessment of what was learned may be appropriate.

Role Playing and Skill Practices

Role plays, sometimes referred to as skill practices, require participants to practice a newly learned skill as they are observed. Participants are provided with assigned roles and specific instructions, which sometimes include an ultimate course of action. The participant then practices the skill with other individuals to accomplish the desired objectives. This exercise is intended to simulate the real-world setting to the greatest extent possible.

The success of this role-play technique also lies in the judgment of those observing. The skill of effective observation is as critical as the skill of the person playing the role. Also, the success of this method depends on the participants' willingness to participate in and adjust to the planned role. If participant resistance is extremely high, the performance in the skill practice may not reflect the actual performance on the job. Nevertheless, these skill practices can be useful—particularly in meetings for which skill building is essential—in helping participants practice discussion skills (e.g. customer service meetings).

Exercises/Activities

Most meetings involve activities or exercises that must be explored, developed, or solved during the meeting. Some of these are constructed in terms of involvement exercises, while others require individual problem-solving skills. When these tools are integrated into the meeting, several specific ways to measure learning are available:

- The results of the exercise can be submitted for review and for possible scoring by a member of the meeting team. This score becomes part of the overall measure of learning.
- The results can be discussed in a group, with a comparison of the different approaches and solutions. The group can give an assessment of how much each individual has learned. This may not be practical in many meeting settings but can work in a few narrowly focused applications.
- The solutions to the problem or exercises can be shared with the group, and the participant can provide a self-assessment indicating the degree to which the skills and/or knowledge have been obtained. This also serves as reinforcement since participants quickly see the correct solution.

Informal Assessments

Now, for the good news: For most meetings, an informal check of learning is sufficient to provide some assurance that participants have acquired the information, knowledge, and skills or that needed changes in attitudes have occurred.

This approach is appropriate when other levels of evaluation are pursued. For example, if a Level 3 (Application) evaluation is planned, conducting a comprehensive Level 2 evaluation might not be as critical. An informal assessment of learning is usually sufficient. After all, if resources are scarce, a comprehensive evaluation at all levels becomes quite expensive. This is an alternative approach to measuring learning when inexpensive, low-key measurements are needed.

The most common informal assessment is participant self-assessment. Participants are provided an opportunity to assess their acquisition of information, knowledge, and skills. A few guidelines can ensure that the process is effective:

- The self-assessment should be made anonymously so that participants feel free to express realistic and accurate assessments of what they have learned.
- The purpose of the self-assessment should be explained, along with the plans for using the data, such as adjustments and changes to the meeting or to future meetings.
- If no improvement has been made or the self-assessment is unsatisfactory, what that means and what the implications will be should be discussed. This will help ensure that accurate and credible information is provided.

Informal assessment has advantages. It is inexpensive, quick, and often user-friendly. In many cases, it is not invasive, rarely interrupting the work flow, because it often takes minimal time and can fit into most meetings' time schedules. Informal assessments can be easily scored, interpreted, and used to make changes or improvements. However, with advantages come disadvantages. This type of assessment is more subjective than formal assessments and, therefore, is less reliable and valid (issues that will be discussed further in the next section). A potential low return rate may develop because participants do not take the exercise as seriously as formal processes. And because it is informal, the conditions in which the data are collected may vary, resulting in potential bias.

ADMINISTRATIVE ISSUES

A few simple administrative issues must be addressed when measuring learning, especially when the process is more structured and formal. Each of these should be part of the overall plan for administering learning measurement:

Reliability and Validity

When formal tests are considered, two important issues are *validity* and *reliability*. Validity is the extent to which an instrument measures what it is designed to measure. Reliability is the extent to which an instrument is stable or consistent over time. In essence, any instrument used to collect data should be both valid (measures what it should measure) and reliable (consistent over time). A reliable instrument means that if the same data were collected at different times and nothing intervened to cause a change in knowledge, then the response should be

		Reliable?	
		Yes	**No**
Valid?	**No**	Undesirable	Worst Case
	Yes	Ideal	Not Possible

Figure 6-1. Relationship Between Validity and Reliability.

the same. Significant deviations mean that the instrument is unreliable. Figure 6-1 shows the relationship between reliability and validity. In the ideal scenario, the instrument has to be both reliable and valid. It is not possible to have a valid instrument if it is not reliable.

The concept of validity and reliability and how to check for an adequate threshold of both are beyond the scope of this book. Other references are available to give more detail (Schrock and Coscarelli, 2000). However, a sensible approach when developing instruments is important. The use of subject-matter experts in the design, development, and use of the instruments is often enough to ensure that the instrument is valid. This is called content validity. Other methods for checking validity become more analytical than most managers and executives want to explore. In terms of reliability, having an appropriate number of questions on a survey and ensuring that no questions are vague and ambiguous can help improve reliability. Table 6-4 provides a few tips for improving validity and reliability.

For most meetings and events, reliability and validity will not be a concern. These two issues become more important when a human resource action (job status change) is taken as a result of a person's passing or failing a test. For example, if an individual is promoted, denied assignment, provided an increase in pay, or is placed in a career ladder because of passing the test or failing it, the instrument

Table 6-4
Tips for Improving Validity and Reliability

Tips for Improving Validity
- Have test items reviewed by content "experts."
- Check for even and consistent representation of course objectives.
- Check with participants for face validity.
- Include an appropriate number of items.
- Reduce potential response bias.
- Administer objectively.

Tips for Improving Reliability
- Provide clear and consistent instructions for test.
- Ensure sufficient time for responses.
- Ensure the same amount of time for responses.
- Ensure consistency in all steps and procedures.

must be defensible. In other words, if a challenge is raised, the reliability and validity must be defendable, up to and including a defense in the courts. In the vast majority of meetings, this will not be the case. Rarely do test failures result in job status changes.

Consistency

Tests, exercises, or assessments for measuring learning must be administered consistently from one group to another. This includes issues such as the time required to respond, the actual learning conditions in which the participants complete the process, the resources available to them, and the assistance from other members of the group. These issues can easily be addressed in the instructions.

Monitoring

When formal testing is used, participants should be monitored as they complete the test or other measurement processes. This ensures that each individual works independently and also that someone is available to provide assistance or answer questions as needed. This may not be an issue in all situations, but should be addressed in the overall plan.

Pilot Testing

Testing an instrument with a small group to ensure validity and reliability is advisable. A pilot test provides an opportunity to clarify confusion that might exist about the instructions, questions, or statements. When a pilot test is pursued, it should be timed to determine how long individuals take to complete it. Also, the individuals who take the pilot should be encouraged to provide input about other ways to ask the questions and the flow of information and provide any other suggestions for improvement.

Readability

As with reaction questionnaires, readability is important. The reading level must be matched with the target audience. This could be a simple step in the process where the readability level can be checked with Microsoft Word® or other software.

Scoring

Scoring instructions have to be developed for the measurement process so that the evaluator will be objective and provide consistent scores. Ideally, the potential bias from this person should be completely removed through proper scoring instructions and other information needed to provide an objective evaluation.

Reporting

In some situations, the participants are provided with the results immediately, particularly with self-scoring tests or with group-based scoring. In other situations, the actual results may not be known until later. In these situations, a method for providing scoring data should be built into the evaluation plan unless it has been predetermined that participants will not know the scores. The worst-case scenario is promising test scores and delivering them late or not delivering them at all.

Confronting Test Failures

Test failures may not be an issue, particularly if the data are collected informally through a self-assessment process. However, when more rigorous and formal methods are used and individuals do not demonstrate the required competencies to pass the test, some consideration must be made for confronting these failures. An important issue is to ensure that the test and the testing procedures are defensible.

USING LEARNING DATA

Data must be used to add value and improve processes. Although several uses of learning data are appropriate, those described in this section are most common.

Ensuring That Learning Has Been Acquired

Sometimes, knowing the extent and scope of learning is essential. Measuring learning, even informally, will provide input on this issue. It shows whether the learning component of the chain of input is successful.

Providing Individual Feedback to Build Confidence

Learning data, when provided directly to participants, provide reinforcement for correct answers and enhance confidence. This reinforces the learning process and provides much-needed feedback to participants involved in meetings and events.

Improving the Meeting

Perhaps the most important use of learning data is to improve the future offering of the meeting. This is process improvement for planners, designers, developers, and speakers. Consistently low responses in certain learning measures may indicate that inadequate facilitation has been provided on that topic. Consistently low scores with all participants may indicate that the objectives and scope of coverage are misdirected or too ambitious.

Evaluating Speakers

Just as reaction data can be used to evaluate speakers, learning measures provide additional evidence of success. The speaker has the responsibility of ensuring that participants have learned the new skills and knowledge needed for meeting success. Learning measures are a reflection of the degree to which the skills and knowledge have been acquired and internalized for application.

Building a Database

In meetings that are repeated, building a database of competency improvement, skills acquisition, or required knowledge may be helpful. These data sets may represent beneficial data to indicate how one meeting compares to another. Over time, they can also be used to set expectations and judge success.

FINAL THOUGHTS

This chapter briefly discusses some of the key issues involved in measuring learning—an important component for the success of meetings. More than any other level, this measurement moves the meetings and events industry from entertainment to learning. Even if it is accomplished informally, learning must be assessed to determine the extent to which meeting participants learn new skills, techniques, processes, tools, and procedures. Should application problems arise later, knowing what went wrong would be difficult without this measure. Also, measuring learning provides an opportunity to make adjustments so that changes can be made to enhance learning and ensure that application can occur. A formal, objective process is usually not needed, except for major meetings with a principal focus on learning. A less-formal, less-structured approach, perhaps a self-assessment activity, is usually appropriate for most meetings and events—often included in the reaction questionnaire.

References

Phillips, J., and Phillips, P.P. *Handbook of Training Evaluation and Measurement Methods*, 4th Edition. Woburn, MA: Butterworth-Heinemann, 2008.

Schrock, S., and Coscarelli, W. *Criterion-Referenced Test Development*, 2nd Edition. Silver Spring, MD: ISPI, 2000.

Senge, P. *The Fifth Discipline: The Art and Practice of the Learning Organization.* New York: Random House, 1990.

Welch, S.J., *Successful Meetings Magazine "23 Secrets of Master Networkers"* (New York, NY: Nielson Business Media, Inc., April 2007).

CHAPTER 7

Measuring Application and Implementation

Some meetings and events are designed to drive action, and they often fail because of breakdowns in application. Participants just do not use what they learned in the meeting, when they should, or at the expected level of performance. Without successful implementation, changes in business impact will not occur. Measuring application and implementation is important to understand the success or lack of success. Data collection methods—such as questionnaires and action planning—are available to measure the application. Along with describing data collection, this chapter addresses the challenges and benefits with this level of evaluation.

THE IMPORTANCE OF MEASURING APPLICATION

Measuring application and implementation is necessary if the participants are expected to do something after the meeting. For some meetings, it is the most critical data set because it provides an understanding of the success of implementation, along with the barriers and enablers that influence success. Without this level of evaluation, no evidence is available to show that the meeting or event made a difference with participants. Here are a few reasons for measuring at this level.

The Value of Information

The value of information increases as progress is made through the chain of impact—from reaction (Level 1) to ROI (Level 5). Therefore, information concerning application and implementation (Level 3) is more valuable to key clients than reaction and learning data. This does not discount the importance of these first two levels, but emphasizes the importance of moving up the chain of impact. Measuring the meeting's application often provides critical data about not only the success of the meetings, but the factors that can contribute to increased success in future meetings.

A Key Transition Time

The three previous measure categories—inputs, reaction, and learning—are assessed before, during, or at the end of the meeting, where attention and focus are placed on the participants' direct involvement in the meeting. Measuring application occurs later and captures the participants' use of information, knowledge, and skills in the work or life context. Essentially, measures at this level reflect the degree of post-meeting success. This key transition period makes measuring application and implementation a critical issue to address.

A Key Focus of Many Meetings

Because most meetings focus directly on the need to use what is learned during the meeting, the client often has concerns about these measures of success. Frequently, executives will request that participants take renewed action, change their approach, shift their tactics, or otherwise implement changes. Major events designed to empower employees, create teamwork, or build a loyal customer base will concentrate on the application of meeting content. A key challenge for meeting planners is to mobilize the audience into action — to get them to do something.

Barriers and Enablers

Often, when a meeting does not deliver the expected follow-up results, the first question asked is, "What happened?" A follow-up question is, "What can we do to improve the meeting?" To respond to either question, the barriers to success are needed. These are the problems encountered during implementation and obstacles to the application of the content. At this level of evaluation, these problems should always be addressed and analyzed. In many cases, the participants provide important recommendations for making improvements.

When a meeting is successful, two obvious questions are "How can we repeat this?" and "how can we improve it in the future?" The answers to these questions are also found at this level of evaluation as enablers are identified. Identifying the factors that directly contribute to meeting success is always necessary. Those same items can be used to replicate the process to produce new or improved results in the future.

CHALLENGES OF MEASURING APPLICATION AND IMPLEMENTATION

Collecting application and implementation data brings into focus some key challenges for meeting professionals. These challenges may inhibit an otherwise successful evaluation. The good news is that these challenges can be addressed adequately with minimum resources.

Linking with Learning

Application data should be linked closely with the learning data discussed in Chapter 6. Essentially, planners must know what actions are needed for participants following the meeting. This information is based on what the participants learned in the meeting. Application data measure the extent to which participants applied what they learned.

Designing Data Collection into Meetings and Events

Application data are collected after the meeting has been conducted, and because of the time difference, securing the appropriate quality and quantity of data is sometimes difficult. Because of this, designing data collection into the meeting from the beginning is one of the most effective ways to secure data. Data collection tools, positioned as application tools, provide a rich source of data. These tools are built in as part of the implementation. For example, many software applications contain overlay software that shows a user performance profile. Essentially, the software tracks the user invisibly, capturing the steps, the pace, the time, and the difficulties encountered while using the software. When a meeting focuses on software use, follow-up application can be captured automatically.

In another example, action plans were designed into a leadership development retreat and positioned as an application tool that also showed the impact of applying the leadership skills. When the process was completed, a credible data set was captured, only because data collection was built into the process from the beginning. Building collection in from the beginning can also help in improving response rates. This approach is covered in detail later in this chapter.

Applying Serious Effort to Level 3 Evaluation

Because some meetings are planned to drive impact data (e.g., sales) and actual ROI, less emphasis may be placed on measuring application and implementation. In some cases, it may be omitted or slighted in the analysis. For example, sales executives expect sales increases after a sales conference is conducted, sometimes ignoring how the sales representatives performed after the meeting. When impact is desired, Level 3 evaluation is needed. To obtain credible, usable data will require a serious effort, perhaps beyond the usual reaction measures.

FUNDAMENTAL ISSUES

When measuring the application and implementation of meetings, several important issues must be addressed. Largely, these are similar to the issues encountered when measuring reaction and learning. A few may differ slightly because of the later collection timeframe.

Methods

When collecting application data, several methods are available. These involve traditional methods of surveys and questionnaires but also include classic methods for qualitative data collection such as observation, interviews, and focus groups. Action planning, where individuals plan their parts of the implementation in the meeting, is also useful. These methods are described in more detail later and are the principal focus of this chapter.

Objectives

As with the other levels, data collection begins with objectives that are set for the meeting's application and implementation. Objectives define expected actions. Without objectives at this level, collecting adequate data will be difficult. Chapter 3 described the basic principles for developing these objectives.

Topics to Explore

The topics addressed at this level parallel many of those identified in Chapters 5 and 6. Therefore, many of the areas can be mapped into this level. However, because of the timeframe, additional opportunities to measure success are available. For example, questions during the meeting about the intent to apply the information, knowledge, and skills are logical issues to measure at this time—when the application and implementation occurs. Application focuses on activity or action, not the consequences (such as the impact), and the number of activities to measure can be mind boggling. Table 7-1 shows some coverage areas for application. These examples can vary.

Sources and Timing

The sources of data are straightforward. The meeting participants are the most likely source. In some situations, the managers of participants may be a source. In other cases, organizational records or systems are the source. In exhibitor studies, the exhibitor would be the source.

The timing of data collection can vary. Since this is a follow up after the meeting, the issue is to determine the best time for a post-meeting evaluation. The challenge is to analyze the nature and scope of the application and determine the earliest time that an action will be taken or completed. This occurs when the application becomes routine, the task is complete, or the implementation is progressing significantly. When to collect data is a judgment call. Collecting as early as possible is important so that potential adjustments can still be made. At the same time, evaluations must allow for desired changes so that the implementation can be measured. For most meetings, this time will be in the three-week to three-month range.

Convenience and constraints also influence the timing of data collection. Perhaps the participants are conveniently involved with another meeting or special event. These would be excellent opportunities to collect data. Constraints are

Table 7-1
Examples of Coverage Areas for Application

Action	Explanation	Example of Measures
Increase	Increasing a particular activity or action.	Increase the use of a probing skill.
Decrease	Decreasing a particular activity or action.	Decrease the number of times the inspection reports are checked.
Eliminate	Stop or remove a particular task or activity.	Eliminate a face-to-face meeting, and replace it with a virtual meeting weekly.
Maintain	Keep the same level of activity for a particular process.	Continue to monitor each complaint.
Create	Design, build, or implement a new procedure, process, or activity.	Create a process for resolving the differences among team members.
Use	Use a particular process, procedure, or activity.	Use the salesforce.com software to track prospects.
Perform	Conduct or do a particular task, process, or procedure.	Perform a post-audit review at the end of each new contract.
Participate	Become involved in various activities, projects, or meetings.	Submit a suggestion for reducing costs.
Enroll	Sign up for a particular program.	Enroll in the career advancement program.
Respond	React to groups, individuals, or systems.	Respond to customer inquiries within 15 minutes.
Network	Facilitate productive relationships with contacts.	Follow-up with contacts on, at least, a quarterly basis.
Initiate	Start a specific task, activity, or action	Initiate at least one cost reduction project in three weeks

sometimes placed on data collection. Clients or other executives are anxious to have the data and to make decisions about the success of the meeting, which moves data collection earlier than the ideal time.

Responsibilities

Measuring application and implementation involves the responsibility and work of others. Because these measures occur after the meeting, an important question may surface in terms of who is responsible for this follow up. Many possibilities exist, from the planner to the client staff, as well as the possibility of external, independent contractors. This matter should be addressed during the planning stage so that no misunderstandings about the distribution of responsibilities occur. More important, those who are responsible must understand the nature and scope of their roles and what is needed to collect data.

Data Collection with Questionnaires and Surveys

Questionnaires have become a mainstream data collection tool for application and implementation measures because of their flexibility, low cost, and convenience. The factors involved in questionnaire design discussed in Chapter 5 apply equally to questionnaire development for measuring application and implementation.

Content

One of the most difficult tasks is to determine specific factors that need to be addressed on a follow-up questionnaire. Although the content items can be the same as those used in reaction and learning questionnaires, additional items are necessary for capturing application and implementation.

A discussion about Progressive Bank is used here to illustrate many of the elements that should be included on follow-up questionnaires. Following a carefully planned growth pattern through acquiring smaller banks, Progressive Bank initiated a meeting to help develop a strong sales culture. An evaluation was planned during the initial meeting design. All branch employees attended the meeting and were asked to provide input on a questionnaire two months after the meeting. Figure 7-1 presents the follow-up questionnaire. Most of the data from the questionnaire covered application and implementation. This type of feedback helped the meeting professionals know which parts of the meeting were most effective and useful. In this section, some of the key questions on the questionnaire will be discussed.

Progress with Objectives. Sometimes, assessing the progress made with the objectives of the meeting in a follow-up evaluation is helpful. While some of the objectives were assessed during the meeting (reaction and learning), the Level 3 and 4 objectives must be revisited on a post-implementation basis as the objectives identify the specific actions that should occur during implementation.

Relevance/Importance of the Meeting. The relevance or importance of a meeting is often assessed during the meeting, as Level 1 data. However, analyzing the relevance or importance after implementation can be helpful. Question 2 verifies that the perceived relevance still exists after implementation.

Knowledge/Skill Use. Perhaps one of the most important questions on the follow-up questionnaire focuses on the application of skills and knowledge. As shown in Question 3 in Figure 7-1, specific skills and knowledge areas are listed, with the question focusing on the amount of change since the meeting was conducted. This is the recommended approach when no pre-meeting data exists.

Sales Culture at Progress Bank
Follow-up Questionnaire

Are you currently in a sales capacity at a branch?   Yes ☐   No ☐

1.   Listed below are the objectives of the sales culture meeting. After reflecting on these, please indicate the degree of success in meeting the objectives. Use the following scale:

   1. No success at all
   2. Limited success
   3. Moderate success
   4. Generally successful
   5. Very successful

As a result of this meeting, participants will:	1	2	3	4	5
a. Identify the needs of customers.	☐	☐	☐	☐	☐
b. Match needs with products.	☐	☐	☐	☐	☐
c. Convince customers to buy/use Progress Bank products and services.	☐	☐	☐	☐	☐
d. Build a productive, long-term relationship with customers.	☐	☐	☐	☐	☐
e. Increase sales of each product line offered in the branch.	☐	☐	☐	☐	☐

2.   Please rate the relevance to your job of each of the following components of the meeting using the following scale:

   1. No relevance
   2. Limited relevance
   3. Moderate relevance
   4. General relevance
   5. Very relevant in every way

	1	2	3	4	5
Job Aids	☐	☐	☐	☐	☐
Group Activities	☐	☐	☐	☐	☐
Incentive Opportunities	☐	☐	☐	☐	☐
Networking Opportunities with Other Branches	☐	☐	☐	☐	☐
Reading Material/Videos	☐	☐	☐	☐	☐
Coaching Sessions	☐	☐	☐	☐	☐
Database Enhancements	☐	☐	☐	☐	☐

3.   Please indicate the change in the application of knowledge and skills as a result of your participation in the sales culture meeting. Use the following scale:

   1. No change
   2. Limited change
   3. Moderate change
   4. Much change
   5. Very much change

Figure 7-1. Sample Questionnaire.

	1	2	3	4	5	No Opportunity To Use Skill
a. Probing for customer needs.	☐	☐	☐	☐	☐	☐
b. Helping the customer solve problems.	☐	☐	☐	☐	☐	☐
c. Understanding the features and benefits of all products and services.	☐	☐	☐	☐	☐	☐
d. Comparing products and services to those of competitors.	☐	☐	☐	☐	☐	☐
e. Selecting appropriate products and services.	☐	☐	☐	☐	☐	☐
f. Using persuasive selling techniques.	☐	☐	☐	☐	☐	☐
g. Using follow-up techniques to stay in touch with the customer.	☐	☐	☐	☐	☐	☐
h. Using new software routines for data access and transactions.	☐	☐	☐	☐	☐	☐

4.   What has changed about your work (actions, tasks, activities) as a result of this meeting?

_____
_____
_____
_____

5.   Please identify any specific accomplishments/improvements that can be linked to this meeting.

_____
_____
_____
_____

6.   Indicate the extent to which you think this meeting has influenced each of these measures in your branch. Use the following scale:

1. No influence
2. Limited influence
3. Moderate influence
4. Much influence
5. Very much influence

	1	2	3	4	5
a. Sales	☐	☐	☐	☐	☐
b. Productivity	☐	☐	☐	☐	☐
c. Customer Response Time	☐	☐	☐	☐	☐
d. Cross-Sales Ratio	☐	☐	☐	☐	☐
e. Cost Control	☐	☐	☐	☐	☐
f. Employee Satisfaction	☐	☐	☐	☐	☐
g. Customer Satisfaction	☐	☐	☐	☐	☐
h. Quality	☐	☐	☐	☐	☐
i. Other _____	☐	☐	☐	☐	☐

Figure 7-1. (Continued)

7.   What barriers, if any, have you encountered that prevented this meeting from being successful. Please explain, if possible.

_____

_____

_____

_____

_____

8.   What has helped this meeting be successful? Please explain.

_____

_____

_____

_____

_____

9.   Which of the following statements best describes the level of management support?

☐ There was no management support.
☐ There was limited management support.
☐ There was a moderate amount management support.
☐ There was much management support.
☐ There was very much management support.

10. What specific suggestions do you have for improving this meeting?

_____

_____

_____

_____

_____

11. Other comments about this meeting:

_____

_____

_____

_____

Figure 7-1. (Continued)

If pre-meeting data have been collected, comparing post-assessments with pre-assessments using the same question is more appropriate. Sometimes, determining the most frequently used skills that are directly linked to the meeting is helpful. For many skills, participants need to experience frequent use quickly after skill acquisition so that the skills become internalized and routine. When this is the case, the questionnaire should include a list of skills, asking participants to indicate their frequency of use.

Changes with Work/Action Items. A participant's work usually changes in some way because of their participation in a meeting. Capturing the specific elements that changed can be important data. As Question 4 illustrates, the participant explores how the application changed his or her work and may include a list of actions, steps, or activities that changed.

Improvements/Accomplishments. Question 5 seeks specific accomplish-ments and improvements that are directly linked to the meeting. This question focuses on specific, measurable consequences that can be easily identified by the participants, represented by one or more business measures. These conse-quences are based on the application data and the changes with work data above. These consequences answer the question, "So what?" Examples that indicate the nature and range of responses requested may be used but may also limit the responses.

Linkage with Measures. Sometimes, determining the degree to which a meet-ing has influenced certain Level 4 impact measures is helpful. As shown in Question 6, participants are asked to indicate the degree to which they think certain measures have been influenced by the meeting. However, when this issue is uncertain, business performance measures known to have been influenced in similar meetings are listed.

Barriers and Enablers. Barriers can influence the successful application of a meeting. Question 7 in Figure 7-1 identify these barriers. As an alternative, the perceived barriers could be listed and participants are asked to check all that apply. Still another variation is to list the barriers with a range of responses, indicating the extent to which the barrier inhibited results.

Just as important as barriers are the enablers—those issues, events, or situations that enabled the meeting's successful application. The same options are available with this question as with the question on barriers. Question 8 captures the enablers.

Management Support. Management support is often critical to the success of a meeting. At least one question should be included on the degree of management support. Sometimes, this question is structured so that various descriptions of management support are detailed, and participants check the one that applies to their situation. Question 9 in Figure 7-1 is an example.

Content Checklist

Developing a checklist of the content issues to include on a follow-up ques-tionnaire may be useful. Table 7-2 shows a checklist of the key issues for the follow-up data that is often needed to measure application and implementation.

Improving Response Rates

For most evaluations at this level, questionnaires and surveys will be used to collect a wide range of information. However, asking for too much detail in the follow-up questionnaire can negatively impact the response rate. The challenge, therefore, is to approach questionnaire and survey design and administration for

Table 7-2
Questionnaire Content Checklist

- ❑ Progress with objectives
- ❑ Knowledge/skill enhancement
- ❑ Materials used
- ❑ Skills used
- ❑ Tasks completed
- ❑ Actions taken
- ❑ Progress made
- ❑ Changes with work
- ❑ Linkage with measures
- ❑ Other benefits
- ❑ Barriers
- ❑ Enablers
- ❑ Management support
- ❑ Suggestions for improvement
- ❑ Other comments

maximum response rate. Here are some of the actions that can be taken to ensure a successful response rate. Although the term questionnaire is used, the list also applies to surveys.

- *Provide advance communication.* If appropriate and feasible, participants and other stakeholders should receive advance communications about the plans for the questionnaire. This minimizes some of the resistance to the process, provides an opportunity to explain in more detail the circumstances surrounding the evaluation, and positions the evaluation as an integral part of the meeting—not an add-on activity. Communicate the purpose, participants and other stakeholders should understand the reason for the questionnaire.
- *Identify who will see the data.* Respondents need to know who will see the data and the results of the questionnaire. If the questionnaire is anonymous, it should clearly be communicated to participants how anonymity will be ensured. If senior executives will see the combined results of the study, the respondent should know.
- *Describe the data integration process.* If the questionnaire is only one of the data collection methods used, the respondents should understand how the questionnaire results will be combined with other data. They should know how the data are weighted and how they will be integrated into the final reporting.
- *Design for simplicity.* Sometimes, a simple questionnaire does not provide the full scope of data necessary for a comprehensive analysis. The simplified approach should be followed when questions are developed and the total

scope of the questionnaire is finalized. Every effort should be made to keep it as brief as possible.

- *Make responding easy.* Whenever possible, the response should be easy. If appropriate, a self-addressed stamped envelope should be included. Perhaps e-mail or Web-based questionnaires could be used, if appropriate and available.

- *Use local management support.* Management involvement at the local level is critical for response-rate success. Managers can distribute the questionnaires themselves, make reference to the questionnaire in meetings, follow up to see whether employees have completed their questionnaires, and generally show support for completing the questionnaire.

- *Let the participants know that they are part of the sample.* For large meetings, a sampling process may be used. When that is the case, respondents should know that they are part of a carefully selected sample and that their input will be used to make decisions regarding a much larger target audience. This action often appeals to a sense of responsibility for participants to provide usable, accurate data for the questionnaire.

- *Consider the use of incentives.* A variety of incentives to complete questionnaires can be offered, and they usually can be grouped into three categories.
  - First, an incentive is provided in exchange for the completed questionnaire. For example, if respondents return the questionnaire personally or through the mail, they will receive a small gift, such as an iPod Shuffle or a jump drive. If anonymity is an issue, a neutral third party can collect the questionnaires and advise the evaluator of the names of respondents.
  - A second category of incentive includes those to make participants feel guilty about not responding. Examples of "make you feel guilty" incentives include money clipped to the questionnaire or a pen enclosed in the envelope. Respondents are asked to "take the money, buy a cup of coffee or tea, and fill out the questionnaire."
  - A third category of incentives is designed to obtain a quick response. This approach is based on the assumption that a quick response will ensure a greater response rate. If an individual puts off completing the questionnaire, the odds of completing it diminish considerably. The initial group of respondents may receive a more expensive gift, or they may be part of a drawing for an incentive.

- *Have an executive sign the introductory letter.* Respondents are always interested in who sent the letter with the questionnaire. For maximum effectiveness, a senior executive who is responsible for the area in which the participants are employed should sign the letter. The employees may be more willing to respond to a senior executive when compared to situations in which a member of the meeting team signs the letter. In ROI evaluations for associations, the letter should be signed by the CEO of the association.

- *Use follow-up reminders.* A follow-up reminder should be sent a week after the questionnaire is received and another sent two weeks later. Depending on the questionnaire and the situation, these times can be adjusted. In some situations, a third follow-up is recommended. Sometimes, the follow-up is sent in a different medium. For example, a questionnaire may be sent through regular mail, whereas the first follow-up reminder is from the immediate manager, and a second follow-up is sent via e-mail.

- *Send a copy of the results to the participants.* Even if it is an abbreviated report, respondents should see the results of the questionnaire. More important, participants should understand that they will receive copies of the impact study (at least in a summary form) when they are asked to provide the data. Following through on the promise will influence response rates for future evaluations.
- *Estimate the time required to complete the questionnaire.* Respondents often have a concern about the time required to complete the questionnaire. A very lengthy questionnaire may quickly turn off the respondents and cause them to discard it. Sometimes, lengthy questionnaires can be completed quickly because many of them have forced-choice questions or statements that make responding easier. However, the number of pages may frighten the respondent. Therefore, indicating the estimated length of time needed to complete the questionnaire—in the letter or noted in the communications—is helpful. A word of caution is necessary, though: the amount of time must be realistic. Purposely underestimating the time can do more harm than good.
- *Show the timing of the planned steps.* Sometimes, the respondents want to know more detail regarding when they can see the results or when the results will be presented to particular groups. A timeline should be presented, showing when different phases of the process—such as when to respond, when the data will be analyzed, when the data will be presented to different groups, and when the results will be returned to the respondents in a summary report. The timetable must be followed to maintain the confidence and trust of the individuals.
- *Make it look professional.* While it should not be a concern in most organizations, unfortunately, there are too many cases in which a questionnaire is not developed properly, does not appear professional, or is not easy to follow and understand. The respondents must gain respect for the process and for the organization.
- *Introduce the questionnaire during the meeting.* Sometimes, it is helpful to explain to the respondents and other key stakeholders that they will be required or asked to provide certain types of data. When this is feasible, questionnaires should be reviewed question by question so that the respondents understand the purpose, the issues, and how to respond.
- *Collect data anonymously or confidentially.* Respondents are more likely to provide frank and candid feedback if their names are not on the questionnaires, particularly when the meeting is going astray or is off-target. Every effort should be made to protect the anonymous input, and explanations should be provided as to how the data are analyzed, minimizing the demographic makeup of respondents so that the individuals cannot be identified in the analysis. Confidentiality means that data sources are protected along with their linkage to data.

Collectively, these items help boost the response rates of follow-up question-naires. Using all these strategies can result in a 60–80% response rate—even for lengthy questionnaires that might take 30 minutes to complete.

For a specific technique, some individuals will respond to it (while others will not), bringing in a few more percentage points of return rate, perhaps 3–8%. A few techniques are very powerful. For example, reviewing a questionnaire at the end of the meeting will often secure about 15–20% when the participants have a chance to understand the reason for the questionnaire, the questions, the data needed, and how the data will be used. As each technique is used, the desired response rate can be achieved, often in the range of 60–90%. This requires determination, focus, and discipline. Too often, meeting planners do not put the effort into collecting data and have a miserable response rate. In reality, this is about changing culture, since the planner essentially creates a dialogue with the participants. When this dialogue is perceived as productive, trusting, and helpful, a tremendous amount of data can be collected.

Data Collection with Interviews

Another helpful data collection method is the interview, although it is not used as frequently as questionnaires. Interviews may be conducted by the planner, the evaluator, or a third party. Interviews can secure data difficult to obtain through written responses. Also, interviews can uncover success stories that can be useful in communicating the success of the meeting. Respondents may be reluctant to describe their success and results in a questionnaire but will volunteer the information to a skillful interviewer who uses probing techniques. The interview is versatile and appropriate for application and implementation data. A major disadvantage of the interview is that it consumes time, which increases the cost of data collection. It also requires preparing interviewers to ensure that the process is consistent.

Types of Interviews

There are two basic types of interviews: *structured* and *unstructured*. A struc-tured interview is similar to a questionnaire. Specific questions are asked with little room to deviate from desired responses. The advantages of structured interviews over questionnaires are that the interview process ensures that the questionnaire is completed and that the interviewer understands the responses supplied by the interviewee.

The unstructured interview permits much probing for additional information. This type of interview uses a few general questions that may lead to more detailed information as data are uncovered. The interviewer must be skilled in the probing process, using probing questions such as:

- Can you provide that in more detail?
- Can you give me an example of what you are saying?

- Can you explain the difficulty that you say you encountered?
- Can you describe the concern in more detail?

Interview Guidelines

The design steps for interviews are similar to those for questionnaires. A brief summary of key issues with interviews is provided here:

- *Develop questions to be asked.* After a decision has been made about the type of interview, specific questions must be developed. Questions should be brief, precise, and designed for easy response.
- *Test the interview protocol.* The interview should be tested on a small number of participants, if possible during the early stages of the meeting. The responses should be analyzed and the interview revised, if necessary.
- *Prepare the interviewers.* The interviewer must have appropriate skills—including active listening, the ability to form probing questions, and the ability to collect and summarize information into a meaningful form.
- *Provide clear instructions.* The interviewer should understand the purpose of the interview and know how the information will be used. Expectations, conditions, and rules of the interview should be thoroughly discussed. For example, the participant should know whether statements will be kept confidential.
- *Administer interviews with a plan in mind.* As with other evaluation instruments, interviews have to be conducted according to a predetermined plan. The timing of the interview, the person conducting the interview, and the location of the interview are relevant when developing an interview plan. For many stakeholders, interviewing only a sample may be necessary to save time and reduce evaluation costs.

DATA COLLECTION WITH FOCUS GROUPS

Focus groups are particularly helpful when in-depth feedback is needed. The focus group, designed to solicit qualitative judgments on a topic or issue, involves a small group discussion conducted by an experienced facilitator. Group members are all required to provide input, as individual input builds on group input.

When compared to questionnaires, surveys, or interviews, the focus group approach has several advantages. The basic premise of using focus groups is that when quality judgments are subjective, several individual judgments are better than one. The group process, whereby participants often motivate one another, is an effective method for generating and clarifying ideas and hypotheses. Compared to interviews, focus groups are inexpensive. They are also flexible and can be planned and conducted quickly.

Applications for Focus Group Evaluation

The focus group is particularly helpful when qualitative information is needed about the success of a meeting or event. For example, a focus group can be used in the following situations:

- To evaluate the application of specific procedures, tasks, schedules, or other components of the meeting or event
- To assess the overall effectiveness of the meeting or event as perceived by participants and exhibitors
- To assess the impact of the meeting or event

Essentially, focus groups are helpful when evaluation information is needed but cannot be collected adequately with questionnaires or surveys.

Guidelines

Although the rules for how to use focus groups for evaluation vary, the following guidelines should be helpful:

- *Ensure that management and the client embrace focus groups.* Because focus groups may be new to your stakeholder group, the process may need clarification. Managers need to understand focus groups and their advantages, raising their confidence in the information obtained from group sessions.
- *Plan topics, questions, and protocol carefully.* As with any evaluation instrument, planning is critical. The specific topics, questions, and issues to be discussed must be carefully planned and sequenced. This enhances the comparison of results from one group to another and ensures that the group process is effective and stays on track.
- *Keep the group size small.* While there is no magical group size, a range of six to twelve seems appropriate for most focus groups. A group has to be large enough to ensure different points of view but small enough to give every participant time to talk freely and exchange comments. Small groups also allow the facilitator to center attention on the key topics.
- *Ensure a representative sample of the target population.* Groups must be stratified appropriately so that participants represent the target population. The group should be homogeneous in experience, rank, and influence within the organization.
- *Facilitators must have appropriate expertise.* The success of a focus group rests with the facilitator, who must be skilled in the focus group process. Facilitators must know how to control aggressive members of the group, diffusing input from those who want to dominate the group. Also, facilitators must create an environment in which participants feel comfortable offering comments. As a result, some organizations use external facilitators.

In summary, the focus group is a relatively inexpensive and quick way to determine the success of implementation. However, for a complete evaluation, focus group information should be combined with data from other data collection methods.

ON-THE-JOB OBSERVATION

Although rarely used when evaluating meetings and events, another data collection method is observing participants in work situations and recording any changes in behavior and specific actions taken. This technique is particularly useful when knowing how the participants use new skills, knowledge, tasks, procedures, or systems is important. The observer may be a member of the planning team, an evaluator, the participant's manager, a member of a peer group, or an external resource, such as a mystery shopper.

Guidelines for Effective Observation

Observation is often misused or misapplied to evaluation situations, forcing some to abandon the process. The effectiveness of observation can be improved with several guidelines:

- *Observers must be fully prepared.* Observers must fully understand what information is needed and what skills are used or what actions are expected. They must be knowledgeable about the content of the meeting.
- *The observations should be systematic.* The observation process must be planned so that it is executed effectively and without surprises. The individuals observed should know in advance about the observation and the reason they are being observed. Ideally, they should be observed invisibly or in an unnoticeable way. The timing of the observations should be part of the plan. There are right times and wrong times to observe a participant. For example, if a participant is observed when work situations are not normal (such as, during a crisis), the data collected may not be a true reflection of routine behavior.
- *Several steps are necessary to accomplish a successful observation.* These include
  - Determine what behavior will be observed.
  - Prepare the forms for the observer's use.
  - Select the observers.
  - Prepare a schedule of observations.
  - Prepare observers for proper observation.
  - Inform participants of the planned observation, providing explanations.
  - Conduct the observations.
  - Summarize the observation data.

- *The observers should know how to interpret and report their observations.* Observations involve judgment decisions. The observer must analyze the behaviors displayed and the actions taken by the participants. Observers should know how to summarize behavior and report meaningful results.
- *The observers' influence should be minimized.* Except for "mystery" or "planted" observers and electronic observations, completely removing the overall effect of an observer is impossible. The presence of the observer must be minimized, and to the extent possible, the observer should blend into the work environment. If not, participants will display the behavior they think is appropriate, performing at their best.

Selection of Observers

Observers are usually independent of the participants. They are typically members of the planning team. An independent observer is usually more skilled at recording behavior, at making interpretations of behavior, and is usually unbiased in these interpretations. Using an independent observer reduces the need for planners to prepare observers and relieves the client of the responsibility. Sometimes, recruiting observers from outside the organization is a better option. On the other hand, the independent observer has the appearance of an outsider, and participants may resent this kind of observer if they know about it. The advantage of this approach is keeping biases from entering the decision making process.

Specific Observation Methods

Five methods of observation are possible, depending on the circumstances surrounding the type of information needed. Each method is briefly described below:

- *Behavior checklist and codes.* A behavior checklist is useful for recording the presence, absence, frequency, or duration of a participant's behavior as it occurs. A checklist does not provide information on the quality, intensity, or possible circumstances surrounding the observed behavior or action. It is useful in helping an observer identify exactly which behaviors should or should not occur. Measuring the duration of a behavior may be more difficult and requires a stopwatch and a place on the form to record time intervals. The number of behaviors listed in the checklist should be small and, if they logically occur in a sequence, listed in that order. A variation of this approach involves coding behaviors on a form. While this method is useful when many behaviors are involved, it is more time-consuming because a code is entered that identifies a specific behavior instead of checking an item.
- *Delayed report method.* With a delayed report method, the observer does not use any forms or written materials during the observation. The information is either recorded after the observation or at particular time intervals

during it. The observer attempts to reconstruct what has been witnessed during the observation period. The advantage of this approach is that the observer is less noticeable, and no forms are completed or notes taken during the observation. The observer becomes a part of the situation and less of a distraction. An obvious disadvantage is that the information reported may not be as accurate and reliable as it would be if noted as it occurred. A variation of this approach is the 360-degree feedback process for a leadership retreat in which surveys are completed on other individuals based on observations within a specific time frame.

- *Video recording*. A video camera records behavior in detail. However, this intrusion may be awkward and cumbersome, and the participants may be unnecessarily nervous or self-conscious while being videotaped. If the camera is concealed, the privacy of the participants may be invaded. Because of this, video recording of on-the-job behavior is not frequently used.
- *Audio monitoring*. Monitoring conversations of participants during implementation is an effective observation technique. This method is particularly helpful in telemarketing jobs. While this approach may stir some controversy, it is an effective way to determine whether skills are applied consistently and effectively. For it to work smoothly, the process must be fully explained and the rules clearly communicated.
- *Computer monitoring*. For employees who work regularly with a keyboard, computer monitoring is an effective way to "observe" participants as they perform job tasks. The computer monitors times, sequence of steps, use of routines, and other activities to determine whether the participant performs the work according to the guidelines of the meeting. As technology continues to be a significant part of the workplace, computer monitoring holds much promise.

THE USE OF ACTION PLANS AND FOLLOW-UP ASSIGNMENTS

In some cases, follow-up assignments can be used to develop implementation and application data. In a typical follow-up assignment, the participant is asked to meet a goal or complete a particular task or make a contact by a set date. A summary of the results of the completed assignment provides further evidence of the success of the meeting and implementation of information, skills, and knowledge gained.

The *action plan* is the most common type of follow-up assignment. With this approach, participants are required to develop action plans as part of the meeting. Action plans contain the detailed steps necessary to accomplish specific objectives related to the meeting. The process is one of the most effective ways to enhance support of a meeting and build the ownership needed for successful application and implementation.

The plan is typically prepared on a printed form, such as the one shown in Figure 7-2. The action plan shows what is to be done, by whom, and the

Name _____ Speaker/Facilitator Signature _____ Follow-Up Date _____

Objective _____ Evaluation Period _____ to _____

SPECIFIC STEPS: *I will do this* ⇗	Date	END RESULT: *So that* ⇗
1.		
2.		
3.		
4.		
5.		
6.		
7.		

Expected Intangible Benefits

Barriers: What Got in the Way?	Enablers: What Helped the Process?

Figure 7-2. Action Plan. Example for application data

date the objectives should be accomplished. The action-plan approach is a straightforward, easy-to-use method for determining how participants will achieve success with implementation. The approach produces data answering questions such as:

- What actions have been taken since the meeting was conducted.
- What workplace improvements have been realized since the meeting was conducted?
- Are the improvements linked to the meeting?
- What may have prevented participants from accomplishing specific action items?

Collectively, these data can be used to assess the success of the meeting implementation. With this information, decisions can be made regarding modification.

Developing the Action Plan

The development of the action plan requires two major tasks: (1) determining the areas for action and (2) writing the action items. Both tasks should be completed during the meeting and, at the same time, be related to workplace, meeting-related activities. A list of areas for action can be developed with the help of the facilitator. The list may include an area needing improvement or an opportunity for increased performance. Examples of typical questions that should be answered before determining the areas for action are listed below:

- Is it related to the meeting?
- How much time will this action take?
- Is this expected?
- Are the information, knowledge, and skills for accomplishing this action item available?
- Who has the authority to implement the actions?
- Will this action have an effect on other individuals?
- Are there any constraints for accomplishing this action item?

Usually, writing specific action items is more difficult than identifying the action areas. The most important characteristic of an action item is that it is written so that everyone involved will know when it is accomplished. One way to help achieve this goal is to use specific action verbs and set deadlines for the completion of each action item. Some examples of action items are:

- Analyze the causes of conflict by [date].
- Identify and secure a new customer account by [date].

- Handle every piece of paper only once to improve my personal time management by [date].
- Probe my employees directly about a particular problem by [date].

If appropriate, each action item should indicate other individuals or resources needed for its completion. Planned changes should be observable. They should be obvious to the participant and others when the change takes place. Action plans, as used in this context, do not require the prior approval or input from the participant's manager, although, as in any case, manager support may be helpful.

Successful Use of Action Plans

The action-plan process can be an integral part of implementation and is not necessarily considered an add-on or optional activity. To gain maximum effectiveness from action plans to collect data for evaluation, the following steps should be implemented:

- *Communicate the action plan requirement early.* One of the most negative reactions to action plans is the surprise in its introduction. When participants realize they must develop detailed action plans, they often resist. Communicating in advance that the process is an integral part of implementation will often minimize resistance. When participants understand the benefits before they attend the first meeting, they take the process more seriously and usually perform extra steps to ensure its success.
- *Describe the action planning process at the beginning of the meeting.* At the beginning of the session, action plan requirements are discussed, including an outline of its purpose, why it is necessary, and the basic requirements during and after the meeting. Some facilitators furnish a separate notepad for participants to collect ideas and useful techniques for their action plans.
- *Teach the action planning process.* A prerequisite for action planning success is understanding how action plans work and how they are developed. A portion of the meeting time is allocated to teaching participants how to develop plans. In this session, the requirements are outlined, special forms and procedures are discussed, and a positive example is distributed and reviewed. Sometimes, an entire module is allocated to this process so that participants understand and use it. Any available support tools—such as key measures, charts, graphs, suggested topics, and sample calculations—should be used in this session.
- *Allow time to develop the plan.* When action plans are used to collect data for meeting evaluation, allowing participants to develop plans during the meeting is important. Sometimes, having participants work in teams so that they can share ideas as they develop specific plans is helpful. In these sessions, facilitators often monitor individual or team progress to keep the process on track and to answer questions.

- *Have the speaker approve the action plans.* The action plan must be related to meeting objectives and, at the same time, represent an important accomplishment when it is completed. Because participants may stray from the intent and purpose of action planning and not give it the attention needed, the speaker or speaker's representative should sign off on the action plan, ensuring that the plan reflects all the requirements and is appropriate for the meeting. In some cases, a space is provided for the signature on the action-plan document.
- *Explain the follow-up mechanism.* Participants must have a clear understanding of action plan timing, implementation, and follow-up. The method by which data will be collected, analyzed, and reported should be openly discussed. Five options are common:
  - The group is convened to discuss progress on the plans.
  - Participants meet with their immediate managers and discuss the success of the plan. A copy is forwarded to the team.
  - Participants send the plan to the evaluator or planner, and it is discussed during a conference call.
  - Participants send the plan directly to the evaluator or planner with no meetings or discussions. This is the most common option.
- *Collect action plans at predetermined follow-up times.* Because an excellent response rate is critical, several steps may be necessary to ensure that action plans are completed and the data are returned to the appropriate individual or group for analysis. Follow-up reminders by mail or e-mail are typical. Others call participants to check progress. Still others offer assistance in developing the final plan. These steps may require additional resources, which must be weighed against the importance of having more data. When the action plan process is implemented as outlined in this chapter, the response rates will normally be very high—in the 60–90% range.
- *Summarize and report the data.* If developed properly, each action plan should contain improvements. Also, each individual has indicated the percentage of improvement directly related to the meeting, either on the action plan or the questionnaire. The data must be tabulated, summarized, and reported in a way that shows successful application and implementation.

Action Plan Advantages and Disadvantages

Although there are many advantages to using action plans, at least two concerns exist:

- The process relies on direct input from the participant, usually with no assurance of anonymity. As such, the information can sometimes be biased and unreliable.
- Action plans can be time-consuming for the participant and, if the participant's manager is not involved in the process, the participant may not complete the assignment.

As the material in this section has illustrated, the action plan approach has many inherent advantages. Action plans are:

- Simple and easy to administer
- Easily understood by participants
- Suitable to a wide variety of meetings and events
- Appropriate for all types of data
- Able to measure reaction, learning, behavior changes, and impact
- Usable with or without other evaluation methods

Because of the flexibility and versatility of the process and the conservative adjustments that can be made in analysis, action plans have become important data collection tools for meeting evaluation.

The Use of Performance Contracts

The performance contract is essentially a slight variation of the action planning process. Based on the principle of mutual goal setting, a performance contract is a written agreement between a participant and the participant's manager. The participant agrees to improve performance in an area of mutual concern related to the specific meeting. The agreement is in the form of a task to be completed or a goal to be accomplished soon after the meeting's completion. The agreement details what is to be accomplished, at what time, and with what results.

Although the steps can vary according to the specific kind of contract and the organization, a common sequence of events follows:

1. The participant becomes involved in a specific meeting.
2. The participant and his or her manager mutually agree on a topic for improvement related to the meeting (What's in it for me?).
3. Specific, measurable goals are set.
4. In the early stages of the meeting, the contract is discussed and plans are developed to accomplish the goals.
5. After the meeting is conducted, the participant works on the contract against a specific deadline.
6. The participant reports the results of the effort to his or her manager.
7. The manager and participant document the results and forward a copy to the planning team, along with appropriate comments.

The process of selecting the area for improvement is similar to the process used in the action planning process. The topic can include one or more of the following areas:

- *Routine performance*—includes specific improvements in routine performance measures, such as sales, efficiency, and error rates
- *Problem solving*—focuses on specific problems, such as an unexpected increase in accidents, a decrease in efficiency, or a loss of morale

- *Innovative or creative applications*—includes initiating changes or improvements in work practices, methods, procedures, techniques, and processes
- *Personal development*—involves learning new information or acquiring new skills to increase individual effectiveness

The topic selected should be stated in terms of one or more objectives. The objectives should state what is to be accomplished when the contract is complete. The objectives should be:

- Written
- Understandable by all involved
- Challenging (requiring an unusual effort to achieve)
- Achievable (something that can be accomplished)
- Largely under the control of the participant
- Measurable and dated

The details required to accomplish the contract objectives are developed following the guidelines for action plans presented earlier. Also, the methods for analyzing data and reporting progress are the same as with action plans.

Barriers to Success

One of the important reasons for collecting data at this level is to uncover the barriers to and enablers of the use of information, skills, and knowledge. Although both groups are important, barriers can kill an otherwise successful meeting. The barriers must be identified and actions must be taken to minimize, remove, or go around the barrier. This problem is serious because barriers exist on every meeting. When barriers can be removed or minimized, the meeting has a much better chance of success. Some would define implementation of a successful meeting as removing the barriers of success.

While a variety of data collection methods can be used, in each method, some step, process, or effort should be made to identify those barriers. When they are identified, they become important reference points for changes and improvements. Table 7-3 shows the typical barriers that will stifle the success of meetings. These are almost universal with any type of meeting, but others may be specific to the particular setting and the type of meeting. The important point is to identify them and then use the data in meaningful ways to try to make them less of a problem.

Along with barriers are the enablers. The enablers are the supporters or enhancers of the transfer of learning. Working with enablers provides an opportunity to make improvements beyond the success that was already achieved. They provide prescriptions for other meetings as well and are very powerful. When learning is not actually used successfully on the job, it is a very serious issue.

Table 7-3
Typical Barriers to Successful Implementation

---

1. My immediate manager does not support the meeting or event.
2. The culture in our work group does not support the meeting or event.
3. No opportunity to use the skills, knowledge, and information from the meeting or event.
4. No time to implement the skills, knowledge, and information from the meeting or event.
5. Did not learn anything that could be applied to my work.
6. Our systems and processes did not support the use of this.
7. The resources are not available to implement this.
8. Changed job and the skills no longer apply.
9. The meeting is not appropriate for our work.
10. Did not see a need to implement the skills, knowledge, or information.
11. Could not change old habits.

Data Use

Data becomes meaningless if it is not used properly. As we move up the chain, the data becomes more valuable in the minds of the sponsors, key executives, and other stakeholders that have a strong interest in the meeting. While data can be used in dozens of ways, the following are the principal uses for data after it is collected.

Report and Review Results

The most obvious use of the data is to report it to the interested stakeholders to inform them of the meeting's progress. This data would even go to the participants who are in some cases providing the data. Figure 7-3 shows how application data might be reported. In this example, six distinct actions need to be taken from this meeting, which was aimed at minimizing sexual harassment complaints. A target value was set, and two different divisions reported results. The results not only showed the success that was achieved but also areas where improvement could continue to be needed.

Adjust Design and Implementation

Sometimes, the data points to problems with the meeting management and implementation. It may indicate that some aspects of the meeting are not working well and have to be redesigned. It may indicate that other processes or partial solutions are needed to achieve the desired success. In either case, efforts may

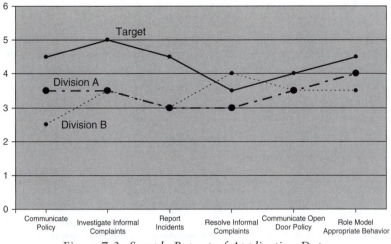

Figure 7-3. Sample Report of Application Data.

have to be taken to adjust the original meeting plan, which included design, development, and implementation.

Identify and Remove Barriers

As described earlier, one of the most important uses of the data is to drive down the barriers—either remove them, minimize them, or provide a way to go around them.

Identify and Enhance Enablers

Enablers are the opposite of barriers. Enablers are the processes, factors, actions, and elements that make the meeting a success. These need to be continued and, in some cases, enhanced so that success improves or continues at the same level.

Recognize Successful Individuals

Every meeting will have individuals who accomplish the goals impressively. They have achieved what they need to and sometimes have exceeded it. Often at this level, many success stories can be developed. These become case studies of success, detailing how some individual or group has achieved extraordinary performance. Recognition of these groups is powerful and serves as a continuing motivator and perhaps subtle communication for those who have not achieved the same success.

Reinforce Desired Actions

Since the data is collected from individuals who are implementing and applying the meeting content, the presence of questions and other data-collection processes serve to reinforce participants of what they should be doing. In a sense, the questionnaire may serve as a reminder of what they should be doing. The interview may signal areas in which they are not doing well. Thus, in essence, data collection alone can drive increased performance.

Improve Management Support

Sometimes, the application and implementation data show a lack of management support or the lack of positive management support. In either case, this data may show how managers need to support and continue to support the meeting. Also, when success is generated, it may provide management with the type of data that they want to see. Although most are interested in the impact, the money, and the ROI, some want to see things working properly, with positive behavior, things in place, processes being accomplished, and tasks being completed. This becomes satisfying data, possibly more so than reaction and learning.

Market Future Meetings or Events

For meetings that are replicated in other places, often within the same organization, the application and implementation data show what individuals have achieved, what they have accomplished, and what they have completed. When combined with qualitative comments, this can lead to powerful, persuasive data for the meeting when it is applied in other locations.

FINAL THOUGHTS

This chapter outlined techniques for measuring application and implementation—a critical issue in determining the success of a meeting. This essential measure determines not only the success achieved, but areas where improvement is needed and areas where the success can be replicated in the future. A variety of techniques are available, ranging from questionnaires to action plans. The method chosen must match the scope of the meeting and resources available to collect data. Complicated meetings may require a comprehensive approach that measures all the issues involved in application and implementation. Simple meetings can have a less formal approach and collect data only from a questionnaire.

CHAPTER 8

Measuring and Isolating the Impact of Meetings and Events

This chapter focuses on tracking business performance measures connected to meetings and events and is the last chapter on collecting data. Executives regard business impact data as, perhaps, the most important data type because of its connection to business success. In many cases, a less-than-desired performance in one or more business measures (a business need) created the need for the meeting or event (e.g., we need to boost sales). This chapter covers the methods needed to collect the business measures and includes monitoring the business records, collecting action plans, and using questionnaires. These three processes account for most opportunities available for collecting impact data.

When a significant increase in business performance is noted after a meeting or event has been conducted, the challenge is to link it to the meeting. Other factors may have contributed to the improvement, as well. This chapter explores useful techniques for isolating the effects of the meeting on the business measure. If this issue is not addressed, the link to business impact is not credible.

IMPORTANCE OF MEASURING BUSINESS IMPACT

Although several obvious reasons exist for measuring impact, several specific issues support the rationale for collecting business impact data related to a meeting or event.

Higher-Level Data

Following the assumption that higher-level data create more value for key stakeholders, the business impact measures offer more valuable data than data collected at lower levels. Impact data represent the consequence of the application and implementation of a meeting or event. They represent the bottom-line measures that are positively influenced when a meeting is successful. For some stakeholders, these are the most valuable data.

A Business Driver for Meetings and Events

For many meetings and events, business impact data represent the initial drivers for the meeting. The problem of deteriorating (or less-than-desired) performance or the opportunity for improvement of a business measure often leads to the need for the meeting. If the business needs defined by business measures are the drivers, then the key measures for evaluating the meeting are those same business measures. These measures often represent hard, indisputable facts that reflect performance that is critical to the business and operating part of an organization. The extent to which measures have changed is the principal determinant of the success of the meeting. These are the measures often desired by the ultimate client—the individual who funds the meeting.

Monetary Data

As stated earlier, business impact measures offer more valuable data than measures at lower levels. Impact data are the consequence of the application and implementation of a meeting. They represent the bottom-line measures that are positively influenced when a meeting is successful. For some stakeholders, these are the most valuable data. At this level, the actual money is developed when necessary for an ROI calculation. Impact data, influenced by the meeting, can be converted to monetary value to show the monetary contribution of the meeting. Although this conversion is actually a separate step, it is derived from the business impact data collected in this step. This makes this level of data collection one of the most critical for ROI analysis.

Easy to Measure

Business impact data are often easy to measure and readily available. Hard and soft data measures at this level reflect key measures found in plentiful numbers throughout an organization. It is not unusual for an organization to have hundreds, or even thousands, of measures reflecting specific business impact items. The challenge is to connect the objectives of the meeting to the appropriate business measures. This is more easily accomplished at the beginning of the meeting due to the availability and ease with which many of the data items can be located.

The irony of this level of data collection is that these data types are the most common. When measuring reaction, learning, or application, the measures usually have to be created. However, at the business impact level, the data have been created, except for rare exceptions where data development is necessary. The good news is that these are common data items tracked and monitored by someone.

TYPES OF IMPACT MEASURES

To help focus on the desired measures, impact measures are separated into two general categories of data described in Chapter 3: hard data and soft data.

Two more specific categories are tangible benefits and intangible benefits. Distinguishing between the categories becomes important when converting data to monetary values, which will be discussed in Chapter 9.

Hard Versus Soft Data

Hard data are the primary measurements of improvement, presented through rational, undisputed facts that are easily collected. Much of the criteria for measuring the effectiveness of management rest on hard data items—such as productivity, profitability, cost control, and quality control. Table 3-6 in Chapter 3, provides examples of hard data grouped into categories of output, quality, costs, and time.

Soft data are more difficult to collect and analyze but are used when hard data are unavailable. Soft data are difficult to convert to monetary values. They are subjectively based, in many cases, and are less credible as a performance measurement. Table 3-7 in Chapter 3 provides a list of typical soft data items grouped into typical categories. The preference of hard data in meetings does not reduce the value of soft data. Soft data are essential for a complete evaluation of a meeting as success may rest on soft data measurements.

Tangible Versus Intangible

The confusion about the categories of soft data and the often reduced value placed on soft data were discussed in Chapter 3. This leads to a critical definition in this book. While the terms hard and soft data can be used to discuss impact data, the terms tangible and intangible can also be used. Tangible data represent a category that can or has been converted to monetary value. Intangibles are defined as data purposely not converted to monetary value (i.e., if data cannot be converted to monetary value credibly with a reasonable amount of resources, then it is left as an intangible). This is consistent with the thinking of many professionals who place tremendous value on the intangible measures.

This approach has several advantages. First, it avoids the sometimes confusing labels of soft and hard. Second, it avoids the image that being soft equates to little or no value. Third, it brings the definition to the situation. In some organizations, a particular data item may be converted to money already and the conversion is credible because it actually becomes tangible. However, in another organization, the same measure has not been converted and cannot be converted with a reasonable amount of resources. Therefore, it is left as intangible. Fourth, it provides a rule that enhances the consistency of the process. This is one of the standards listed in Chapter 2. Having this rule ensures that if two people conducted the same evaluation, they would get the same or similar results.

SPECIFIC MEASURES LINKED TO MEETINGS

An important issue that often surfaces when considering ROI applications is to identify specific measures often driven by specific meetings. While there are no standard answers, Table 8-1 represents a summary of some typical payoff measures for specific types of meetings. The measures are broad for some meetings. For example, an association general meeting may pay off in a variety of measures,

Table 8-1
Typical Measures for Meetings and Events

Project	Key Impact Measurements
Anti-social behavior conferences	Complaints, turnover, absenteeism, productivity, employee satisfaction
Association meetings	Productivity, sales, quality, time, costs, customer service, turnover, absenteeism, job satisfaction
Business coaching conferences	Productivity/output, quality, time savings, efficiency, costs, employee satisfaction, customer satisfaction
Career-focused meetings	Enrollments, promotions, recruiting expenses, turnover, job satisfaction
Communications meetings	Errors, stress, conflicts, productivity, job satisfaction
Compliance meetings	Penalties/fines, charges, settlements, losses
Dealer meetings	Sales, market share, cost of sales, quality efficiency, customer loyalty
Diversity meetings	Turnover, absenteeism, complaints, charges, settlements, losses
Employee retention conferences	Turnover, engagement, job satisfaction
Engineering/technical conferences	Productivity/output, quality, customer satisfaction, turnover, absenteeism, job satisfaction
Executive conferences	Productivity, sales, quality, time, costs, customer service, market share, turnover, absenteeism, job satisfaction
Franchise meetings	Productivity, sales, quality, time, costs, customer service, market share, turnover, absenteeism, job satisfaction
Golfing events	Sales, market share, customer loyalty, new accounts, upselling
Indoctrination/orientation meetings	Early turnover, training time, productivity, performance
Labor-management conferences	Work stoppages, grievances, absenteeism, job satisfaction
Leadership retreats/staff retreats	Productivity/output, quality, efficiency, cost/time savings, employee satisfaction, engagement
Management conferences	Productivity, sales, quality, time, costs, customer service, turnover, absenteeism, job satisfaction

Table 8-1
(Continued)

Project	Key Impact Measurements
Medical meetings	Medical costs, quality, compliance, efficiency, patient satisfaction
Personal productivity meetings	Time savings, productivity, stress reduction, job satisfaction
Project management conferences	Time savings, quality improvement, budgets
Quality meetings	Defects, rework, response times, cycle times, costs
Safety meetings	Accident frequency rates, accident severity rates, first aid treatments
Sales meetings	Sales, market share, customer loyalty, new accounts, brand awareness
Supervisor/team leader meetings	Productivity, sales, quality, time, costs, customer service, turnover, absenteeism, job satisfaction
Team-building sessions	Productivity, sales, quality, time, costs, customer service, turnover, absenteeism, job satisfaction
Wellness/fitness meetings	Stress, turnover, medical costs, accidents, absenteeism

such as improved productivity, enhanced revenues, improved quality, cycle-time reduction, direct cost savings, and employee job satisfaction. In other meetings, the influenced measures are narrow. For example, a meeting on diversity typically influences turnover, complaints, absenteeism, and employee satisfaction. The measures influenced depend on the objectives and the design of the meeting. The table also illustrates the immense number of measures that can be driven or influenced. A word of caution is needed. Presenting specific measures linked to a typical meeting may give the impression that these are the only measures influenced. In practice, a particular meeting can have many outcomes.

The good news is that most meetings and events are driving business measures. The measures are based on what is being changed in the various business units, divisions, regions, and individual workplaces. These are the measures that matter to senior executives. The difficulty often comes in ensuring that the connection to the meeting exists. This is accomplished through a variety of techniques, which isolate the effects of the meeting on the particular business measures and will be discussed later.

BUSINESS PERFORMANCE DATA MONITORING

Data to measure business performance are available in every organization. Monitoring performance data enables management to measure performance in terms of output, quality, costs, time, job satisfaction, and customer satisfaction, among other measures. In determining the source of data in the evaluation, the first consideration should be existing databases, reports, and scorecards. In most organizations, performance data suitable for measuring meeting-related improvement are available. If not, additional record-keeping systems will have to be developed for measurement and analysis. At this point, the question of economics surfaces. Is it economical to develop the record-keeping systems necessary to evaluate a meeting? If the costs are greater than the expected benefits, developing those systems is pointless.

Identify Appropriate Measures

Existing performance measures should be thoroughly researched to identify those related to the proposed objectives of the meeting. Often, several performance measures are related to the same item. For example, the effectiveness and efficiency of a sales force can be measured in several ways:

- Number of units sold
- Sales by product line
- Total sales
- Profit of the sale
- Customer satisfaction
- Customer loyalty
- Percentage of goal met
- Market share
- Wallet share
- Sales cost per unit
- Total cost of sales
- Customer churn

Each of these, in its own way, measures the effectiveness or efficiency of the sales team. All related measures should be reviewed to determine those most relevant to the meeting.

Convert Current Measures to Usable Ones

Occasionally, existing performance measures are integrated with other data, and keeping them isolated from unrelated data may be difficult. In this situation, all existing, related measures should be extracted and tabulated again to make them more appropriate for comparison in the evaluation. At times, conversion factors may be necessary. For example, the average number of new sales orders per month may be presented regularly in the performance measures for the sales department. In addition, the sales costs per sales representative are also presented. However, in the evaluation of a meeting, the average cost per new sale is needed. The average number of new sales orders and the sales cost per sales representative are required to develop the data necessary for comparison.

Develop New Measures

In some cases, data needed to measure the effectiveness of a meeting are not available, and new data are needed. The evaluator or planner must work with the client organization to develop record-keeping systems, if economically feasible. In one organization, the sales staff's delayed responses to customer requests were an issue. This problem was discovered based on customer feedback. The feedback data prompted a meeting to reduce the response time. To help ensure the success of the meeting, several measures were planned, including measuring the actual time to respond to a customer request. Initially this measure was not available. As the meeting was implemented, new software was used to measure the time.

Several questions regarding this issue were addressed:

- Which department/section will develop the measurement system?
- Who will record and monitor the data?
- Where will it be recorded?
- Will input forms be used?
- Who will report it?

These questions will usually involve other departments or a management decision that extends beyond the scope of evaluators. Often the administration, operations, or the information technology unit will be instrumental in helping determine whether new measures are needed and, if so, how they will be developed. This action should be a last resort.

THE USE OF ACTION PLANS TO MEASURE BUSINESS IMPACT DATA

For many meetings, business data are readily available. However, at times, data will not be easily accessible to the planner. Sometimes, data are maintained at the individual, work unit, or department level and may not be known to anyone outside that area. Tracking down those data sets may be too expensive and time consuming. When this is the case, other data collection methods such as action plans may be used to capture data sets and make them available for the planner. Action plans can capture application and implementation data, as discussed in Chapter 7. They can also be a useful tool for capturing business impact data. For business impact data, the action plan is more focused and credible than a questionnaire. The basic design principles involved in developing and administering action plans are the same for business impact data as they are for application and implementation data. However, a few elements unique to business impact are presented in this section.

Set Goals and Targets

As shown in Figure 8-1, an action plan can be developed with a direct focus on business impact data. The plan presented in this figure requires participants to

Name: _____ Speaker/Facilitator Signature _____ Follow-Up Date _____

Objective: _____ Evaluation Period _____ to _____

Improvement Measure: _____ Current Performance _____ Target Performance _____

Action Steps	Analysis
1. _____	A. What is the unit of measure? _____
2. _____	B. What is the value (cost) of one unit? $ _____
3. _____	C. How did you arrive at this value? _____
4. _____	
5. _____	D. How much did the measure change during the evaluation period? (monthly value) _____
6. _____	E. List the other factors that have influenced this change. _____
7. _____	F. What percent of this change was actually caused by this meeting? _____ %
Intangible Benefits:	G. What level of confidence do you place on the above information? (100% = Certainty and 0% = No Confidence) _____ %

Comments: _____

Figure 8-1. Action Plan. Example for Impact Data

develop an overall objective for the plan, which is usually the primary objective of the meeting. In some cases, a meeting may have more than one objective, which requires more action plans. In addition to the objective, the improvement measure and the current levels of performance are identified. This information requires that the participant anticipate the application of skills and set goals for specific performances that can be realized.

Complete the Action Plan

The action plan is completed during the meeting, often with input and assistance from the speaker or facilitator. The facilitator actually approves the plan, indicating that it meets the requirements of being specific, motivating, achievable, realistic, and time-based (SMART). The plan can actually be developed in less than a one-hour timeframe and often begins with action steps related to the meeting. These action steps are Level 3 activities that detail application and implementation. All these steps build support for, and are linked to, the business impact measures defined on the plan.

Define the Unit of Measure

Next, the unit of measure must be defined. In some cases, more than one measure may be used and will subsequently be contained in additional action plans. The unit of measure is necessary to break the process into the simplest steps so that its ultimate value can be determined. The unit may be output data, such as an additional unit manufactured or package delivered, or it can be sales and marketing data, such as additional sales revenue or a one percent increase in market share. In terms of quality, the unit can be one reject, one error, or one defect. Time-based units are usually measured in minutes, hours, days, or weeks. Other units are specific to their particular types of data, such as one grievance, one complaint, one absence, or one less person on welfare. The point is to break down impact data into the simplest terms possible.

Place a Monetary Value on Each Improvement

During the meeting, participants are asked to locate, calculate, or estimate the monetary value for each improvement outlined in their plans. The unit value is determined using a variety of methods such as standard values, expert input, external databases, or estimates. The process used in arriving at the value is described in the instructions for the action plan. When the actual improvement occurs, participants will use these values to capture the annual monetary benefits of the plan (More information on converting data to money is covered in the next Chapter).

In the worst-case scenario, participants are asked to calculate the value. Using standard values or having participants contact an expert are the best actions.

When participant estimates are necessary, participants must show the basis of their calculations, and space for this information should be provided.

Implement the Action Plan

Participants implement the action plan after the meeting is conducted. The participants follow action plan steps, and the subsequent business impact results are achieved.

Provide Specific Improvements

At the end of the specified follow-up period—usually 3 months or 6 months—the participants indicate the specific improvements made, usually expressed as a daily, weekly, or monthly amount. This determines the actual amount of change that has been observed, measured, or recorded. Participants must understand the need for accuracy as data are recorded. In most cases, only the changes are recorded, as those amounts are needed to calculate the monetary values of the meeting. In other cases, before and after data may be recorded, allowing the evaluator to calculate the differences.

Isolate the Effects of the Meeting

Although the action plan is initiated because of the meeting, the actual improvements reported on the action plan may be influenced by other factors. Accordingly, the meeting should not be given full credit for all the improvement. For example, an action plan to implement leadership skills could only be given partial credit for a business improvement because other variables might have influenced the impact measures. While several ways are available to isolate the effects of a meeting, participant estimation is usually most appropriate in the action planning process. Participants are asked to estimate the percentage of the improvement directly related to the meeting. This question can be asked on the action plan form or in a follow-up questionnaire. Sometimes, preceding this question with a request to identify all the other factors that might have influenced the results is beneficial. This allows the participants to think through the relationships before allocating a portion to the meeting.

Provide a Confidence Level for Estimates

The process described above to isolate the amount of the improvement directly related to the meeting is not precise. Participants are asked to indicate their level of confidence in their estimates. Using a scale of 0–100%—where 0% means no confidence and 100% means the estimates represent absolute certainty—participants have a way to express their uncertainty with the estimates.

Collect Action Plans at Specified Time Intervals

An excellent response rate is essential, so several steps may be necessary to ensure that the action plans are completed and returned. Usually, participants will see the importance of the process and will develop their plans during the meeting. Some organizations use follow-up reminders by mail or e-mail. Others call participants to check progress. Still others offer assistance to complete the final plan. These steps may require additional resources, which must be weighed against the importance of having more precise data. Specific ways to improve response rates were discussed in Chapter 7.

Summarize the Data and Calculate the ROI

If developed properly, each action plan should have annualized monetary values associated with the improvements. Also, each individual should have indicated the percentage of the improvement directly related to the meeting. Finally, participants should have provided a confidence percentage to reflect their uncertainty with the estimates and the subjective nature of some of the data that they provided.

Because this process involves estimates, it may not appear accurate. Several adjustments during the analysis make the process credible and more accurate. These adjustments reflect the guiding principles of the ROI Methodology.

Advantages of Action Plans

The action-planning process has several inherent advantages as a useful way to collect business impact data. Most of the data are taken directly from participants and often have the credibility needed for the analysis. Also, much of the responsibility for the analysis and evaluation is shifted to the participants as they address three of the most critical parts of the process. In effect, they collect data to show improvements, isolate the effects of the meeting, and convert data to monetary values. This enables the evaluation to be conducted with limited resources and shifts much of the responsibility to those who apply and implement the ideas, information, and knowledge from the meeting.

THE USE OF PERFORMANCE CONTRACTS TO MEASURE BUSINESS IMPACT

The performance contract is a variation of the action plan. Based on the principle of mutual goal setting, a performance contract is a written agreement between a participant and the participant's manager. The participant agrees to improve performance in an area of concern related to the meeting. The agreement is in the form of a goal to be accomplished during or after the meeting. The agreement details what is to be accomplished, at what time, and with what results.

Although the steps can vary according to the organization and the specific contract, a common sequence of events follows:

1. The employee (participant) becomes involved in the meeting.
2. The participant and (his or her) immediate manager mutually agree on a measure or measures for improvement related to the meeting (What's in it for me?).
3. Specific, measurable goals for improvement are set, following the SMART requirements.
4. In some part of the meeting, the contract is discussed, and plans are developed to accomplish the goals.
5. During implementation, the participant works on the contract against a specific deadline.
6. The participant reports the results of the effort to his or her manager.
7. The manager and participant document the results and forward a copy to the planning team along with appropriate comments.

The process of selecting the area for improvement is similar to the process used when preparing an action plan.

THE USE OF QUESTIONNAIRES TO COLLECT BUSINESS DATA

As described in previous chapters, the questionnaire is one of the most versatile data collection tools and can be appropriate for Level 1, 2, 3, and 4 data. Chapter 7 presented a sample questionnaire in which application and implementation data (Level 3) are collected. Some of the questionnaire issues discussed in the previous chapter apply equally in collecting business impact data. Essentially, the design principles and the content issues are the same. However, questionnaires developed for a business impact evaluation will contain additional questions to capture impact data items.

Using questionnaires for impact data collection brings both good and bad news. The good news is that questionnaires are easy to use and the cost is minimal. Data analysis is efficient, and the time to provide the data is often short, making them among the least disruptive data collection methods. However, the bad news is that the data can be distorted, inaccurate, and sometimes missing. The challenge is to take all the steps necessary to ensure that questionnaires are complete and accurate and are returned. Unfortunately, because of the disadvantages, questionnaires represent one of the weakest methods of data collection. Paradoxically, it is the most used method because of its advantages.

The philosophy in the use of the ROI Methodology is to make the weakest method as credible as possible. Therefore, the challenge is to make questionnaires credible and useful by ensuring that they capture all the necessary data, participants provide accurate and complete data, and the return rates are in the 70–80% range.

The reason return rates need to be so high is based on Guiding Principle 6 in the ROI Methodology—no data, no improvement. If an individual provides no improvement data, the assumption is that the person had no improvement. This is a conservative principle but necessary for the credibility of the results. Therefore, using questionnaires will require effort, discipline, and personal attention to ensure proper response rates. Remembering that this is the least preferred method is important, and questionnaires are only used when the other methods do not work (i.e., business performance data cannot be easily monitored or action plans are not feasible). Three scenarios for questionnaire use are possible.

When You Do not Have a Clue

In the worse-case situation, the meeting planner does not have a clue which measures have been driven or influenced by the meeting. For some, this situation may be inconceivable, but in practice it occurs routinely. Consider the tremendous amount of money poured into meetings and events with most of them implemented without knowing how they will add value or improve a specific measure. When this is the case, the data collection instrument would follow the series of questions shown in Figure 8-2. This is much like a fishing expedition as the meeting planner attempts to uncover a particular business measure connected to the meeting. Still, it could be a useful exercise with some surprising results.

Question 1 is an attempt to connect the meeting to the work environment—it is the transition. It is essentially a Level 3 question about application. The goal is to get the participant to reflect on actions taken because of the meeting. Question 2 examines consequences, defining or explaining more specifically the outcomes of their actions, implementation, and behaviors. The influence could

---

Scenerio 1. When You Do not Have a Clue

1. How did you use the material from this meeting?
2. What influence did it have in your work? Team?
3. What specific measure was influenced? Define it.
4. What is the unit value of the measure? (Profit or Cost)
5. What is the basis of this value?
6. How much did the measure change since the meeting was conducted?
7. What is the frequency of the measure? (Daily, weekly, monthly, etc.)
8. What is the total annual value of the improvement?
9. List the other factors that could have caused this total improvement?
10. What percent of the total improvement can be attributed to this meeting?
11. What is your confidence estimate, expressed as a percent, for the above data? 0% = no confidence; 100% = certainty

---

Figure 8-2. Chain of Impact Questions When the Measure Is Unknown.

be with individual work, the team, or even the organization. Question 3 asks for the specifics, defining the measure. In many cases, more than one measure may be involved, and these questions can have multiple responses. Question 4 is the actual unit value, which is profit if it is a sales-related output measure or costs if it is a quality, productivity, or time measure. This is a difficult challenge, but it is achievable in most organizations because the unit values are already developed. Question 5 gauges the credibility of the data provided in Question 4. The participant explains how he or she arrived at the unit value. If Question 5 is left blank, the data item is thrown out (but the participants know this from the instructions given). In essence, this would be an unsupported claim that is omitted from the analysis (Guiding Principle 8).

Question 6 documents the change, the difference in the pre-meeting measure and the post-meeting measure. Question 7 details the specific frequency. The frequency is necessary to calculate the total annual improvement asked for in Question 8. This is the first-year value of improvement. Most meetings will only pay off on the first year of value. Question 9 requires participants to think through other factors that might have influenced the specific measure they reported. This is a way of validating the reported change. Initially, the participant may think that the improvement is all directly connected to this meeting. In reality, other factors are there. This question provides an opportunity for participants to reflect on the links to other factors. Question 10 then asks the participants to decide, after thinking about other possible factors, what percentage of the improvement came directly from the meeting, isolating the effects of the meeting from other influences. Because this is an estimate, it is adjusted for error, asked for in Question 11. Participant estimate as an isolation technique is described later in the chapter.

Participants must not be surprised with these questions. They must know that they are coming, and every effort must be made to solicit a response. Still, many professionals may consider this series of questions a futile exercise—that participants cannot provide responses. Fortunately, the research does not support this position. In hundreds of studies in which this kind of approach is taken, participants can and will provide data connected to the meeting, assuming that a connection to a business measure exists.

The skeptics often think that participants are unknowing, uncooperative, and irresponsible, validating their point that the data would not be forthcoming. However, participants will provide data for four basic reasons:

1. They are the most credible source, since they are directly involved and understand the full scope of the meeting and its consequences.
2. It is their work, and they know more about it than anyone. Their performance is being reported and analyzed.
3. This process recognizes their roles as experts. The question suggests that they are in a position to know, and they appreciate the recognition that they have the expertise to provide the data.
4. They are responsible. For the most part, participants will provide data if they understand why the data are needed and how they will be used.

Of course, not every participant will warm up to this exercise. It works extremely well for professional, engineering, administrative, management, and technical personnel. Operators, laborers, and entry-level clerical staff may have more difficulty. But in most situations, the participants are responsible and knowledgeable and care about the process. Because of this, the quality and quantity of the data may be surprising.

When the Measure Is a Defined Set

A slightly modified approach to these questions is to assume that the meeting is influencing a set of measures in a distinct category or group. Figure 8-3 shows such an example. Question 1 lists a group of measures that logically could be directly connected to the meeting. (This is a little easier than the previous scenario

---

Scenario 2, When the Measure Is in a Defined Set

1. To what extent did this meeting positively influence the following measures:

	Significant Influence				No Influence	
	5	4	3	2	1	n/a
productivity	O	O	O	O	O	O
sales	O	O	O	O	O	O
quality	O	O	O	O	O	O
cost	O	O	O	O	O	O
efficiency	O	O	O	O	O	O
time savings	O	O	O	O	O	O
employee satisfaction	O	O	O	O	O	O
customer satisfaction	O	O	O	O	O	O
other	O	O	O	O	O	O

2. What other measures were positively influenced by this meeting?
   _____

3. Of the measures listed below, which **one** is most directly linked to the project? (check only one)
   ❏ productivity   ❏ sales   ❏ quality
   ❏ cost   ❏ efficiency   ❏ time
   ❏ employee satisfaction ❏ customer satisfaction ❏ other

4. Please define the measure above.
   _____

Figure 8-3. Chain of impact questions when the measure is in a defined set.

where the set of measures was not known.) This series of questions requires participants to think about specific outcomes but is triggered by potential or possibility. This is even more powerful when the measures are focused on the possible or probable outcomes of the meeting. The other questions and analysis are similar to what was contained in the previous scenario. This approach has the advantage of being more credible because it connects to a given set of measures.

To complete this questionnaire, questions 4–11 from Figure 8-2 are repeated.

When the Measure Is Known

Fortunately, with some meetings, the actual measures are known. These are the measures tied to the meeting in the beginning and are often the measures that drive the meeting. When these are known, the questionnaire can be focused, specific, and credible. Essentially, questions 3–11 in Figure 8-2 are asked when the measure is known. The important point here is that the participant defines the measure precisely and in some cases it is given to them on the questionnaire. This scenario is more credible than the previous two, as it focuses on a specific measure that was defined in the beginning and has driven the meeting.

Response Rates

To ensure an appropriate response for all three scenarios, the techniques outlined in Chapter 7 apply equally to follow-up questionnaires where business impact data are collected. Questionnaires must be thoroughly explained and, if possible, reviewed during the meeting. The list of techniques presented in the previous chapter will not be repeated.

ISOLATE THE EFFECTS OF THE MEETING

In almost every situation, multiple influences drive business measures. With multiple influences, measuring the effect of each influence is imperative, at least to the extent that it is attributed to the meeting. Without this isolation step, meeting success will be in question. The results will be overstated if *all* the change in the business impact measure is attributed to the meeting. When this issue is ignored, the impact study is considered invalid and inconclusive. This places tremendous pressure on meeting planners to show the business value of the meetings when compared to other factors.

The cause-and-effect relationship between a meeting and business impact can be confusing and difficult to prove but can be shown with an acceptable degree of accuracy. The challenge is to develop one or more specific techniques to isolate the effects of the meeting early in the process, usually as part of an evaluation plan conducted before the meeting is planned. Up-front attention ensures that appropriate techniques will be used with minimum costs and time commitments.

Use of Control Groups

The most accurate approach for isolating the impact of a meeting is the use of control groups in an experimental design process. This approach involves the comparison of one group attending the meeting (experimental group) and a control group that is not involved. The composition of both groups should be as identical as possible and, if feasible, participants for each group should be assigned randomly. When this is achieved, and both groups are subjected to the same environmental influences, the difference in the performance of the two groups can be attributed to the meeting.

Case Study—International Software Company

International Software Company (ISC) produces payroll software for companies with a small number of employees. Packaged as standard payroll processing software, several enhancements can be purchased to perform other routines involving employee statistics and data. In some cases, data gets into staffing and manpower-planning issues. The company enjoys a customer database of more than 1,500 users. For the most part, the customers use only the payroll functions.

Each year ISC hosts a conference where the users discuss issues they have encountered with implementation, new uses of the software, and how it can be adjusted, modified, or enhanced to add value to the organization. This is also an opportunity for ISC to get referrals and sell enhanced versions of the software. The audience for this project is the individuals who attend the users' conference. Attendees of the conference must be current purchasers of the software and use it primarily for the payroll option.

The solution is the two-day conference designed to improve customer satisfaction with the current use of the software, upgrade particular software users to other options, and obtain referrals for other potential clients. There is no charge for the participants to attend; however, the participants must handle their own travel arrangements and hotel accommodations.

Several measures are monitored in a control group arrangement to ensure the success of this program.

1. Enhanced sales of upgrading options to current customers (increased sales of existing clients).
2. Referrals for new clients.
3. Increase in customer satisfaction as measured on the annual satisfaction survey.

Four specific criteria were used to select individuals for the comparison group. The user group attendees became the experimental group, and a comparison group of users that did not attend the conference became the control group. The two groups were matched using the following criteria:

1. The type of organization. This was basically matching the type of business by standard industrial classification.
2. The extent of use. The extent to which the customers are using upgraded software options beyond the standard, basic payroll processing.
3. The actual sales volume to date, which reflected the number of employees.
4. The actual longevity of the customer measured in years of using the current software.

One hundred twenty-four users attended the conference, and a matching group of 121 were selected with the criteria outlined above. The experiment lasted for one year to track the three measures identified to compare the performance in the years after the program (i.e., the average referrals from other channels compared with referrals coming through the conference as well as the actual upgrade from other users groups compared to those who attended the conference). Finally, the customer satisfaction data were compared for the two groups.

Concerns about Control Groups

One concern with the use of a control group is that it may create an image of a laboratory setting, which can make some executives and administrators uncomfortable. To avoid this stigma, some organizations conduct a pilot meeting using participants as the experimental group. A similarly matched, non-participating control group is assigned but does not attend or receive any communication about the meeting. The terms pilot and comparison group are less threatening than experimental group and control group.

The control group approach does have some inherent problems that may make it difficult to apply in practice. The first major problem is assigning the groups. Having identical control and experimental groups is impossible. Dozens of factors can affect performance, some of them individual, others contextual. To address this problem on a practical basis, it is best to select four to six variables that will have the greatest influence on performance, using the concept of Pareto principle. With the 80/20 rule, the factors that might account for 80% of the difference and the most important factors are used.

For example, in a sales meeting for Dell Computer Corporation, a control group arrangement was used. The meeting involved regional sales managers, account managers, account executives, account representatives, and sales representatives. The output measures were quota attainment, total revenue attainment, profit margin, and sales volumes. An experimental group was involved in the meeting and was carefully matched with a control group that was not involved. The equivalent number of participants for the control group was assigned at random using the company database. To ensure that the control group and the meeting group were equivalent, assignments were made on three criteria: job positions, job levels, and experience.

Another major problem with control groups is that the process is inappropriate for many situations. Withholding the meeting from one group while it is implemented in another may not be appropriate. This is particularly important for critical solutions that are needed immediately. This barrier keeps many control groups from being implemented.

Making it Work

Several questions should be explored to determine if a control group is feasible:

1. Is the population large enough to divide into groups?
2. Is the population homogeneous—representing similar jobs and similar environments?
3. What is the particular measure that the meeting or event is influencing?
4. What criteria may be affecting this measure? These criteria are used to select the comparison groups.
5. Using the Pareto Principle (focus on the most important factors), which of the factors account for most of the difference between the groups?
6. Can the meeting or event be withheld from a particular group? Sometimes this is a naturally occurring situation because it may take a long time to roll out a series of repeat meetings. Individuals who participate in the last meeting may be as many as three to six months behind those who were involved in the first meeting, creating an opportune time to compare the last group with the first group.
7. Is a pilot meeting planned? Could the pilot group be matched with other groups for comparison purposes?

Several important rules are appropriate when working with control groups:

1. Keep the groups separated by different locations, buildings, cities, or shifts, if possible.
2. Minimize communication between the groups.
3. Do not let the control or experimental group know they are part of an experiment and being compared with others.
4. Monitor data on a short-term basis to check for improvements for both groups.
5. Watch out for the Hawthorne effect from the experimental group (e.g., minimize the attention paid to the group other than that required by the meeting design).
6. Minimize the effect of the self-fulfilling prophecy by not creating expectations beyond the norm that may drive results (e.g., do not tell people they are a special group and top performance is expected).

Because the use of control groups is an effective approach for isolating impact, it should be considered as a technique when a major ROI impact study is planned. In these situations, isolating the meeting's impact with a high level of accuracy is important, and the primary advantage of the control group process is accuracy. Additional information on the use of control groups is found in other references, (Phillips and Phillips, 2008).

Use of Trend Line Analysis

Another useful technique for approximating the impact of a meeting is trend line analysis. With this approach, a trend line is drawn to project the future performance of a measure, before the meeting is conducted, using previous performance as a base. After the meeting is conducted, actual performance is compared to the trend line projection. Any improvement in performance above what the trend line predicted can then be reasonably attributed to the meeting, if certain conditions are met. While this is not an exact process, it provides a reasonable estimate of the meeting's impact.

When to Use it

To use this technique, two conditions must be met:

- The trend that has developed prior to the meeting is expected to continue if the meeting had not been conducted (i.e., would this trend continue on the same path established before the participants attended the meeting?). The process owner(s) should be able to provide input to reach this conclusion. If the answer is "no," the trend-line analysis will not be used. If the answer is "yes," the second condition is considered.
- No new variables or influences entered the process during the evaluation period. The key word is "new," realizing that the trend has been established because of the influences already in place, and no additional influences enter the process beyond conducting the meeting. If the answer is "yes," another method would have to be used. If the answer is "no," the trend line analysis develops a reasonable estimate of the impact of this meeting.

Pre-meeting data must be available before this technique can be used, and the data should have some reasonable degree of stability. If the variance of the data is high, the stability of the trend line becomes an issue. The trend line can be projected directly from historical data using a simple routine that is available with many calculators and software packages, such as Microsoft Excel™.

Case Studies

Figure 8-4 shows an example of a trend line analysis taken from sales data from a division of a consumer producer's company. Data are presented before and after a sales meeting in July. As shown in the figure, an upward trend on the data began prior to the sales meeting. Although the meeting apparently had an effect

Figure 8-4. Trend Line Analysis.

on shipment productivity, the trend line shows that some improvement would have occurred anyway, based on the trend that had been established. The meeting planner may have been tempted to measure the improvement by comparing the average six months' sales prior to the meeting (87.3 million) to the average six months after the meeting (92.3 million), yielding a 7.1 million difference. However, a more accurate comparison is the six-month average after the meeting compared to the trend line (92.3 million). In this analysis, the difference is 2.1 million. Using this more conservative measure increases the accuracy and credibility of the process to isolate the impact of the meeting.

Figure 8-5 shows the trend line analysis for sexual harassment complaints at a healthcare chain, Faith Hospitals. It shows the dramatic effect of a series of seventeen meetings held with all employees and managers of this firm, which employs more than 8,000. The meeting was designed to explain the organization's policy for addressing sexual harassment issues and explored what constitutes illegal and inappropriate sexual comments and activities. As the figure illustrates, the complaints on a monthly basis were rising. Yet, after the meeting, they dropped dramatically.

Using the trend line, the number is forecasted to be much higher one year after the meeting. However, the actual number is much lower. When the actual differences are compared, it revealed that approximately thirty-two complaints

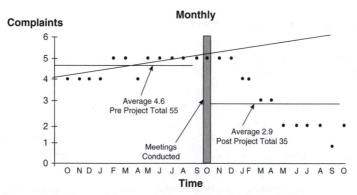

Figure 8-5. Formal Internal Complaints of Sexual Harassment.

were prevented as a result of this meeting. To ensure this could be used, two conditions were validated. The human resources staff, including the individuals who investigate these complaints, confirmed that these two conditions were validated. It was determined that the contributions of the meeting resulted in thirty-two avoided complaints.

Using Estimates

Unfortunately, the most common method of isolating the effects of a meeting is the use of estimates. Estimating the amount of improvement connected to a particular meeting is the least effective method from an analytical viewpoint. Because it is the weakest method, every step should be taken to make it as credible as possible. The good news is that this can be a credible process if some precautions are taken, as described in this section.

The beginning point in using this method is ensuring that the isolation is performed by the most credible source, and that is often the participant. The individual who provides this information must be able to understand how the meeting affects the impact measures. Essentially, there are four categories of input. Often, the most credible are the participants directly involved in the meeting and the managers of the participants, if they are close to the situation. Customers give credible estimates in unique situations where they are involved. External experts may also be helpful. These are all described in this section.

An easily implemented method for isolating the impact of a meeting is to obtain information directly from participants. The effectiveness of this approach rests on the assumption that participants are capable of determining or estimating how much of a performance improvement is related to the meeting. Because their actions have produced the improvement, participants may have highly accurate input on the issue. They should know how much of the business impact change was caused by implementing the meeting content. Although an estimate, this value will usually have considerable credibility with management because they know participants are at the center of the change or improvement.

Questionnaire or Interview Approach

Participant estimation is obtained by asking participants this series of questions in an interview or questionnaire:

- What other factors have contributed to this improvement in performance?
- What is the link between these factors and the improvement?
- What percentage of this improvement can be attributed to the meeting?
- What confidence do you have in this estimate, expressed as a percentage? (0% = No confidence; 100% = Complete confidence)
- What other individuals or groups could estimate this percentage to determine the amount attributed to this meeting?

Table 8-2
Example of a Participant's Estimation

Factor That Influenced Improvement	% of Improvement Caused by	Confidence Expressed as a %	Adjusted % of Improvement Caused by
Meeting	60	80	48
Process changes	15	70	10.5
Environmental changes	5	60	3
Compensation changes	20	80	16
Other	–	–	–
Total	100%		

Table 8-2 illustrates this approach with an example of one participant's estimates. Participants who do not provide information on the questions are excluded from the analysis. Also, erroneous, incomplete, and extreme information should be discarded before analysis. To be conservative, the confidence percentage should be factored into the values. The confidence percentage is a reflection of the error of the estimate. Therefore, an 80% confidence level equates to a potential error range of ±20%. With this approach, the level of confidence is multiplied by the estimate. In the example, the participant allocated 60% of the improvement to the meeting and was 80% confident in the estimate. The confidence percentage was multiplied by the estimate to develop a usable value of 48%. This adjusted percentage was then multiplied by the actual amount of the improvement (post-meeting – pre-meeting value) to isolate the portion attributed to the meeting. The adjusted improvement could then be converted to monetary value and, ultimately, used in the ROI calculation.

Focus Group Approach

A focus group works extremely well for this challenge if the group size is relatively small—in the 8–12 range. If much larger, the groups should be divided into multiple groups. Focus groups provide the opportunity for members to share information equally, avoiding domination by any one individual. The process taps the input, creativity, and reactions of the entire group.

The focus group should take about one hour (slightly more if there are multiple factors affecting the results or there are multiple business measures). The facilitator should be neutral to the process (i.e., the same individual who organized the meeting or event should not conduct this focus group). Focus group facilitation and input must be objective.

The task is to link the meeting or event to business performance. The group is presented with the improvement and they provide input on isolating the effects of the meeting or event. The following steps are recommended to arrive at the most credible value:

1. **Explain the task.** The task of the focus group meeting is outlined. Participants should understand that there has been improvement in performance. While many factors could have contributed to the performance, the task of this group is to determine how much of the improvement is related to the training.

2. **Discuss the rules.** Each participant should be encouraged to provide input, limiting his or her comments to two minutes (or less) for any specific issue. Comments are confidential and will not be linked to a specific individual.

3. **Explain the importance of the process.** The participant's role in the process is critical. Because it is their performance that has improved, the participants are in the best position to indicate what has caused this improvement; they are the experts in this determination. Without quality input, the contribution of this training (or any other processes) may never be known.

4. **Select the first measure and show the improvement.** Using actual data, show the level of performance prior to and following the meeting or event. The change in business results is reported.

5. **Identify the different factors that have contributed to the performance.** Using input from experts—others who are knowledgeable about the improvements—identify the factors that have influenced the improvement (e.g., advertising has changed, a new system has been implemented, or technology has been enhanced). If these are known, they are listed as the factors that may have contributed to the performance improvement.

6. **The group is asked to identify other factors that have contributed to the performance.** In some situations, only the participants know other influencing factors and those factors should surface at this time.

7. **Discuss the linkage.** Taking each factor one at a time, the participants individually describe the linkage between that factor and the business results. For example, for the meeting influence, the participants would describe how the meeting has driven the actual improvement by providing examples, anecdotes, and other supporting evidence. Participants may require some prompting to provide comments. If they cannot provide dialogue of this issue, there is a good chance that the factor had no influence.

8. **The process is repeated for each factor.** Each factor is explored until all the participants have discussed the linkage between all the factors, and the business performance improvement. After this linkage has been discussed, the participants should have a clear understanding of the cause and effect relationship between the various factors and the business improvement.

9. **Allocate the improvement.** Participants are asked to allocate the percent of improvement to each of the factors discussed. Participants are provided a pie chart, which represents a total amount of improvement for the measure in question, and are asked to carve up the pie, allocating the percentages

to different improvements with a total of 100%. Some participants may feel uncertain with this process, but should be encouraged to complete this step using their best estimate. Uncertainty will be addressed next.

10. **Provide a confident estimate.** The participants are then asked to review the allocation percentages and, for each one, estimate their level of confidence in the allocation estimate. Using a scale of 0–100%, where 0% represents no confidence and 100% is certainty, participants express their level of certainty with their estimates in the previous step. A participant may be more comfortable with some factors than others so the confidence estimate may vary. This confidence estimate serves as a vehicle to adjust results.

11. **Participants are asked to multiply the two percentages.** For example, if an individual has allocated 35% of the improvement to the meeting or event and is 80% confident, he or she would multiply 35% by 80%, which is 28%. In essence, the participant is suggesting that at least 28% of the teams' business improvement is linked to the meeting or event. The confidence estimate serves as a conservative discount factor, adjusting for the error of the estimate. The pie charts with the calculations are collected without names and the calculations are verified. Another option is to collect pie charts and make the calculations for the participants.

12. **Report results.** If possible, the average of the adjusted values for the group is developed and communicated to the group. Also, the summary of all the information should be communicated to the participants as soon as possible.

Participants who do not provide information are excluded from the analysis.

Estimates from Others

In lieu of, or in addition to, participant estimates, the participants' managers may be asked to provide input as to the meeting's influence on improved performance. In some settings, the participants' managers may be more familiar with any other influencing factors. Therefore, they may be better equipped to provide impact estimates. The recommended questions to ask managers, after describing the improvement, are similar to those asked of the participants.

Another helpful approach in some narrowly focused meetings is to solicit input on the impact of meetings directly from customers. In these situations, customers are asked why they chose a particular product or service or to explain how their reaction to the product or service was influenced by meeting participants. This technique often focuses directly on what the meeting was designed to improve. Routine customer surveys provide an excellent opportunity to collect input directly from customers concerning their reactions to an assessment of new or improved products, services, processes, or procedures. Pre- and post-data can pinpoint the changes related to an improvement driven by a customer-focused meeting.

External or internal experts can sometimes estimate the portion of results that can be attributed to a meeting. When using this technique, experts must be carefully selected based on their knowledge of the process, meeting, and situation. For example, an expert in quality might be able to provide estimates of how much change in a quality measure can be attributed to a meeting conducted to improve quality and how much can be attributed to other factors.

FINAL THOUGHTS

The good news is that business impact data are often readily available and credible. After describing the types of data that reflect business impact, this chapter provided an overview of several data collection approaches that can be used to capture business data. Several options are available. Some methods are gaining more acceptance for use in impact and ROI analysis. Performance monitoring, follow-up questionnaires, action plans, and performance contracts are used regularly to collect data for impact evaluation. Because credibility of data will always be an issue when this level of data is collected and analyzed, this chapter also presents a variety of techniques that can be used to isolate the effects of a meeting or event. The techniques represent the most effective approaches available to address this issue and are used by some of the most progressive organizations. Too often, results are reported and linked to the meeting without any attempt to isolate the exact portion that can be attributed to it. If meeting and event professionals are committed to improving the images of their functions, as well as meeting their responsibilities for obtaining results, this issue must be addressed early in the process for all major meetings and events.

REFERENCES

Phillips, Jack J. and Phillips, Patricia Pulliam. *The Handbook of Training Evaluation and Measurement Methods*, 4th Edition, Butterworth-Heinemann, 2008.

Phillips, Jack J., Myhill, Monica, McDonough, James B. *Proving the value of Meetings and Events: How and why to Measure ROI*, Meeting Professionals International and ROI Institute, Birmingham, AL, 2007.

Phillips, Patricia Pulliam, Phillips, Jack J., Stone, RonDrew, Burkett, Holly. The ROI Field Book: Strategies for Implementing ROI, Butterworth-Heinemann, Burlington, MA, 2007.

CHAPTER 9

Monetary Benefits, Costs, and ROI

To calculate the ROI, two additional steps are necessary: calculating the monetary benefits by converting data to monetary values and tabulating the fully loaded costs of the meeting or event. While results at lower evaluation levels are important, converting the positive outcomes into monetary amounts and weighing them against the costs of the meeting are more valuable from an executive viewpoint. This is the ultimate evaluation level in the framework presented in Chapter 2.

This chapter presents the techniques to convert data to monetary values. The good news is that most measures that matter have already been converted to money and are considered standard values. If they are not available, several easy-to-use techniques can be used to convert data to monetary values.

This chapter also explores the costs of meetings and events, identifying the specific costs that should be captured and some economical ways in which they can be developed. Some costs are hidden and not usually counted. The conservative philosophy presented here is to account for all costs, direct and indirect. The monetary values for the benefits are combined with meeting cost data to calculate the return on investment. This chapter also explores the techniques and issues involved in calculating the ROI. It explains how meeting and event planners are pushing the evaluation envelope to the development of monetary values and calculating ROI.

THE IMPORTANCE OF MONETARY BENEFITS AND ROI

The rationale for ROI is not always clearly understood. A meeting could be labeled a success without a positive ROI, just by using business impact data that shows the amount of improvement directly attributed to the meeting. For example, a change in sales, quality, cycle time, market share, or customer satisfaction could represent significant improvements linked directly to a meeting. For most meetings, this evaluation would be sufficient. However, a few executives and clients need the actual monetary value and ROI.

Value Sometimes Equals Money

For some executives, the most important value is money. There are many different types of value. However, money is becoming one of the most important values as the economic benefits of meetings are desired. This is particularly true for executives, sponsors, clients, administrators, and top leaders. They are concerned about the allocation of funds and want to see the contribution of a meeting in monetary values. Anything short of this value for these key stakeholders would be unsatisfactory.

This quest for value has been evolving for some time. Figure 9-1 shows how the evolution has moved from "show me" to "show me the real money and make me believe it." For some time, executives and managers have asked meeting professionals to show them data, any type of data but, particularly, impact data. They may ask, how will this meeting help the organization reach its goals? How will it improve the business? These are key questions for individuals who fund meetings and events. That request evolved into "show me the money;" show the actual monetary impact that the meeting will have on the organization. Then when business measures were offered, next came the request to show the real money. The challenge at this stage is to isolate the effects of the meeting or event on the money so that the amount of money generated can be connected directly to the meeting or event.

Finally, the ROI question evolved: show the ROI—"show me the real money and make me believe it." In this scenario, the key client is the person who funds the meeting or event, and that might not be the typical person labeled client. For corporate meetings and events, this person has control of the budget for the meeting or event. In other words, this person could choose to invest in the meeting or event or to invest in some other process, such as advertising or promotion, to

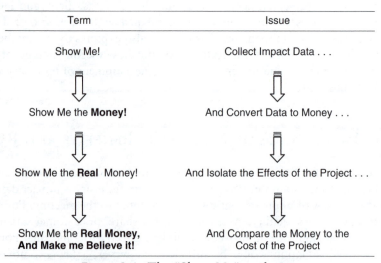

Term	Issue
Show Me!	Collect Impact Data . . .
⇩	⇩
Show Me the **Money!**	And Convert Data to Money . . .
⇩	⇩
Show Me the **Real** Money!	And Isolate the Effects of the Project . . .
⇩	⇩
Show Me the **Real Money, And Make me Believe it!**	And Compare the Money to the Cost of the Project

Figure 9-1. The "Show Me" evolution.

achieve the same or better results. For an association, the key client is the head of the association who wants to understand the impact of a specific meeting versus another meeting for the participants of an association meeting, the key client is the person who must pay for the registration fee and the travel expenses, this may be the participant's manager who is concerned about how will this meeting help the participant in the future. This "show me" evolution is alive and well in the meetings and events industry, and the quest for ROI is now at the top of the list.

For some meetings, the impact is more understandable when the monetary value is developed. For example, consider the impact of a leadership retreat aimed at middle managers. As part of the retreat, the managers were asked to address at least two measures that matter to them and need to improve for those managers to meet specific goals. These could represent dozens, if not hundreds, of different measures. When the meeting impact was captured, most of these measures had changed, leaving a myriad of improvements, difficult to appreciate without a conversion to monetary value. When the first-year monetary value was developed for each of the improved measures, the results provided the meeting professional and client with a sense of the impact of the meeting. Without converting to monetary values, understanding the contribution was difficult.

Money is Necessary for ROI

Monetary value is required to develop ROI. As described in earlier chapters, a monetary value is needed to compare to costs to develop the benefit-cost ratio, the ROI (as a per cent), and the payback period. These three measures are explained in this chapter. In fact, the monetary benefits become half of the equation and are absolutely essential.

Monetary Value is Needed to Understand Problems

In all businesses, costs are necessary for understanding the magnitude of any problem. Consider, for example, the cost of employee turnover. The traditional records and even those available through an analysis of cost statements will not show the full value or cost of turnover. A variety of estimates and expert input may be needed to supplement cost statements to arrive at a particular value. That's the monetary value needed in a fully loaded format to understand the problem. For a meeting or event that reduces employee turnover, the payoff is the fully loaded cost of the turnover prevented. Many organizations have developed a number of standard cost items that represent undesired issues.

For meetings that focus on compliance, the monetary value is expressed in terms of fines and avoided or reduced penalties. The problem essentially is expressed as money when at the same time, some intangible benefits—such as image, reputation, morale, and perhaps stress—could also be influenced by a meeting devoted to a compliance issue.

Key Steps to Convert Data to Monetary Values

Before describing specific techniques to convert both hard and soft data to monetary values, five general steps should be completed for each data item.

1. *Focus on a unit of measure.* First, define a unit of measure. For output data, the unit of measure is the item produced (one item assembled), service provided (one package shipped), or sale completed. Time measures might include the time to complete a meeting, cycle time, or customer-response time, and the unit is usually expressed in minutes, hours, or days. Quality is a common measure, with a unit being defined as one error, reject, defect, or reworked item. Soft data measures vary, with a unit of improvement representing such things as a complaint or a one-point change in the customer satisfaction index. Table 9-1 provides examples of these units.

2. *Determine the value of each unit.* Now, the challenge. Place a value (V) on the unit identified in the first step. The techniques described in this chapter provide an array of approaches for making this determination or conversion. When more than one value is available, usually the most credible or the lowest value is used in the calculation.

3. *Calculate the change in performance data.* Calculate the change in output data after the effects of the meeting have been isolated from other influences. The change (Δ) is the performance improvement, measured as hard or soft data, that can be directly attributed to the meeting. The value may represent the performance improvement for an individual, a team, a group of participants, or several groups of participants.

Table 9-1
Breaking Down the Units of Measure

Units of Measure

One new customer	One discrimination complaint
One sale made	One lost time accident
One package delivered	One grievance
One patient served	One unplanned absence
One student enrolled	One voluntary turnover
One loan approved	One minute of downtime
One unit produced	One hour of wait time
One project completed	One day of delay
One call escalation	One hour of cycle time
One reject	One hour of employee time
One rework	One hour of overtime
One error	One customer complaint

4. *Determine an annual amount for the change.* Annualize the Δ value to develop a total change in the performance data for at least one year (ΔP). Using annual values has become a standard approach for meeting professionals seeking to capture the benefits of a meeting, although the benefits may not remain constant throughout the entire year. First year benefits are used even when the meeting produces benefits beyond one year. This approach is considered conservative. More will be discussed about this later.

5. *Calculate the annual value of the improvement.* Arrive at the total value of improvement by multiplying the annual performance change (ΔP) by the unit value (V) for the group in question. For example, if one group of participants is involved in the meeting being evaluated, the total value will include total improvement for all participants in the group. This value for annual meeting benefits is then compared to the costs of the meeting, usually with the ROI formula presented in this chapter.

Table 9-2 shows how the steps are applied to a meeting of franchise owners for a flooring company. The calculations are based on one of the measures influenced by the meeting.

Table 9-2
Converting Sales Data to Monetary Values

Setting: Annual Franchise Meeting for Flooring Company

Step 1	*Define the Unit of Measure.* Weekly sales per office location.
Step 2	*Determine the Value of Each Unit.* The profit margin is needed. This value is a standard value already developed by the accounting staff. (V = 30% of sales)
Step 3	*Calculate the Change in Performance Data.* Six months after the meeting, total sales per week increased by $2100 per office. With 155 office locations, this represents a total value of $325,500. Franchise owners estimated that 32% of this value is related to the meeting. This was after an adjustment for confidence. (Isolating the effects of the meeting) The adjusted dollar amount (Δ) is $325,500 × 0.32 = $104,160.
Step 4	*Determine an Annual Amount for the Change.* The weekly value yields an annual improvement of $5,416,320. (ΔP = 104,160 × 52)
Step 5	*Calculate the Annual Value of the Improvement.* Annual Value = ΔP times V = $5,416,320 × 30% = $1,624,86

STANDARD MONETARY VALUES

Most hard data items have been converted to monetary values and have standard values. By definition, a standard value is a monetary value placed on a unit of measurement that is accepted by key stakeholders. These standards have been developed because they are often the measures that matter in the organization. They are important. They reflect problems, and because of that, efforts have been made to convert them to monetary values to show their impact on the operational and financial well-being of the organization. The best way to understand the magnitude of any problem is to place a monetary value on it.

Spanning the last two decades, a variety of organizations have focused only on the cost of quality. Organizations have been obsessed with placing a value on mistakes or the payoff of avoiding these mistakes. This is one of the most important outgrowths of quality management systems—the standard cost of items. In addition, process improvement meetings—such as reengineering, reinventing the corporation, transformation, continuous process improvement, and many others—have had a measurement component in which the cost of a specific measure has been developed. Finally, cost controls, cost containment, and cost management systems have been developed such as activity-based costing. These have forced organizations, departments, and divisions to place costs on activities and, in some cases, relate those costs directly to the revenue or profits of the organization.

Standard values are usually available for the hard data categories of output, quality, and time and Figure 9-2 shows how they have been converted to the other hard data category, cost. Output is converted to either profits or cost savings. Output in the form of sales, new customers, market share, and customer loyalty add value through additional profits obtained from additional sales. Outputs where profits are not connected, such as the output of an individual work group,

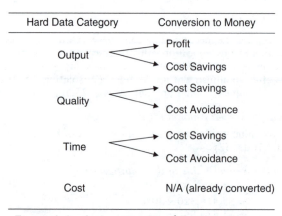

Figure 9-2. Converting Hard Data to Money.

can be converted to savings. For example, if the outputs of a work group can be increased as a result of a particular meeting with no additional resources needed to drive the output, then the corresponding value is in the cost savings. That is, additional output presented or the cost per unit of output actually goes down, resulting in a cost savings. When quality is improved, the result is either cost savings when quality is a problem or in cost avoidance if the meeting or event is preventive—preventing a mistake or a quality issue.

Time is converted in the same way. If time is reduced, it is converted to a cost savings. If the time does not increase when normally it should, it represents cost avoidance. Therefore, the ultimate payoff of typical hard data items are profits, cost savings, or cost avoidance. This logic also explains why most ROI studies pay off on cost savings or cost avoidance instead of profits. Those meetings and events directly related to customers and sales are normally converted to profits. Others are converted to cost savings or cost avoidance. The additional details on how these conversions are made are presented next. However, almost all hard data items have been converted to monetary values as standard values.

Converting Output Data to Money

When a meeting produces a change in output, the value of the increased output can usually be determined from the organization's accounting or operating records. For organizations operating on a profit basis, this value is typically the marginal profit contribution of an additional unit of production or service provided. For example, a team within a major appliance manufacturer was able to boost the sales of small refrigerators after a business development conference. The unit of improvement was the profit margin of one refrigerator. For organizations that are performance-driven rather than profit-driven, this value is usually reflected in the savings accumulated when an additional unit of output is realized for the same input. For example, in the visa section of a government office, an additional visa application was processed at no additional cost. Therefore, an increase in output translated into a cost savings equal to the unit cost of processing a visa application.

Perhaps no area is filled with more standard values the sales and marketing area. Table 9-3 shows a sampling of measures in the sales and marketing area that are routinely calculated and are considered to be standard values (Farris *et al.*, 2006). For example, the first two entries go together. The sales cannot be used in an ROI value until they have been converted to profit. Sales are usually adjusted by the profit percentage to generate the actual value of the improvement. Other profit margins can be developed for a particular unit, a product line, or even a customer. Retention rates and return rates are routinely developed as are the lifetime value of a customer. Even these days, the market share and loyalty are developed because they all translate directly into additional sales. For the most part—with the exception of workload and inventories—the value is developed through profits. Even market share and customer loyalty are valued based on sales or additional sales obtained from the customer.

Table 9-3
Examples of Standard Values from Sales and Marketing

Metric	Definition	Converting Issues
Sales	The sale of the product or service recorded in a variety of different ways: by product, by time period, by customer.	This data must be converted to monetary value by applying the profit margin for a particular sales category.
Profit Margin (%)	for the product, Cost customer, and time period.	The most common way factored to convert sales to data.
Unit Margin	Unit Price less the Unit Cost	This shows the value of incremental sales.
Channel Margin	Channel profits as a percent of channel selling price.	This would be used to show the value of sales through a particular marketing channel.
Retention Rate	The ratio of customers retained to the number of customers at risk of leaving.	The value is the money saved to retain a new replacement customer.
Churn Rate	Churn rate is the complement of the retention rate. It is the percent of customers leaving compared to the number who are at risk of leaving.	The value is the money saved for acquiring a new customer.
Customer Profit	The difference between the revenues earned from and the cost associated with the customer relationship during the specified period.	The monetary value add is the additional profit obtained from customers. It all goes to the bottom line.
Customer Value Lifetime	The present value of the future cash flows attributed to the customer relationship.	This is bottom line as customer value increases, it adds directly to the profits. Also, as a new customer is added, the incremental value is the customer lifetime average.
Cannibalization Rate	The percent of the new product sales taken from existing product lines.	This needs to be minimized because it is an adverse effect on existing product with the value add being the loss of profits from the sales loss.
Workload	Hours required to service clients and prospects.	The salaries and commissions and benefits from the time the sales staff spends on the workloads.

Table 9-3
(Continued)

Metric	Definition	Converting Issues
Inventories	The total amount of product or brand available for sale in a particular channel.	Since the inventories are valued at the cost of carrying the inventory, space, handling, and the time value of money. Insufficient inventories is the cost of expediting the new inventory or loss sales because of the inventory outage.
Market Share	The sales revenue as a percent of total market sales.	The actual sales are converted to money through the profit margins. This is a measure of competitiveness.
Loyalty	This includes the length of time the customer stays with the organization, the willingness to pay a premium, and the willingness to search.	The additional profit from the sale or the profit on the premium

Adapted from Farris *et al.*, (2006; 46–47).

Converting Quality to Monetary Values

Quality and the cost of quality are important issues in most manufacturing and service firms. Because many meetings are designed to increase quality, the meeting planner may have to place a value on the improvement of certain quality measures. With some quality measures, the task is easy. For example, if quality is measured with the defect rate, the value of the improvement is the cost to repair or replace the product. The most obvious cost of poor quality is the scrap or waste generated by mistakes. Defective products, spoiled raw materials, and discarded paperwork are all the result of poor quality. Scrap and waste translate directly into a monetary value. In a production environment, for example, the cost of a defective product is the total cost incurred up to the point that the mistake is identified, minus the salvage value. In the service environment, a defective service is the cost incurred up to the point that the deficiency is identified, plus the cost to correct the problem, plus the cost to make the customer satisfied, plus the loss of customer loyalty.

Employee mistakes and errors can be expensive. The most costly rework occurs when a product or service is delivered to a customer and must be returned for correction. The cost of rework includes both labor and direct costs. In some organizations, rework costs can be as much as 35 per cent of operating expenses. As with output data, the good news is that a tremendous number of quality measures have been converted to standard values. Quality costs can be grouped into six major categories:

1. *Internal failure* represents costs associated with problems detected prior to product shipment or service delivery. Typical costs are for reworking.
2. *Penalty costs* are fines or penalties levied on organizations as a result of unacceptable quality.
3. *External failure* refers to problems detected after product shipment or service delivery. Typical items are technical support, complaint investigation, remedial upgrades, and repairs.
4. *Appraisal costs* are the expenses involved in determining the condition of a particular product or service. Typical costs are testing and related activities, such as product-quality audits.
5. *Prevention costs* include efforts undertaken to avoid unacceptable product or service quality. These efforts include service quality administration, inspections, process studies, and improvements.
6. *Customer dissatisfaction* is perhaps the costliest element of inadequate quality. In some cases, serious mistakes result in lost business.

As with output data, the good news is that a tremendous number of quality measures have been converted to standard values. Table 9-4 shows a sampling of the quality measures that are typically converted to actual monetary value.

The typical definition of these measures can vary slightly with the organization, and the magnitude and the costs can vary significantly. The most common method for converting cost is to use internal failure, external failure, appraisal, or penalty costs. This exhibit shows the tremendous variety of quality measures that are monitored and represents only a small sampling from a typical organization. Some larger organizations literally track thousands of quality measures as standard values have been developed for many of them (Muir, 2006).

Table 9-4
Examples of Standard Quality Measures

Defects	Failure
Rework	Customer Complaint
Variances	Delay
Waste	Missing Data
Processing Errors	Fines
Date Errors	Penalties
Incidents	Inventory Shortages
Accidents	Unplanned Absenteeism
Grievances	Involuntary Employee Turnover
Down Time – Equipment	Risk
Down Time – System	Days Sales Uncollected
Repair Costs	Queues

Converting Employee Time to Money

Saving employee time is an objective for some meetings and events. In a team environment, a meeting may enable the team to complete tasks in less time or with fewer people. On an individual basis, a new technology tool introduced during a meeting may be designed to help professional, sales, and managerial employees save time when performing daily tasks. The value of the time saved is an important measure, and determining the monetary value for it is relatively easy. The monetary savings are found by multiplying the hours saved by the labor cost per hour. For example, after attending a time management meeting, participants estimated that they saved an average of 74 minutes per day, worth $31.25 per day, or $7500 per year. The time savings were based on the average salary plus benefits for the typical participant.

When developing time savings, caution is needed. Savings are only realized when the amount of time saved translates into other productive work. Having participants estimate the percentage of their time saved that is used on productive work may be helpful, followed by a request for examples of how the time was used. If a team-based meeting sparks a new process that eliminates several hours of work each day, the actual savings will be based on a reduction in staff or overtime pay. Therefore, an important preliminary step in developing time savings is determining whether the expected savings will be genuine. This will only happen if the time saved is put to productive use.

Finding Standard Values

As this section has illustrated, standard values are available for all types of hard data and are available in all types of functions and departments. Essentially, every major department will develop standard values that are tracked and monitored in that area. Table 9-5 shows the typical functions in a major organization where

Table 9-5
Locating the Standard Values

Standard Values Are Everywhere
• Finance and Accounting
• Production
• Operations
• Engineering
• IT
• Administration
• Sales and Marketing
• Customer Service and Support
• Procurement
• Logistics
• Compliance
• Research and Development
• HR

standard values would be tracked. Sometimes, it is a matter of understanding the data set that they monitor, collect, and publish. Thanks to enterprise-wide systems software, these functions, including the standard values in some cases, are integrated and available for access to a variety of people. Access may be an issue, and access may need to be addressed or changed to ensure that the data can be obtained.

Some evaluators, using the ROI methodology, have taken the extra step of collecting the standard values from the systems within their organizations and developing a handbook of values. This involves tapping into the databases or departmental files of these functions and others. The result is an interesting list of what things are worth. When this has been compiled previously, it has become a much-sought-after document as others looking at cross-functional processes need the value of the measures as well. This would be an excellent project for wide-scale ROI implementation.

DATA CONVERSION WHEN STANDARD VALUES ARE NOT AVAILABLE

When standard values are not available, several techniques for converting data to monetary values exist. Some are appropriate for a specific type of data or data category, while others may be used with virtually any type of data. The challenge is to select the strategy that best fits the situation. These strategies are presented next, beginning with the most credible approach.

Using Historical Costs from Records

Sometimes, historical records contain the value of a measure and reflect the cost (or value) of a unit of improvement. This strategy relies on identifying the appropriate records, files, and statements and tabulating the actual cost components for the item in question. For example, a large construction firm organized a meeting to improve safety. The meeting was designed to improve several safety-related performance measures, ranging from safety fines to total workers' compensation costs. By examining the company's records using one year of data, the average cost for each safety measure was developed. This involved the direct costs of medical payments, insurance payments, insurance premiums, investigation services, and lost-time payments to employees as well as payments for legal expenses, fines, and other direct services. Also, the amount of time used to investigate, resolve, and correct any of the issues had to be included. This time involved not only the health and safety staff, but other staff members, as well. In addition, the cost of lost productivity, the disruption of services, morale, and dissatisfaction is also estimated to obtain a fully loaded cost. Corresponding costs for each item are then developed.

This quick example shows the difficulty in working to keep systems and databases to find a value for a particular data item. This raises several concerns about this method. Sorting through databases, cost statements, financial records, and a variety of activity reports takes a tremendous amount of time, time that may not be available. Keeping this part of the process in perspective is helpful. This is only one step in the ROI Methodology (converting data to monetary value) and only one of the measures that may need to be converted to monetary value. Resources need to be conserved. Fortunately, other methods are available.

In some cases, data are not available to show all the costs for a particular item. While some direct costs are associated with a measure, often the same numbers of indirect or invisible costs, or costs that cannot be obtained easily, are associated with the meeting. Calculating the cost of an involuntary turnover is one example.

Figure 9-3 shows the fully loaded costs of turnover and can be compared to the Iceberg Principle (Ahlrichs, 2000). The visible part of the iceberg is the *green*

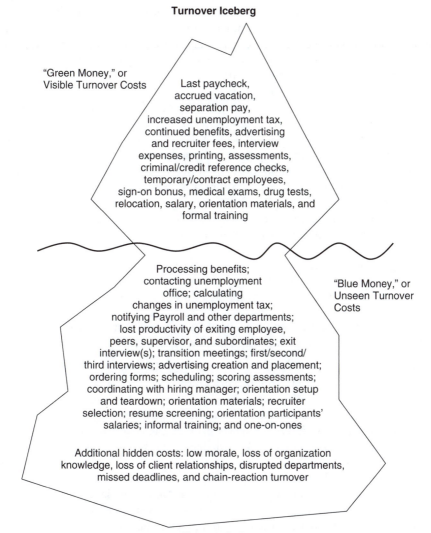

Figure 9-3. Fully Loaded Turnover Costs.

money—these are the costs that are in the records, reports, and cost statements. Although capturing them all would be difficult, still more difficult and often unavailable are the *blue money* items. These are the invisible costs—the part of the iceberg that cannot be seen from a surface observation. Often labeled hidden or indirect, they can be significant and make converting data to monetary values not only a time-consuming process but one that will involve estimates and expert input.

In some cases, the effort just to secure data from databases becomes difficult. With the proliferation of data warehousing and data capturing systems, combined with existing legacy systems that may not talk to each other, finding the values for a particular cost item becomes a sometimes insurmountable task.

Compounding the problem of time and availability is access. Sometimes, monetary values may be needed from a system or record set that is under someone else's control. In a typical meeting implementation, the evaluator or planner may not have full access to cost data. Cost data are more sensitive than other types of data and are often protected for many reasons, including the competitive advantage. Therefore, easy access becomes difficult and, sometimes, is even prohibited unless an absolute need to know exists.

Finally, an acceptable level of accuracy is needed in this analysis. While a measure calculated in the current records may give the impression that it is based on accurate data, this may be an illusion. When data are calculated, estimations are involved, access to certain systems is denied, and different assumptions are necessary (which can be compounded by different definitions of systems, data, and measures). Because of these limitations, the calculated values may be suspect unless care is taken to ensure that they are accurate.

Calculating the monetary value of data using records should be done with caution and only when these two conditions exist:

1. The client approves spending additional time, effort, and money to develop a monetary value from the current records and reports.
2. The measure is simple and available in a few records.

Otherwise, moving to another method is preferred. Other methods may be more accurate and certainly less time-consuming than this particular approach.

Using Input from Experts to Convert Data

Using input from experts might be a viable and very attractive option to convert data to money. Internal experts provide the cost (or value) of one unit of improvement. Individuals with knowledge of the situation and the respect of management must be willing to provide estimates—as well as the assumptions made in arriving at the estimates. Most experts have their own methodology for developing these values. So when requesting their input, explaining the full scope of what is needed, providing as many specifics as possible, is critical.

Internally, experts are not difficult to find. Sometimes, it is the obvious department, where the data originated or the department that was involved in collecting the data. For example, the quality department generates quality measures, the IT department generates IT data, the sales department generates sales data, and so forth. In some cases, the expert(s) is the individual or individuals who send the report. The report is sent either electronically or entered into a database and the origins are usually known. If it is sent on a routine basis, the person sending the report may be the expert or at least can lead to the expert.

In some cases, the expert(s) is the individual or individuals who send the report. The report is sent either electronically or entered into a database, and the origins are usually known. If it is sent on a routine basis, the person sending the report may be the expert, or at least can lead the evaluator or planner to the expert. Sometimes, an individual's job title can indicate whether he or she is a possible expert. For example, in an insurance firm, interest arose in determining the value or the cost of a customer appeal. In that company, when a claim was turned down, the customer could appeal the process. A meeting was implemented to lower the number of customer appeals and the payoff of the meeting had to be developed based on the reduction of appeals. To find the value, the planner contacted the individuals with the job title of customer appeals coordinator and in a focus group developed the data directly from them.

When it is not so obvious in the directory, asking may be helpful—asking a few questions may lead to the person who knows. Internally, for almost every data item generated, someone is considered an expert about that data.

Externally, the experts—consultants, professionals, or suppliers in a particular area—can be found in some obvious places. For example, the costs of accidents could be estimated by the workers' compensation carrier or the cost of a grievance could be estimated by the labor attorney providing legal services to defend the company in grievance transactions.

The credibility of the expert is the critical issue when using this method. Foremost among credibility measures is the individual's experience with the process or the measure. This individual must be knowledgeable of the processes for this measure and, ideally, work with it routinely. Also, this person must be unbiased. Experts have to be neutral in terms of the measure's value. They should not have a personal or professional interest in this value being larger or smaller than it should be. This can be very subtle. For example, a labor relations internal expert (the individual who coordinates grievances for the company) may exaggerate the cost of a grievance to show the impact of his or her particular job. However, since they work with this, they may have the most knowledge, and the bias may have to be filtered in some way. In a case like this, contacting an external expert who is not connected with the issue may be more appropriate. Part of the expertise may be based on the credentials of the person: Does he have a degree in this area? Does she hold certification in a related area? This type of information can confirm the person's expertise.

When internal experts have a strong bias regarding the measure or are not available, external experts are sought. External experts must be selected based on their experience with the unit of measure. Fortunately, many experts are available who work directly with important measures, such as employee attitudes, customer satisfaction, turnover, absenteeism, and grievances. They are often willing to provide estimates of the cost (or value) of these intangibles. Because the accuracy and credibility of the estimates are directly related to the expert's reputation, his or her reputation is critical.

In addition, the credentials of external experts—publications, degrees, and other honors or awards—are important for validating and supporting their expertise. For people who are tapped often, their track records of estimating are important. If the value they estimate has been validated in more detailed studies and found to be consistent, this track record could be the most credible confirmation of their expertise to provide this data.

Using Values from External Databases

For some data, using cost (or value) estimates based on the work and research of others may be appropriate. This technique taps external databases that contain studies and research from meetings, focusing on the cost of data items. Fortunately, many databases include cost studies of data items related to meetings, and most are accessible through the Internet. Data are available on the cost of customer complaints, turnover, absenteeism, accidents, and even customer satisfaction. The difficulty is in finding a database with studies or research appropriate to the specific measure. Ideally, the data should come from a similar setting in the same industry, but that is not always possible. Sometimes, data on all industries or organizations are sufficient, perhaps with some adjustments to suit the context of the meeting. For some, the Web holds the most promise for finding monetary values for data not readily available from standard values and experts. Tremendous progress has been made—and continues to be made—in Web searches to develop monetary values.

Here are a few guidelines. General Web directories and portals may be very helpful. Although they have quite a bit in common with Web search engines, general Web directories such as Yahoo, Open Directory, and Look Smart also differ greatly. Even though the databases may include less than 1% of what search engine databases cover, general Web directories still serve unique research purposes and in many cases may be the best starting point (Hock, 2004).

A specialized directory is more appropriate for accessing immediate expertise in Web resources on a specific topic. These sites bring together well-organized collections of Internet resources on specific topics and provide an important starting point.

The search engines hold more promise for searches because of their vast coverage. General Web search engines such as Altavista, AllTheWeb, and Google stand in contrast to a Web directory in three primary ways:

1. They are much larger, containing billions instead of a few million records.
2. Virtually no human selectivity is involved in determining which Web pages are included in the search engine's database.
3. They are designed for searching (responding to a user's specific query), rather than browsing and, therefore, provide much more substantial searching capabilities than directories.

Groups, mailing lists, and other interactive forums create a class of Internet resources that too few researchers take advantage of—useful for a broad range of applications, including finding the value of data. These tools can be gold mines.

A range of news resources are also available on the Internet, including news services, news wires, newspapers, news consolidation services, and more. Because some studies around particular values are newsworthy, these may be excellent sources for capturing the values of data. Overall, Web searches are an important tool for the evaluator when it comes to collecting the data.

A typical concern of Web searches is the quality of the content. Some think that the Internet has low-quality content, although in reality, it is no different from other sources. Right alongside high-quality publications often available on news stands are those with low-quality content. Here are a few guidelines:

- *Consider the source.* From what organization does the content originate? Look for the organization to be identified both on the Web page itself and at the URL. Is the content identified as coming from known sources, such as a news organization, the government, an academic journal, a professional association, or a major investment firm? The URL will identify the owner, and the owner may be revealing in terms of the quality.
- *Consider the motivation.* What is the purpose of this site—academic, consumer protection, sales, entertainment, or political? The motivation can be helpful in assessing the degree of objectivity.
- *Look for the quality of the writing.* If the content contains spelling and grammatical errors, then this can mean content quality problems as well.
- *Look at the quality of the source documentation.* First, remember that even in academic circles, the number of footnotes is not a true measure of the quality of the work. On the other hand, if facts are cited, does the page identify the origin of the facts? Check out some of the cited sources to see if the facts were accurately quoted.
- *Are the site and its content as current as they should be?* If the site reports on current events, the need for currency and the answer to the question of currency will be apparent.
- *Verify the facts used in the data conversion using multiple sources, or choose the most authoritative source.* Unfortunately, many facts given on Web pages are simply wrong from carelessness, exaggeration, guessing, or for other reasons. Often they are wrong because the person creating the page content did not check the facts.

These are helpful ways to help focus only on the quality content, which is critical when determining the monetary value of a particular measure.

When searching for monetary values, critical thinking should be applied to the information found and the claims that are made. The Web has some special and unique attributes and using it to research calls for a certain set of critical thinking questions. Table 9-6 has a few questions that provide a quick reference list for the serious searcher to get to the right information with the right quality and in the right time (Berkman, 2004).

Table 9-6
Using the Web Appropriately

Asking the Right Questions

Before going to the Web for business research, ask yourself:

- Why am I choosing the Web to perform this research?
- For example, if it's because the Web is fast, why is that good?
- If it's because it's free, why is free information best? How much would I pay for good information?
- Is a search engine the best tool to find what I'm looking for on the Web?
- Where else might I find the same type of information?
- Would a library or a fee-based database contain the data?

When you find a source of interest on the Web, ask yourself:

- Who put this information on the Web? Why?
- If it's free, why did the creator allow free access?
- Who gains from having this information on the Web?

When evaluating the authority of the publisher/creator of the information, ask yourself:

- What are the qualifications of this person or organization?
- Why should I trust them/it?
- Why are these opinions being offered?

If a search engine doesn't return the information you're looking for, ask yourself:

- Did I use all the appropriate keywords and phrases?
- Did I follow the search engine's instructions?
- Could the search engine have failed to index the site that includes the information?
- Could the information be online, but as part of the "Invisible Web" that's inaccessible to search engines?
- Could it mean that the information isn't on the Web? If so, might it be available from other sources (the library, a journal database, a book or directory, an association, expert, etc.)?
- Could it be that what I'm looking for isn't the kind of information that's easily found on the Web? If so, am I better off trying a different type of resource altogether?
- Could it mean that the information simply doesn't exist?

When you find statistical data, ask yourself:

- What/who/where is the original source/creator of the data?
- Is this the most recent version/series of the data?
- Do I have the larger context from which this data was derived?
- Where can I find the methodologies and assumptions used to create these statistics?

On an online news site, ask yourself:

- What makes this a legitimate news-gathering and reporting site?
- What is a legitimate news-gathering and reporting site?
- Can I distinguish editorial from advertising on this site?

Adapted from Berkman (2004).

Linking with Other Measures

When standard values, records, experts, and external studies are not available, a feasible approach might be to find a relationship between the measure in question and some other measure that may be easily converted to a monetary value. This involves identifying existing relationships, if possible, that show a strong correlation between one measure and another with a standard value.

For example, a classical relationship, depicted in Figure 9-4, shows a correlation between increasing customer satisfaction and revenue. In a meeting designed to improve customer satisfaction, a value is needed for changes in the customer satisfaction index. A predetermined relationship showing the correlation between improvements in customer satisfaction and increases in revenue can link the changes directly to turnover. Using the profit margin (a standard value), the revenue can easily be developed as described earlier. Therefore, a change in customer satisfaction is converted to a monetary value or, at least, an approximate value using this relationship. However, it is important not to double count this value. If the sales increase was counted already, then the customer satisfaction value (converted to money) should not be used. Instead it should be left as an intangible.

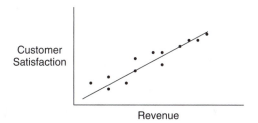

Figure 9-4. Relationship Between Customer Satisfaction and Revenue.

Using Estimates

If none of the previous methods were appropriate or feasible, then estimates may be collected. Estimates may come from participants, managers, or others within the organization (not to be confused with the experts described earlier). A word of caution: An estimate from a non-expert may not be credible. As a result, the data item may not be converted to money but be left as an intangible benefit. Intangible benefits will be discussed in more detail later.

Using Estimates from Participants.   In some cases, participants in the meeting should estimate the value of improvement. This technique is appropriate when participants are capable of providing estimates of the cost (or value) of the unit of measure improved with the meeting. When using this approach, participants should be provided with clear instructions, along with examples of the type of information needed.

Using Estimates from the Management Team. Sometimes, participants may be incapable of placing a value on the improvement. Their work may be so far removed from the value of the process that they cannot reliably provide estimates. In these cases, the team leaders, supervisors, or managers of participants may be capable of providing estimates. In some cases, senior management provides estimates of the value of data. With this approach, senior managers interested in the meeting are asked to place a value on the improvement based on their perception of its worth. This approach is used when the value is difficult to calculate or when other sources of estimation are unavailable or unreliable.

All the formulas presented in this chapter use annualized values so that the first-year impact of the meeting is calculated. Using annualized values is an accepted practice for developing the ROI. This approach is a conservative way to develop the ROI, since some meetings have added value in the second or third year.

SELECTING THE CONVERSION METHOD

With so many techniques available, the challenge is selecting one or more strategies appropriate for the situation and available resources. Developing a table or list of values or techniques appropriate for the situation may be helpful. Credibility is the key issue.

Use the Technique Appropriate for the Type of Data

Some strategies are designed specifically for hard data, while others are more appropriate for soft data. The type of data often dictates the strategy. Standard values are developed for most hard data items. Company records and cost statements are used with hard data. Soft data are often involved in external databases, linking with other measures, and using estimates. Experts are used to convert both types of data to monetary values.

Move from Most Accurate to Least Accurate

Table 9-7 shows the techniques presented in order of accuracy, beginning with the most accurate. Working down the list, each technique should be considered for its feasibility in the situation. The technique with the most accuracy is always recommended if it is feasible for the situation.

Consider the Resources

Sometimes, the availability of a particular source of data will drive the selection. For example, experts may be readily available. Some standard values are easy to find; others are more difficult. In other situations, the convenience

Table 9-7
The Accuracy of the Techniques to Convert to Money

Accuracy	Technique Using:	Comment
Most Accurate	Standard Values	80% of the measures that matter have standard values, monetary values that are accepted by stakeholders.
	Company Records and Cost Statements	Use only if complete and fully loaded. Unfortunately it usually takes much time to do this
	Experts	Must have a comprehensive knowledge of the issue and can be unbiased and neutral.
	External Databases of Other Studies	The Internet has opened many opportunities. The studies must have similar settings.
	Linking with Other Measures	More relationships are being developed.
Least Accurate	Estimates	Use most credible source.

of a technique may be an important selection factor. The Internet is making external database searches more convenient.

As with other processes, keeping the time invested in this phase to a minimum is important, so that the total effort for the ROI study does not become excessive. Some techniques can be implemented in much less time than others. Too much time on this step may dampen otherwise enthusiastic attitudes about the use of the methodology.

When Estimates are Sought, Use the Source with the Broadest Perspective on the Issue

According to Guiding Principle 3, the most credible data source must be used. The individual providing estimates must be knowledgeable of the processes and the issues surrounding the value of the data. For example, consider estimating the cost of a customer complaint. Although a customer service representative may have insight into what has caused a particular complaint, he or she may be limited in terms of a broad perspective of its impact. A high-level manager may be able to understand the total impact of the complaint and how impact will affect other areas. Thus, a high-level manager would be a more credible source because of the broader perspective.

Use Multiple Techniques When Feasible

Sometimes, having more than one technique for obtaining values for the data is beneficial. When multiple sources are feasible, they should be used to serve as comparisons or to provide additional perspectives. The data must be integrated using a convenient decision rule, such as the lowest value. A conservative approach of using the lowest value is recommended as Guiding Principle 4, but only the sources have equal or similar credibility.

Converting data to monetary value has its challenges. As the specific method is selected and used, several adjustments or issues need to be considered to make it the most credible and applicable value with the least amount of resources.

Apply the Credibility Test

The techniques presented in this chapter assume that each data item collected and linked to a meeting can be converted to a monetary value. Although estimates can be developed using one or more strategies, the process of converting data to monetary values may lose credibility with the target audience, which may question its use in analysis. Highly subjective data, such as changes in employee attitudes or a reduction in the number of employee conflicts, are difficult to convert. The key question to ask when making this determination is: "Could these results be presented to senior management with confidence?" If the process does not meet this credibility test, the data should not be converted to monetary values but listed as intangible benefits. Other data, particularly hard data items, would normally be used in the ROI calculation, leaving the highly subjective data expressed in intangible terms.

This issue of credibility when combined with resources is illustrated clearly in Figure 9-5. This is a logical way to either convert data to a monetary value or leave it as an intangible and it addresses both the minimum resources. Essentially, if no standard value exists, many other ways are available to capture or convert the data to monetary value. However, there is a question of resources: Can it be done with minimum resources? Some of the techniques mentioned in this chapter—such as searching records, maybe even searching the Internet—cannot be used with minimum resources. However, an estimate obtained from a group or a few individuals would use minimum resources. Then we move to the next challenge, credibility. Our standard credibility test is simple—if an executive who is interested in the meeting will buy into the monetary value for the measure in two minutes, then it is credible enough to be included in the analysis—if not, then move it to the intangibles. Incidentally, the intangibles are very important and are covered in much more detail in the next chapter.

Review the Client's Needs

The accuracy of data and the credibility of the conversion process are important concerns. Planners sometimes avoid converting data because of these issues. They are more comfortable reporting that a special conference on youth unemployment reduced the youth unemployment rate from 26% to 18%, without attempting to place a value on the improvement. They may assume that the sponsor will place a value on the reduction. Unfortunately, the target audience for

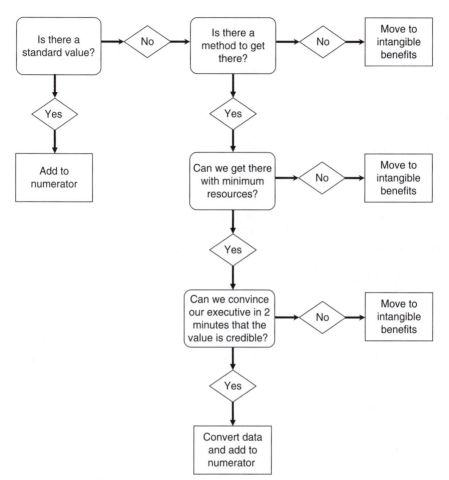

Figure 9-5. Data Conversion Four-Part Test.

the conference may know little about the cost of unemployment and will usually underestimate the actual value of the improvement. Consequently, some attempt should be made to include this conversion in the ROI analysis.

Is This Another Project?

Because the efforts involved in developing a credible monetary value may be extensive and yet desired by the client, an appropriate response to this question is: Yes, it can be done; no, it cannot be done using minimum resources; and yes, it will be another project.

Essentially, bringing up the issue of converting data to monetary value in terms of the resources required is appropriate. Although it is part of the planning for a study, the resources required can be discussed. If the client is interested in converting data to money when they have not been converted before, then this realistically should be considered a separate project. This keeps the conversion from bogging down the ROI evaluation and places the proper emphasis and resources on the process of doing a credible job on the conversion.

Consider the Short-Term/Long-Term Issue

When data are converted to monetary values, usually one year of data are included in the analysis—this is Guiding Principle 9, which states that for short-term solutions, only the first-year benefits are used. In rare occasions, some meetings may be considered long-term solutions. The issue of whether it is short-term or long-term is defined in the context of the time it takes to fully participate in the meeting. If an individual participating in a series of meetings that take months to complete, then the series is probably not a short-term solution. In general, it is appropriate to consider a meeting to be a short-term solution when it is one meeting.

When it is long-term, no set time is used, but the time value should be set before the evaluation. Input should be secured from all stakeholders, including the client, champion, planner, designer, and evaluator. After some discussion, the estimates of the time factor should be very conservative and should perhaps be reviewed by finance and accounting. When it is a long-term solution, the concept of forecasting will need to be used to estimate multiple years of value. No client will wait several years to see whether a meeting was a success. Some assumptions have to be made and forecasting must be used.

Consider an Adjustment for the Time Value of Money

Since a meeting investment is made during one time period and the return is realized at a later time, some organizations adjust the benefits to reflect the time value of money using discounted cash-flow techniques. The actual monetary benefits of the meeting are adjusted for this time period. The amount of adjustment, however, is usually small when compared with the typical benefits of meetings.

Although this may not be an issue for every meeting, it should be considered on each ROI evaluation of a meeting, and a standard discount rate should be used. Consider an example of how this is calculated. Assume that a meeting cost $100,000, and a two-year period will be used before the full value of the investment will be recovered. In other words, this is a long-term solution with a two-year pay off. Using a discount rate of 6%, the amount of cost for the meeting for the first year would be $100,000 × 106% = $106,000. For the second year it is $106,000 × 106% or $112,360. Thus, the meeting cost has been adjusted for a two-year value with a 6% discount rate. This assumes that the client could have used the money for some other investment and obtained at least a 6% return on that investment, hence, another cost is added for this missed opportunity.

Monitoring Meeting Costs

Monitoring the cost of the meeting or event is an essential step in developing the ROI calculation because it represents the denominator in the ROI formula. It is just as important to capture costs as it is to capture benefits. In practice, however, costs are often more easily captured than benefits, and meeting planners have an excellent track record for capturing costs. The direct cost of the meeting is usually calculated in the proposal for the meeting.

Of course, one of the most important reasons for monitoring costs is creating budgets for meetings and events. The initial cost of some meetings is usually calculated during the proposal for the meeting. This cost is usually based on those from previous meetings, a history that is generated throughout a process of monitoring costs. The only way to have a clear understanding of costs so that they can be used in future meetings and budgets is to track them using different categories.

Costs should be monitored in an ongoing effort to control expenditures and keep the meeting within budget as well. Monitoring cost activities not only reveals the status of expenditures, but also gives visibility to expenditures and influences the team to spend wisely. And of course, monitoring costs in an ongoing fashion is much easier, more accurate, and more efficient than trying to reconstruct events to capture costs retrospectively. Developing accurate costs by different categories builds a database for understanding and predicting costs in the future.

Fundamental Cost Issues

The first step in monitoring costs is to define and discuss several issues relating to a cost-control system. The key issues are presented in this section.

Monitor Costs, Even if They are not Needed.   For some meetings, the pressure to show the costs in detail or in categories is not necessary. However, because of the reasons listed above and explained in this chapter, beginning the discipline of developing these costs is important. In the future, they will be needed. Also, even if fully loaded costs (direct and indirect) are not needed, monitoring these costs helps to understand and appreciate the total costs involved. Then the decision can be made later as to how and when to use the costs and whether to push the evaluation to the ROI level.

Costs will not be Precise.   Although the indirect costs need to be realistic, they do not have to be absolutely precise. Some costs, particularly those in the indirect category, will not be known exactly, and estimates will have to be used. In some situations, the estimates have already been developed as activity-based costs or have been put into standard cost systems. If they have not, estimates from credible sources will suffice. Keeping in mind the resources required for this analysis is important. Spending an excessive amount of time trying to pinpoint the precise cost may be a misuse of resources.

Fully Loaded Costs.   When using a conservative approach to calculating ROI, costs should be fully loaded. This is Guiding Principle 10. With this approach, all costs that can be identified and linked to a meeting are included. The philosophy is simple: For the denominator, "When in doubt, put it in" (that is, if it is questionable whether a cost should be included, including it is recommended, even if the cost guidelines for the organization do not require it). When an ROI is calculated and reported to target audiences, the process should withstand even the closest scrutiny in terms of its credibility. The only way to meet this test is to ensure that all costs are included. Of course, from a realistic viewpoint, if the controller or chief financial officer insists on not using certain costs, then leaving them out or reporting them as an alternate scenario is best.

Reporting Costs Without Benefits.   Communicating the costs of a meeting without presenting the benefits is dangerous. Unfortunately, meeting professionals have fallen into this trap for years. Because costs can easily be collected, they are presented to management in many ingenious ways, such as the cost of the meeting, cost per day, and cost per participant. While these may be helpful for efficiency comparisons, presenting them without benefits may be troublesome. When most executives review meeting costs, a logical question comes to mind: What benefit was received from the meeting? This is a typical management reaction, particularly when costs are perceived to be very high.

For example, in one organization, all the costs associated with a major transformation meeting were tabulated and reported to the senior management team to let them know the total investment in the meeting. The total figure exceeded the perceived value of the meeting, and the executive group's immediate reaction was to request a summary of (monetary and non-monetary) benefits derived from the meeting. The conclusion was that few, if any, economic benefits were achieved. As a result, future meetings were drastically reduced. While this may be an extreme example, it shows the danger of presenting only half the equation. Because of this, some organizations have developed a policy of not communicating cost data unless the benefits can be captured and presented along with the costs. Even if the benefits are subjective and intangible, they are included with the cost data. This helps maintain a balance between the two issues.

MAJOR COST CATEGORIES

Table 9-8 shows the recommended cost categories for a fully loaded, conservative approach to estimating costs. Each category is described below.

Initial Analysis and Needs Assessment

An often ignored item is the cost of conducting the initial analysis and needs assessment to determine the need for the meeting or event. In a comprehensive meeting, this may involve data collection, problem solving, assessment, and

Table 9-8
Cost Categories

Recommended Cost Categories		
Cost Item	Prorated	Expensed
Needs assessment		√
Design, development, and production	√	
Acquisition costs	√	
Administration expenses		√
Marketing/promotion		√
Legal fees/insurance		√
Registration expenses		√
Meeting delivery expenses		
• Salaries/benefits of staff time		√
• Fees to others		√
• Meeting Materials		√
• Travel (staff and participants)		√
• Lodging for staff and participants		√
• Food & beverages		√
• Facility rental(s)		√
• Audio visual rental and rervices		√
• Transportation		√
• Translation and interpretation		√
• Exhibitions		√
• Tips and gratuities		√
• Participant and staff salaries and benefits – contact time		√
• Participant and staff travel time		√
Support and overhead	√	√
Evaluation and reporting		√

analysis. In some meetings, this cost is near zero because the meeting is conducted without an assessment. However, as more meeting professionals place increased attention on accountability needs assessment and analysis will become a significant cost in the future. All costs associated with the analysis and assessment should be captured to the fullest extent possible. Estimates are appropriate. These costs include time, direct expenses, and internal services and supplies used in the analysis.

Design, Development, and Production

One of the more significant items is the costs of designing, developing, and producing the meeting. These costs include time in both the design and development and the purchase of supplies, technology, and other materials directly related to production. Design, development, and production costs are usually fully charged to the meeting. However, in some situations, the major expenditures may be prorated over several meetings, if the content or developments is used in other meetings.

Acquisition Costs

In lieu of development costs, some planners purchase materials, software, and equipment from other sources to use directly or in a modified format. The acquisition costs for these items include the purchase price, support materials, and licensing agreements. Some meetings have both acquisition costs and development costs. Acquisition costs can usually be prorated if the acquired solutions can be used in other meetings.

Administrative Expenses

Specific administrative expenses directly connected to the meeting are included in this category. These may include on-site registration assistance, wages for temporary employees or contract labor, copying, and other miscellaneous expenses for support of the meeting.

Marketing and Promotion

This category includes all the promotion and marketing for the meeting. For internal corporate meetings, these costs may be minimal, involving just the preparation of the agenda description and the distribution of the material. For open meetings, including association meetings, marketing and promotion can be expensive. These costs would include all the brochures, acquisition of mailing lists, postage and delivery expenses, other media outlets (including internet advertising), and email distribution.

Legal Fees and Insurance

This category covers all the legal expenses connected to the meeting, including contract negotiations and contract disputes. It also includes the cost of insurance, including general liability, cancellation, and other insurance categories.

Registration Expenses

These include the direct costs of registration including contract/temporary help, administrative expenses, materials, and other miscellaneous costs. If any of these costs were included in the administrative expenses, they should only be included once in the total costs.

Meeting Delivery Expenses

Usually, the largest cost segment in a meeting is associated with implementation and delivery. The major categories are reviewed below:

- Salaries and benefits of staff time for participants (for time attending the meeting), planners, coordinators, organizers, and internal speakers.
- Fees paid to others including facilitators, presenters, and entertainers.
- Meeting materials, which includes handouts, signage, decorations, CD ROMs, and flash drives.
- Travel for participants, staff, facilitators, and presenters
- Lodging for staff, facilitators, presenters, and participants
- Food and beverages for all events
- Facility rentals
- Audio/visual rental services
- Transportation
- Translation and interpretation
- Exhibitions
- Tips and gratuities
- Participants and staff's travel time (if appropriate)

Support and Overhead

Another charge is the cost of support and overhead, the additional costs of the meeting not directly related to a particular meeting. The overhead category represents any cost not considered in the above calculations. Typical items include the cost of administrative/clerical support, telecommunication expenses, office expenses, salaries of client managers and meeting managers, and other fixed costs. This is usually an estimate allocated in some convenient way based on the number of meeting days, then estimating the overhead and support needed each day. This becomes a standard value to use in calculations.

Evaluation and Reporting

The total evaluation cost should be included in the meeting costs to complete the fully loaded cost. Evaluation costs include the cost of developing the evaluation strategy, designing instruments, collecting data, analyzing data, preparing a report, and communicating the results. Cost categories include time, materials, purchased instruments, surveys, and any consulting fees.

Final Note on Cost Categories

The costs detailed in this section represent all costs—direct and indirect. Although these are not routinely accumulated or reported for normal management and control purposes, they should be included if an ROI calculation is planned for a meeting. Also, some of the costs are not exclusively attached to the organization planning the meeting. Therefore, ROI evaluations from multiple perspectives must be considered. For example, when calculating the ROI of an association meeting, the ROI for the association only includes the costs accrued by the association, whether direct or indirect. An ROI calculation from the participant's perspective would include the costs incurred by the participant, and the ROI from the exhibitor's perspective would only include the exhibitor's expenses. Additional information for ROI from different perspectives will be discusses later in this chapter.

Cost Accumulation and Estimation

Meeting costs can be classified in two basic ways. One is with a description of the expenditures—such as labor, materials, supplies, and travel. These are expense-account classifications, which are standard with most accounting systems. The other way to classify is with categories in the meeting planning steps—such as initial analysis, development, and implementation. An effective system monitors costs by account categories according to the description of those accounts but also includes a method for accumulating costs in the functional categories of steps in the process.

Calculating the ROI

As discussed earlier, ROI is becoming a critical measure demanded by many stakeholders, including clients and senior executives. It is the ultimate level of evaluation showing the actual payoff of the meeting, expressed as a percentage and based on the same formula used for other types of investments. Because of its perceived value and familiarity to senior management, it is becoming a common requirement for meeting evaluation. When ROI is required or needed, it must be calculated. Otherwise, it may be optional, unless some compelling reason exists to take the evaluation to this level.

All the formulas presented in this chapter use annualized values so that the first-year impact of the meeting can be calculated. Using annualized values is an accepted practice for developing the ROI. This approach is a conservative way to develop the ROI, since some meetings add value in the second or third year.

When selecting the approach to measure ROI, communicating to the target audience the formula used and the assumptions made in arriving at the decision to use this formula are important. This helps avoid misunderstandings and confusion surrounding how the ROI value was actually developed. Although several approaches are described in this chapter, two stand out as preferred methods: the benefit-cost ratio and the basic ROI formula. These two approaches are described next.

Benefit-Cost Ratio

The benefit-cost ratio compares the monetary benefits of the meeting to the costs, using a simple ratio. In formula form, the ratio is:

$$BCR = \frac{\text{Meeting Benefits}}{\text{Meeting Costs}}$$

In simple terms, the BCR compares the annual economic benefits of the meeting to the costs of the meeting. A BCR of one means that the benefits equal the costs. A BCR of two, usually written as "2:1," indicates that for each dollar spent on the meeting, two dollars in benefits are realized. For example, an annual agents' conference for an insurance company was conducted. In a follow-up evaluation, the first-year payoff for the meeting was $2,091,880. The total, fully loaded meeting costs were $1,369,745. Therefore, the ratio was:

$$BCR = \frac{\$2,091,880}{\$1,369,745} = 1.53$$

For every dollar invested in this meeting, 1.53 dollars in benefits were received (Phillips, Myhill, and McDonough, 2007).

ROI Formula

Perhaps the most appropriate formula is the net meeting benefits divided by the costs. This is the traditional financial ROI and is directly related to the BCR. The ratio is expressed as a percentage when the fractional values are multiplied by one hundred. In formula form, the ROI is:

$$ROI(\%) = \frac{\text{Net Meeting Benefits}}{\text{Meeting Costs}} \times 100$$

Net benefits are meeting benefits minus costs. In the agents' conference described earlier, the benefits were $2,091,880. The costs were $1,369,745. Therefore, the return on investment was:

$$ROI(\%) = \frac{\$2,091,880 - \$1,369,745}{\$1,369,745} \times 100 = 53\%$$

The ROI value is related to the BCR. Just subtract the number 1 from the BCR and multiply by one hundred to calculate the ROI percentage. For example, a BCR of 2.45 is the same as an ROI value of 145% ($1.45 \times 100\%$).

This formula is essentially the same as the ROI for capital investments. For example, when a firm builds a new plant, the ROI is developed by dividing annual earnings by the investment. The annual earnings are comparable to net meeting benefits (annual benefits minus the costs). The investment is comparable to fully loaded meeting costs, which represent the investment in the meeting.

Table 9-9
Misuse of Financial Terms

Term	Misuse	CFO Definition
ROI	Return on Information Return on Involvement Return on Intelligence Return on Inspiration	Return on Investment
ROE	Return on Expectation Return on Event Return on Excellence	Return on Equity
ROA	Return on Anticipation	Return on Assets
ROCE	Return on Client Expectation	Return on Capital Employed
ROP	Return on People	??
ROO	Return on Objectives	??
ROM	Return on Meeting	??

An ROI on a meeting of 50% means that the costs are recovered and an additional 50% of the costs are reported as "earnings." Using the ROI formula essentially places meetings and events investments on a level playing field with other investments using the same formula and similar concepts. The ROI calculation is easily understood by key management and financial executives who regularly use ROI with other investments.

The monetary benefits can be based on profits of cost savings, sales, or customer service. In practice, more opportunities for cost savings occur than for profits. Cost savings can be generated when improvement in productivity, quality, efficiency, cycle time, or actual cost reduction occurs as a result of a meeting or event.

Table 9-9 shows some misuse of financial terms in the literature. Terms such as return on intelligence (involvement or information), abbreviated as ROI, do nothing but confuse the CFO, who is thinking that ROI is the actual return on investment described above. Sometimes, return on expectations or event (ROE), return on anticipation (ROA), or return on client expectations (ROCE) are used, confusing the CFO, who is thinking return on equity, return on assets, and return on capital employed, respectively. Use of these terms will do nothing but confuse and perhaps lose the support of the finance and accounting staff.

ROI from Different Perspectives

Most of the analysis and comments contained in this book have perfected the use of ROI from one perspective, the organizations funding a meeting. This will be the case for many corporate meetings, as the corporation is concerned about its ROI. However, an ROI from the association's perspective may be needed, as well as the ROI from the attendee's or participant's perspective. In addition, an ROI calculation from the exhibitor or sponsor perspective may be needed.

All perspectives work well with this analysis. All the costs from the perspective are captured, and all the benefits connected to that same perspective are captured. The costs versus the benefits are compared for each perspective. Even in the corporate environment, multiple perspectives may be appropriate. Franchise meetings, in which the franchise owner pays some or part of the expenses to come to the meeting, may be an ideal setting for multiple perspectives. The company is interested in the ROI for organizing the conference. The franchisee is concerned about the ROI for those attending the conference. Multiple perspectives must be considered when appropriate.

ROI Objectives

Specific expectations for ROI should be developed before an evaluation study is undertaken. Four strategies have been used to establish a minimum acceptable objective, or hurdle rate, for ROI in a meeting. The first approach is to set the ROI using the same values used to invest in capital expenditures, such as equipment, facilities, and new companies. For North America, Western Europe, and most of the Asian Pacific area (including Australia and New Zealand), the cost of capital is low and this internal hurdle rate for ROI is usually in the 15–20% range. Therefore, using this strategy, the meeting professional would set the expected ROI at the same value expected from other investments.

A second strategy is to use an ROI minimum that represents a higher standard than the value required. This target value is above the percentage required for other types of investments. The rationale: the ROI Methodology for meetings is still relatively new and often involves subjective input, including estimations.

A third strategy is to set the ROI value at a break-even point. A zero per cent ROI represents break-even. The rationale for this approach is an eagerness to recapture the cost of the meeting only. This is the ROI objective for many government planners. If the funds expended for the meeting can be recovered, additional value has been realized in the intangible measures, which are not converted to monetary values.

Finally, a fourth, and sometimes recommended, strategy is to let the client set the minimum acceptable ROI value. In this scenario, the individual who initiates, approves, sponsors, or supports the meeting, establishes the acceptable ROI.

ROI is not for Every Meeting

The ROI Methodology should not be applied to every meeting. Creating a valid and credible ROI study takes time and resources. ROI is appropriate for meetings that:

- Are important to the organization in meeting its operating goals. These meetings are designed to add value. ROI may be helpful to show that value.
- Are closely linked to the strategic initiatives. Anything this important needs a high level of accountability.

- Are expensive. An expensive meeting, using large amounts of resources, should be subjected to this level of accountability.
- Are highly visible and sometimes controversial. These meetings often require this level of accountability to satisfy the critics.
- Have large audiences.
- Command the interest of top executives and administrators. If top executives are interested in knowing the impact, the ROI Methodology should be applied.

These are only guidelines and should be considered within the context of the situation and the organization. Other criteria may also be appropriate.

It is also helpful to consider the meetings where the ROI Methodology is not appropriate. ROI is seldom appropriate for meetings that:

- are short in duration,
- are inexpensive,
- are legislated or required by regulation and would be difficult to change anything as a result of this evaluation,
- are required by senior management. It may be that these meetings will continue, unchanged, regardless of the findings,
- serve as basic or required information for specific jobs. It may be more appropriate to measure only at Levels 1, 2, and 3 to ensure that participants know how to use the information and are using it properly.

This is not meant to imply that the ROI Methodology cannot be implemented for these types of meetings. However, when considering limited resources for measurement and evaluation, careful use of these resources and time will result in evaluating more strategic meetings.

Final Thoughts

With some meetings, ROI is an important value. Meeting and events professionals are being aggressive in defining the monetary benefits of a meeting and developing ROI. They are no longer satisfied to simply report the meeting success with application and impact data. Instead, they take additional steps to convert impact data to monetary values and weigh them against the meeting costs. In doing so, they achieve the ultimate level of evaluation: the return on investment. This chapter presented several strategies used to convert business results to monetary values, offering an array of techniques to fit any situation or meeting.

Costs are important, and because of the scrutiny involved in ROI calculations, all costs should be included, even if this goes beyond the requirements of the policy. After the benefits are collected and converted to monetary values and the meeting costs are tabulated, the ROI calculation becomes an easy step. Plugging the values into the appropriate formula is the final step. This chapter presented the two basic approaches for calculating the return; the ROI formula and the benefit-cost ratio.

REFERENCES

Ahlrichs, N.S. *Competing for Talent*. Palo Alto, CA: Davies-Black, 2000.

Berkman, R. *The Skeptical Business Searcher: The Information Advisor's Guide to Evaluating Web Data, Sites, and Sources*. Medford, NJ: Information Today, Inc., 2004.

Farris, P.W., Bendle, N.T., Pfeifer, P.E., and Ribstein, D.J. *Marketing Metrics: 50+ Metrics Every Executive Should Master*. Upper Saddle River, NJ: Wharton School Publishing, 2006.

Hock, R. *The Extreme Searcher's Internet Handbook*. Medford, NJ: CyberAge Books, 2004.

Muir, A.K. *Lean Six Sigma Statistics: Calculating Process Efficiencies in Transactional Projects*. New York: McGraw-Hill, 2006.

Phillips, J.J., Myhill, M., and McDonough, J.B. *Proving the Value of Meetings and Events: How and Why to Measure ROI*. Birmingham, AL: ROI Institute and MPI, 2007.

CHAPTER 10

Intangible Benefits

The results of meetings and events include both tangible and intangible measures. The tangible measures are converted to monetary values and included in the ROI calculation. Intangible measures are the benefits (or detriments) directly linked to a meeting that cannot or should not be converted to monetary values. By definition, from the guiding principles of the ROI Methodology, an intangible benefit is a measure that is purposely not converted to money (i.e., if a conversion cannot be accomplished with minimum resources and with credibility, it is left as an intangible). Table 10-1 lists common examples of these measures. Some measures make the list because of the difficulty in measuring them; others because of the difficulty in converting them to money. Others are on the list for both reasons. Several typical intangible benefits are examined in detail later in the chapter.

Table 10-1
Common Intangible Benefits

Typical Intangible Measures Linked with Meetings	
Adaptability	Employee complaints
Awards	Engagement
Brand Awareness	Execution
Career minded	Image
Caring	Innovation
Collaboration	Job satisfaction
Communication	Leadership
Conflicts	Networking
Cooperation	Organizational climate
Corporate social responsibility	Organizational commitment
Creativity	Partnering
Culture	Reputation
Customer complaints	Resilience
Customer response time	Stress
Customer satisfaction	Talent
Decisiveness	Teamwork

Wearing the intangible label does not mean these items cannot be measured or converted to monetary values. In one study or another, each item in the table has been monitored successfully and monetarily quantified. However, in a typical meeting evaluation, these variables are considered intangible benefits because of the difficulty in measuring the variable or the difficulty in converting the data to monetary values.

WHY INTANGIBLE BENEFITS ARE IMPORTANT

While the concept of intangible benefits is not new, they are becoming increasingly important. Intangible benefits drive funding, they drive the economy, and organizations are built on them. In every direction we look, intangible benefits are becoming not only increasingly important but critical to organizations. Here are some reasons why they have become so important.

The Invisible Advantage

When the success behind well-known organizations is examined, intangible benefits are there. A highly innovative company continues to develop new and improved products; a company with involved and engaged employees attracts and keeps talent. An organization shares knowledge with employees, giving them a competitive advantage. Still another organization is able to develop valuable strategic partners and alliances. These intangible benefits often do not appear in cost statements and other record-keeping, but they are there, and they make a huge difference.

For some, they are invisible, yet their presence is known. Trying to measure them, identify them, and react to them may be difficult, but the ability to do this exists. These intangible benefits are transforming the way organizations work, the way employees are managed, the way products are designed, the way services are sold, and the way customers are treated. The implications are profound, and an organization's strategy must deal with these intangible benefits.

The Intangible Economy

The intangible economy has evolved from changes that date back to the Stone Age. The Stone Age evolved into the Iron Age and then evolved into the Agricultural Age. In the late 19th century and during the early 20th century, the world moved into the Industrial Age. From the 1950s forward, the world has moved into the Technology and Knowledge Age, and these translate into intangible benefits. During this time, a natural evolution of the technologies has occurred. During the Industrial Age, companies and individuals invested in tangible assets. In the Technology and Knowledge Age, companies invest in intangible assets, such as brands or systems. The future holds more of the same—as intangible benefits continue to evolve as an important part of the overall economic system (Boulton *et al.*, 2000).

More Intangible Benefits are Converted to Tangible Measures

The good news to report in this chapter, and building on Chapter 9, is that more data, previously regarded as intangible, are now converted to monetary values. Because of this, classic intangible benefits are now accepted as tangible measures, and their values are more easily understood. Consider, for example, customer satisfaction. Just a decade ago, few organizations had a clue as to the monetary value of customer satisfaction. Now, more firms have taken the extra step to link customer satisfaction directly to revenues, profits, and other measures this classic intangible has become tangible. Companies are clearly seeing the tremendous value that can be derived from intangible benefits. As this chapter will illustrate, more data are being accumulated to show the monetary values, moving some intangible measures into the tangible category.

Intangible Benefits Drive Meetings and Events

Some meetings and events are implemented because of the intangible benefits. For example, the need to have greater collaboration, partnering, communication, teamwork, or customer service will drive meetings. The need to develop brands, image, and reputation create the need for meetings and events, and above all, networking is an objective for most meetings. In the public sector the need to reduce poverty, to employ disadvantaged citizens, and to save lives often drive meetings and events. From the outset, the intangible benefits are the important drivers and become the most important measures.

MEASURING THE INTANGIBLE BENEFITS

Although intangible benefits may not be perceived as high in value as tangible measures, they are critical to the overall evaluation process. In some meetings, intangible benefits are more important than monetary measures. Therefore, these measures should be monitored and reported as part of the ROI evaluation. In practice, every meeting, regardless of its nature, scope, and content, will produce intangible measures. The challenge is to identify them effectively and report them appropriately.

Often, we explore the issue of measuring the difficult to measure. Responses to this exploration usually occur in the form of comments instead of questions. "You cannot measure it," is a typical response. We disagree. We think anything can be measured. What the frustrated observer suggests is that it is not something you can count, examine, and see in quantities, such as items produced. In reality, a quantitative value can be assigned or developed for any intangible. If it exists, it can be measured.

Several approaches are available for measuring intangible benefits. Some typical intangible benefits can be counted such as an employee complaint. Unfortunately, most intangible benefits are based on attitudes and perceptions and must be measured in some way. One approach is to list the intangible measure and have the participants indicate the extent to which the meeting has influenced the measure, using a five-point scale. Table 10-2 lists six intangible items from a national sales meeting. The respondent is asked to indicate the meeting's influence on each measure. Scales can be created in many ingenious ways. When repeated, used, refined, and modified, these often become industry standards.

Table 10-2
An Example of Measuring Intangible Benefits

Indicate the extent to which you think your application of the information, knowledge, skills, and contacts learned in the meeting had a positive influence on the following measures.

Please check the appropriate response beside each measure.

Business Measure	Not Applicable	Applies But No Influence	Some Influence	Moderate Influence	Significant Influence	Very Significant Influence
A. Customer satisfaction	☐	☐	☐	☐	☐	☐
B. Stress	☐	☐	☐	☐	☐	☐
C. Communication	☐	☐	☐	☐	☐	☐
D. Brand awareness	☐	☐	☐	☐	☐	☐
E. Engagement	☐	☐	☐	☐	☐	☐
F. Teamwork	☐	☐	☐	☐	☐	☐

Still other ratings can come through an assessment on a scale of 1 to 10 after reviewing a description of the intangible. Table 10-3 lists three intangible items with a full description, and the respondent is asked to indicate the level of that factor in place (Ulrich and Smallwood, 2003). Scales can be created in many ingenious ways and when repeated, used, refined, and modified, often become standards in the industry.

Another approach to measuring the intangible is to connect it to a another measure, which is easier to value. This was described in the previous chapter. As shown in Figure 10-1, most hard-to-value measures are linked to an easy-to-value measure. Although this link can be developed through logical deductions and conclusions, having empirical evidence through a correlation analysis is the best approach. However, a detailed analysis would have to be conducted to ensure that a causal relationship exists. Just because a correlation is apparent does not mean that one caused the other. Additional analysis and supporting data could pinpoint the actual causal effect.

Table 10-3
Measuring the Intangible

Intangible Measure	Assessment (1 = Low; 10 = High)

Clarity

We are precise about the decisions we are making.

We never begin a meeting without being clear about what decisions we will make by the end of the meeting.

We don't have reviews without knowing what the decision will be as a result of the review.

We can dissect big ideas (such as quality or market share) into specific decisions with clear alternatives. We create decision pyramids of the little decisions that will lead to other decisions.

Accountability

We know who is responsible for a decision and hold that person (or team) accountable if they do or don't make and execute a decision.

Consensus does not mean everyone gets equal vote.

Somebody (individual or team) must make the decision, but should involve others in it. Ideally, the decision should have the support of those who care about it, and general acceptance on the part of those who don't.

Timeliness

We have deadlines for decisions to be made and we stick to those deadlines. (It's often useful to set a limit of 14 days to closure on most decisions.)

We are decisive and demanding on getting decisions done and if a team lags, the manager makes it.

Adapted from Ulrich and Smallwood (2003).

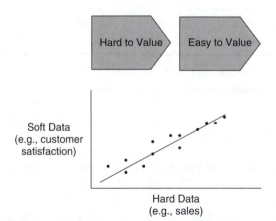

Figure 10-1. The Link Between Hard-to-Value and Easy-to-Value Items.

Through the difficulties of measuring intangible benefits, remembering that these are usually combined with a variety of tangible measures to reflect performance is helpful. Also, intangible benefits are often associated with non-profit, non-government, or public sector organizations.

CONVERTING TO MONEY

Converting hard-to-value measures to money is challenging, to say the least. There are examples of this in many other books (Phillips and Phillips, 2007). The interest in the monetary contribution is expanding. The client who often funds or supports a particular meeting sometimes seeks monetary values, among other measures. "Show me the money!" is a familiar request from many stakeholders.

The approaches to converting a measure to monetary value were detailed in Chapter 9. These will not be repeated here. However, showing the path most commonly used to capture values for intangible benefits is helpful. Figure 10-2 shows the typical approach of converting intangible benefits to monetary values.

The first issue is to locate the data or to measure it in some way, making sure that it is accurate, reliable, and reflects the concept. Next, an expert may be able to place a monetary value on the item based on experience, knowledge, credentials, and previous track record. Stakeholders may provide their input, although the input should be factored for bias. Some stakeholders are biased in one way or the other—they want the value to be smaller or larger, depending on their particular motives. These may have to be adjusted or thrown out all together, based on the biased approaches. Finally, the data are analyzed using the conservative processes described in Chapter 8, often adjusting for the error in the process. If the conversion cannot be accomplished with minimum resources and with credibility, it is left as an intangible.

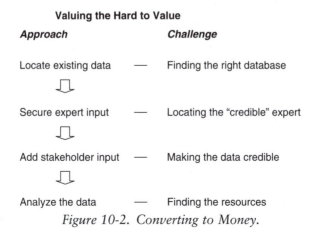

Figure 10-2. Converting to Money.

IDENTIFYING INTANGIBLE BENEFITS

Intangible measures can be taken from different sources and at different times in the meeting lifecycle, as depicted in Figure 10-3. They can be uncovered early in the process, during the initial discussion of the need for the meeting. For example, employee satisfaction, an intangible measure, is identified as a measure that will be influenced by the meeting. It will be monitored with no plans to convert it to a monetary value. From the beginning, this measure is destined to be a non-monetary, intangible benefit reported along with the ROI results.

A second opportunity to identify intangible benefits is in the planning process, when the evaluation plan is developed. The planning team can usually identify the intangible measures expected to be influenced by the meeting. For example, a team-building meeting in a large multinational company was planned, and an ROI analysis was desired. The meeting planner and other staff members identified potential intangible measures that were perceived to be influenced by the meeting, including collaboration, communication, and teamwork.

A third opportunity to identify intangible measures presents itself during data collection. Although the measure is not anticipated in the initial meeting design, it may surface on a questionnaire, in an interview, or during a focus group. Questions are often asked about other improvements linked to the meeting, and participants frequently provide several intangible measures for which no plans are available to assign a value. For example, in the evaluation of a customer service meeting, participants were asked what specifically had improved about their work area and relationships with customers as a result of the meeting. Participants provided more than a dozen intangible measures attributed to the meeting.

During data analysis and reporting, the fourth opportunity to identify intangible measures occurs when attempting to convert data to monetary values. If the conversion loses credibility, the measure should be reported as an intangible benefit. For example, in a sales meeting, customer satisfaction was identified early in the process as a measure of the meeting's success. A conversion to monetary values was attempted, but lacked accuracy and credibility. Therefore, customer satisfaction was reported as an intangible benefit.

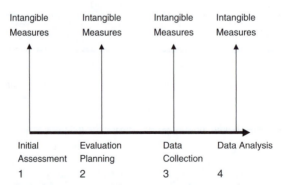

Figure 10-3. Identifying Intangible Measures During the Meeting Lifecycle.

ANALYZING INTANGIBLE BENEFITS

For each intangible measure identified, some evidence of its connection to the meeting must be shown. However, in many cases, no specific analysis is planned beyond tabulating responses. Early attempts to quantify intangible data sometimes results in aborting the entire process, and no further data analysis is conducted. In some cases, isolating the effects of the meeting may be undertaken using one or more of the methods outlined in Chapter 8. This step is necessary when clients need to know the specific amount of change that has occurred in the intangible measure as a result of the meeting. In most situations, however, the direct link to the meeting can be obtained by asking a specific question, "To what extent has this meeting influenced this measure?" A five-point scale could be used for responses.

Intangible data often reflect improvement. However, neither the precise amount of improvement nor the amount of improvement directly related to a meeting is usually necessary. Since the value of this data is not included in the ROI calculation, intangible measures are not normally used to justify the continuation of an existing meeting. A detailed analysis is not required. Intangible benefits are often viewed as additional evidence of the meeting's success and are presented as supportive, qualitative data. The demander of this chapter explores several intangibles, showing how they are measured and converted to money. This is only a sample of the progress made in this area.

CUSTOMER SERVICE AND BRANDING

Because of the importance of building and improving customer service and developing a brand, a number of related measures are typically monitored and reported to track the payoff of meetings. Several types of customer focused meetings have a direct influence on these measures.

These metrics make the list of intangible benefits because they are perceived as difficult to measure and to convert the data to monetary value. However, in the last two decades, much work has been done in this area, and some of these measures are routinely considered tangible because they are converted to money using one or more of the measures described in Chapter 9. In that chapter, the technique, linking to other measures, clearly illustrates the most common way in which customer service intangible measures are converted to money. To convert a brand to money essentially follows a sequence shown in Figure 10-4. The first issue is to create an awareness of a particular product, brand, or service. The next step is to develop attitudes, which define the beliefs, opinions, and intentions about the product, service, or brand, and this leads to usages that describe the purchase habits and loyalty of a customer.

This important link is ingrained in most marketing and promotion, meetings, and processes. This has led to a variety of measures that are becoming standard in the industry. Table 10-4 shows customer intangible benefits and underscores the array of possibilities all aimed at developing awareness, attitudes, and usage.

Awareness, Attitudes, and Usage: Typical Questions

Type	Measures	Typical Questions
Awareness ⇩	Awareness and Knowledge	Have you heard of Brand X?
		What brand comes to mind when you think "luxury car?"
Attitudes ⇩	Beliefs and Intentions	Is Brand X for me?
		On a scale of 1 to 5, is Brand X for young people?
Usage ⇩	Purchase Habits and Loyalty	Did you use Brand X this week?
		What brand did you last buy?

Figure 10-4. Customer Service Links.

(Adapted from Farris *et al.* (2006)).

Table 10-4
Customer Service Intangibles

Metric	Definition	Issues	Purpose
Awareness	Percentage of total population that is aware of a brand.	Is this prompted or unprompted awareness?	Consideration of who has heard of the brand.
Top of Mind	First brand to consider.	May be subject to most recent advertising or experience.	Saliency of brand.
Knowledge	Percentage of population with knowledge of product, recollection of its advertising.	Not a formal metric. Is this prompted or unprompted knowledge?	Extent of familiarity with product beyond name recognition.
Beliefs	Customers'/consumers' view of product, generally captured via survey responses, often through ratings on a scale.	Customers/consumers may hold beliefs with varying degrees of conviction.	Perception of brand by attribute.
Purchase Intentions	Probability of intention to purchase.	To estimate probability of purchase, aggregate and analyze ratings of stated intentions (for example, top two boxes).	Measures pre-shopping disposition to purchase.
Willingness to Recommend	Generally measured via ratings across a 1–5 scale.	Nonlinear in impact.	Shows strength of loyalty, potential impact on others.

Table 10-4
(Continued)

Metric	Definition	Issues	Purpose
Customer Satisfaction	Generally measured on a 1–5 scale, in which customers declare their satisfaction with brand in general or specific attributes.	Subject to response bias. Captures views of current customers, not lost customers. Satisfaction is a function of expectations.	Indicates likelihood of repurchase. Reports of dissatisfaction show aspects that require improvement to enhance loyalty.
Willingness to Search	Percentage of customers willing to delay purchases, change stores, or reduce quantities to avoid switching brands.	Hard to capture.	Indicates importance of distribution coverage.
Loyalty	Measures include willingness to pay premium, willingness to search, willingness to stay.	"Loyalty" itself is not a formal metric, but specific metrics measure aspects of this dynamic. New product entries may alter loyalty levels.	Indication of base future revenue stream.

Adapted from Farris *et al.* (2006).

Perhaps the most common is customer satisfaction, which is generally measured on a 1 to 5 scale, although other scales are used. A tremendous amount of research has been accumulated about the value of satisfied customers and the tremendous loss connected with dissatisfied customers. Using elaborate processes of decision tree analysis, probability theories, expected value, and correlations, organizations have developed detailed monetary values showing that movement in sales and profits are connected to a variety of measures, but most importantly to customer satisfaction. Within a given organization, more specific measures can be developed, such as customer response time, sensitivity to costs and pricing issues, and creativity with customer responses. Of particular importance is the timing issue. Providing prompt customer service is a critical issue for most organizations. Therefore, organizations monitor the time taken to respond to specific customer service requests or problems. Although reducing response times is often an objective of a meeting, the measure is not usually converted to a monetary value. Thus, customer response time is reported as an important intangible measure.

TEAMWORK

To evaluate the success of teams within an organization, several key measures are monitored. Although the output and quality of the teamwork are often measured as hard data and converted to monetary values, other interpersonal measures may be tracked and reported separately. This made our list because of the difficulty in measuring and the difficulty in converting to money. The good news is that significant progress has been made to evaluate a variety of team effectiveness measures. Standard instruments are available and processes are in place to measure the quality of the team process. Just the volume of the materials, books, and articles focused on teams and how they can work effectively underscores the importance of this intangible.

Cross-functional, high-performance, and virtual teams are important assets for organizations striving to improve performance. Sometimes, team members are surveyed before and after a meeting to see whether the level of teamwork has increased. The monetary value of increased teamwork is rarely developed as a measure; rather, it is usually reported as an intangible benefit.

Cooperation/Conflict

The success of a team often depends on the cooperative spirit of team members. Some instruments measure the level of cooperation before and after a meeting, but since converting the findings to monetary values is so difficult, the measure is always reported as an intangible.

In some team environments, the level of conflict is measured. A decrease in conflict may reflect a successful meeting. In most situations, a monetary value is not placed on such a reduction, and it is reported as an intangible benefit.

Decisiveness/Decision Making

Teams make decisions, and the expedience and quality of the decision-making process often become important issues. Decisiveness is usually measured by how quickly decisions are made. Survey measures may reflect the perception of the team or, in some cases, monitor precisely how quickly decisions are made. The quality of the decisions reflects value as well. Some meetings are expected to influence this process, with improvements usually reported as intangible benefits.

Communication

Communication is critical in every team. Several instruments are available to qualify and quantify communication among a team. Positive changes in communication skills or perceptions of skills driven by a meeting are not usually converted to monetary values but reported as intangible benefits.

The difficulty in turning team effectiveness into monetary value stems from the tremendous variety of team processes, settings, and participants. Essentially, the output of team effectiveness, including teamwork, is measured by the output of the teams, and this can vary significantly. Consider the typical organization in which teams are working throughout every functional area. The measures that are improved are essentially all the measures in the organization. The challenge is to link the team process directly to the measure in question using one or more of the isolation techniques described in Chapter 8. Then a monetary value is placed on the measure using one or more of the techniques used in Chapter 9.

INNOVATION AND CREATIVITY

Innovation and creativity are both related to human capital. In this knowledge-based and technology-based economy, they are becoming important factors in organizations' success.

Innovation

For most organizations, innovation is a critical issue. Because innovation comes from employee creativity, it is a human capital issue. Just how important is innovation? Let's put it in perspective. If it were not for the intellectual curiosity of employees—thinking things through, trying out new ideas, and taking wild guesses in all the research and development (R&D) labs across the country—the United States would have half the economy that it has today. In a recent report on R&D, the American Association for the Advancement for Science estimates that as much as 50% of U.S. economic growth during the half century since the Fortune 500 came into existence has been due to advances in technology (Brown, 2004).

After a few years of retrenchment and cost cutting, senior executives across a variety of industries share the conviction that innovation, the ability to define and create new products and services and quickly bring them to market, is an increasingly important source of competitive advantage. Executives are setting aggressive performance goals for their innovation and product-development organizations, targeting 20–30% improvements in such areas as time to market, development costs, product cost, and customer value (Kandybihn and Kihn, 2004).

Innovation is both easy and difficult to measure. Measuring the outcomes in areas such as new products, new processes, improved products and processes, copyrights, patents, inventions, and employee suggestions is easy. Many companies track these items. They can be documented to reflect the innovative profile of an organization. Unfortunately, comparing these data with previous data or benchmarking with other organizations is difficult because these measures are typically unique to each organization.

Perhaps the most obvious measure is tracking the patents that are not only used internally but are licensed for others to use through a patent and license exchange. For example, IBM has been granted more patents than any other company in the world—over 25,000 U.S. patents. IBM's licensing of patents and technology generates several billion dollars in profits each year. While IBM and

Microsoft® are at the top of the list, most organizations in the new economy monitor trademarks, patents, and copyrights as important measures of the innovative talent of employees.

The development of patents comes from the inventive spirit of employees, and remembering this is helpful. The good news is that employees do not have to be scientists or engineers to be inventive. Even though at times, invention is thought of only in the context of technology, computing, materials, energy, and so forth, it is trans-disciplinary and, therefore, can be extracted from any technological realm and applied to problems in any area (Schwartz, 2004).

Creativity

Creativity, often considered the precursor to innovation, refers to the creative experience, actions, and input of organizations. Measuring the creative spirit of employees may prove more difficult. An employee suggestion system, a long-time measure of the creative processes of the organization, flourishes today in many firms and is easily measured. Employees are rewarded for their suggestions if they are approved and implemented. Tracking the suggestion rates and comparing them with other organizations is an important benchmarking item for creative capability. Other measures, such as the number of new ideas, comments, or complaints, can be monitored and measured in some way. Formal feedback systems often contain creative suggestions that can lead to improved processes.

Some organizations measure the creative capabilities of employees using inventories and instruments that are often distributed in meetings and training sessions. In other organizations, statements about employee creativity are included in the annual employee feedback survey. Using scaled ratings, employees either agree or disagree with the statements. Comparing actual scores of groups of employees over time reflects the degree to which employees perceive the improvement of creativity in the workplace. Having consistent and comparable measures is still a challenge. Other organizations may monitor the number, duration, and participation rate for creativity training meetings. The last decade has witnessed a proliferation of creativity tools, meetings, and activity.

EMPLOYEE ATTITUDES

Employee Satisfaction

An important item monitored by most organizations is employee job satisfaction, and some meetings and events are designed to improve job satisfaction. Using feedback surveys, executives monitor the degree to which employees are satisfied with their employer, policies, the work environment, supervision and leadership, the work itself, as well as other factors. Sometimes, a composite rating is developed to reflect an overall satisfaction value or an index for the organization, division, department, or region.

While job satisfaction has always been an important issue in employee relations, in recent years it has taken on a new dimension because of the linking of job satisfaction to other measures. A classical relationship with job satisfaction is in the attraction and retention of employees. Firms with excellent job satisfaction ratings often attract potential employees. It becomes a subtle, but important, recruiting tool. "Employers of Choice" and "Best Places to Work," for example, often have high job satisfaction ratings. This relationship between job satisfaction and employee retention has attracted increased emphasis in recent years because turnover and retention are critical issues. The previous chapter presented the classic relationship between on-the-job satisfaction and employee turnover. These relationships are now easily developed using human capital management systems, with modules to calculate the correlation between the turnover rates and the job satisfaction scores for the various job groups, divisions, and departments.

Job satisfaction has taken on new dimensions in connection with customer service. Dozens of applied research meetings are beginning to show a high correlation between job satisfaction scores and customer satisfaction scores. Intuitively, this seems obvious. A more satisfied employee is likely to provide more productive, friendly, and appropriate customer service. Likewise, a disgruntled employee will provide poor quality service. Job attitudes (job satisfaction) relate to customer impression (customer satisfaction), which relates to revenue growth (profits). Therefore, if employee attitudes improve, revenues increase. These links, often referred to as a service-profit-chain, create a promising way to identify important relationships between attitudes and profits in an organization.

Organizational Commitment

In recent years, organizational commitment (OC) measures have complemented or replaced job satisfaction measures. Organizational commitment measures go beyond employee satisfaction to include the extent to which the employees identify with organizational goals, mission, philosophy, value, policies, and practices. The concept of involvement and becoming committed to the organization is a key issue. Organizational commitment more closely correlates with productivity and other performance improvement measures, while job satisfaction usually does not. Organizational commitment is often measured the same way as job satisfaction, using attitude surveys and a 5-point or 7-point scale taken directly from employees. As organizational commitment scores improve (taken on a standard index), a corresponding improvement in productivity should exist.

Employee Engagement

A different twist to the organizational commitment measure is the measure that reflects employee engagement. This involves the measures that indicate the extent to which employees are actively engaged in the organization. Consider the case of the Royal Bank of Scotland Group (RBS). With more than 115,000 employees, RBS considered measuring the effectiveness of its investment in people and its impact on business performance to be a strategic imperative and consequently had been building, validating, and introducing a human capital model that demonstrably links people strategies to performance (Bates, 2003).

RBS moved beyond monitoring employee satisfaction and commitment to measuring whether employees actively improved business results, using an employee engagement model to assess the employees' likelihood of contributing to the bank's profits. This model linked the separate HR information in a consistent way, which was then linked to key business indicators. The outputs enabled the business to understand how to influence the bank's results through its people.

To test and validate the model, RBS' HR Research and Measurement team reviewed all the survey instruments used in HR activities (joiner, leaver, "pulse," employee opinion), along with the HR data available in its HRMS database. The HR team decided to put the employee engagement model into practice in the processing and customer contact centers. In these functions, productivity measures are very important, as these affected customer service. Using the amount of work processed as a throughput measure, they found that productivity increased in tandem with engagement levels. The team was also able to establish a link between increasing engagement and decreasing staff turnover.

Hundreds of organizations now use engagement data, not only reflecting the extent to which employees are engaged and connected with productivity and turnover, but also as selection criteria in the competition for the "Best Places to Work" in *Fortune*.

LEADERSHIP

Leadership is perhaps the most difficult measure to address and it is the focus of many meetings and events. On the surface, it seems easy to measure the outcome because effective leadership leads to effective organizations, but putting a monetary value on the consequences of new leadership behavior is not as easy as it appears. Leadership can (and usually does) make the difference in the success or failure of an organization. Without the appropriate leadership behaviors throughout the organization, resources can be misapplied or wasted, and opportunities can be missed. The news and literature are laced with examples of failed leadership at the top. Instances are everywhere of particular top executives having ineffective leadership styles in the way that they manage the team, employees, shareholders, investors, and the public. Some of these failed leadership stories have been painful and high-profile. At the same time, positive examples exist of how a particular leader, such as Jack Welch, has brought extraordinary success throughout the organization over a sustained period. These leaders often are documented in books, articles, and various lists of admired people and clearly make the difference in their organizations. Obviously, the ultimate measure of leadership is the overall success of the organization. Whenever overall measures of success have been achieved or surpassed, they are always attributed to great leadership—perhaps rightfully so. However, attempting to use that kind of success as the only measure of leadership is a cop-out in terms of accountability.

Other measures must be in place to develop system-wide monitoring of the quality of leaders and leadership in the organization.

360-Degree Feedback

Measuring leadership can be achieved in many different ways. Perhaps the most common way is 360-degree feedback. Here, a prescribed set of leadership behaviors desired in the organization is assessed by different sources to provide a composite of the overall leadership capability. The sources often come from the immediate manager of the leader, a colleague in the same area, the employees under the direct influence of the leader, internal or external customers, and a self-assessment. Combined, these assessments form a circle of influence (360 degrees).

The measure is basically an observation of behavior captured in a survey, often reported electronically. This 360-degree feedback has been growing rapidly in the United States, Europe, and Asia as an important way to capture overall leadership behavior change. Since behavior change usually has consequences measured as business impact, leadership improvement should be linked to the business in some way. Leadership development meetings aimed at improving leadership behavior and driving business improvement often have high payoff with ROI values in the range of 500–1000% (Phillips and Schmidt, 2004). This is primarily because of the multiplicative effect as leaders are developed and a change of behavior influences important measures in the leader's team.

Leadership Inventories

Another way to measure leadership is to require the management team to participate in a variety of leadership inventories, assessing pre-determined leadership competency statements. The inventories reflect the extent to which a particular leadership style, approach, or even success is in place. These inventories, while popular in the 1970s and 1980s, are often being replaced by the 360-degree feedback process described earlier.

Leadership Perception

Quality of leadership can also be captured from the perspective of employees. In some organizations employees rate the quality of leadership using several dimensions. Top executives are the typical focal point for this evaluation, along with the employees' immediate managers. The measure is usually taken along with the annual feedback survey in the form of direct statements about the leader; the respondent agrees or disagrees using a 5-point scale. This survey attempts to measure the extent to which the followers in a particular situation perceive the quality, success, and appropriateness of leadership behavior as it is practiced.

Networking

The concept of networking, particularly social networks, has been a topic for study for many years. According to *Successful Meetings*, participants attend meetings for education and networking (Welch, 2007). Networking makes our list of intangibles because so many meetings seem to enhance or facilitate networking, and networking is difficult to measure and often very difficult to convert to monetary value. Inside an organization, social networks are the way in which much of the work gets done. When any person views an organizational chart, the first thing that comes to mind is: Who are the real players? and How do they work together? The lines on the organizational chart, while showing connections between boxes, do not really capture the way in which things are accomplished. From one organization to another, networking is an important way in which ideas are shared and information is exchanged. Recently, the book *The Tipping Point* brought to the forefront the importance of networking (Gladwell, 2001). Through many stories and examples, Gladwell shows how social networks dramatically influence the adoption of ideas and the development of trends in our society.

While networking occurs naturally, for some organizations, it is enhanced through planned activities. Meetings and meetings are implemented to foster networking within the organization and with other organizations. Some events in the meetings and events industry are designed to be networking events.

Is there a value in networks? Is there a value in something that seems to be invisible? When many managers, executives, and other professional employees are so busy meeting goals, deadlines, quotas, standards, and their key performance indicators, do they have time for informal networking on their long lists? Only if there is value in the networking.

Several studies have highlighted the value of networking. One study showed that there was a clear connection between networking and performance. This study showed that teams that were allowed to network seamlessly were higher performers than those that were not allowed to network (Cross and Parker, 2004). Another study conducted with Accenture's Institute for Strategic Change showed that the power of networks was an important lever for improving organizational performance. In this study, technology use and individual expertise did not distinguish the high performers from the low performers. What distinguished high performance were larger and more diversified personal networks than those of the average or low performers (Cross *et al.*, 2003). Many other research projects show the value of networking (Tapscott and Williams, 2006).

Still other research underscores the importance of social networks for meetings and events. When the concept of sharing information and sharing knowledge is considered, it is assumed that this would occur primarily through the Internet, websites, and search engines. However, in reality, they are often underused because more people turn to colleagues for information. One such study showed that engineers and scientists were roughly five times more likely to turn to a person for information than to an impersonal source, such as a database or a file cabinet (Linden *et al.*, 2002). But these studies beg the question: Can you actually convert networking to monetary value?

Since networking is so difficult, the impact and outcomes are often unique to the individual. The payoff of a particular networking activity is based on what outcome or consequence comes from that mutual relationship.

It is virtually impossible to track certain measures and attribute a net amount of improvement to networking, although it may be possible in certain unique situations. While meaningful measures of networking may be just keeping records of how the network is evolving, a social network analysis survey may be developed whereby individual networking is tracked. This collects information about the individual, the area, and what specifically is being gained from the networking. Obviously, this is a cumbersome process and is now being replaced by technology.

One organization, nTAG, has developed networking badges for each participant at a networking event. The badges are designed to communicate with each other. When one person is talking to another directly, it is documented on the records of both individuals. It records not only who the conversation is with but for how long it is conducted. It can also automatically generate follow-up information to track the outcome of that particular networking event. This is an excellent example of how technology is helping to measure a hard to measure item.

In summary, networking is a powerful process. On the one hand it seems to be invisible, yet it is an important factor in generating ideas, developing new techniques, and improving organizations.

FINAL THOUGHTS

Get the picture? Intangible measures are crucial to reflecting the success of a meeting or event. While they may not carry the weight of measures expressed in monetary terms, they are nevertheless an important part of the overall evaluation. Intangible measures should be identified, explored, examined, and monitored for changes linked to meetings. Collectively, they add a unique dimension to the evaluation report since most, if not all, meetings involve intangible variables.

REFERENCES

Bates, S. Linking People Measures to Strategy. *Research Report* R-1342-03-RR. New York: The Conference Board, 2003.

Boulton, R.E.S., Libert, B.D., and Samek, S.M. *Cracking the Value Code.* New York: Harper Business, 2000.

Brown, S.F. "Scientific Americans." *Fortune*, September 20, 2004, p. 175.

Cross, R., Davenport, T., and Cantrell, S. *Rising Above the Crowd: How High Performance Knowledge Workers Differentiate Themselves.* Accenture Institute for Strategic Change Working Paper, 2003.

Cross, R., and Parker, A. *The Hidden Power of Social Networks.* Boston, MA: Harvard Business School Press, 2004.

Farris, Paul W., Bendle, Neil T., Pfeifer, Phillip E., and Ribstein, David J. *Marketing Metrics: 50 + Metrics Every Executive Should Master.* Upper Saddle River, NJ: Wharton School Publishing, 2006.

Gladwell, M. *The Tipping Point*. Boston, MA: Little, Brown, 2001.

Linden, A., Ball, R., Waldir, A., Haley, K. *Gartner's Survey on Managing Information*. Number: COM-15-0971. Stamford, CT: Gartner, Inc., 2002.

Kandybihn, A. and Kihn, M. "Raising Your Return on Innovation Investment." *Strategy + Business*, 2004, (35).

Phillips, J.J. and Phillips, P.P. *Show Me the Money: How to Determine ROI in People, Projects, and Programs*. San Francisco, CA: Berrett-Koehler, 2007.

Phillips, J.J. and Schmidt, L. *The Leadership Scorecard*. Woburn, MA: Butterworth-Heinemann, 2004.

Schwartz, E.I. *Juice: The Creative Fuel that Drives World-Class Inventors*. Boston, MA: Harvard Business School Press, 2004.

Tapscott, D. and Williams, A.D. *How mass Colloboration Changes Everything*. New York: Penguin, 2006.

Ulrich, D., and Smallwood, N. *Why the Bottom Line Isn't*. Hoboken, N.J.: John Wiley & Sons.

Welch, S. J. "23 Secrets of Master Networkers." *Successful Meetings*. April 2007, p. 28.

CHAPTER 11

Reporting Results

With results in hand, what's next? Should the results be used to improve the meeting, change the design, show the contribution, justify new meetings, gain additional support, or build goodwill? How should the data be presented? The worst course of action is to do nothing. Communicating results is as important as achieving results. This chapter provides useful information to help present evaluation data to the various audiences using both oral and written reporting methods.

WHY THE CONCERN ABOUT COMMUNICATING RESULTS?

Communicating results is critical to the accountability of meetings and events. While communicating achieved results to stakeholders after the follow-up evaluation is important, early communication is also important. Continuous communication ensures that information is flowing so that adjustments can be made, and that all stakeholders are aware of the success and issues surrounding the success of the meeting.

As Mark Twain once said, "Collecting data is like collecting garbage—pretty soon we will have to do something with it." Evaluation data mean nothing unless the findings are communicated promptly to the appropriate audiences so that they will be aware of the results and can take action if necessary. Here are a few important reasons why communication is necessary.

Communication is Necessary to Make Improvements

Because information is collected at different points during the meeting cycle, the communication or feedback to involved groups is the only way they can take action and make adjustments if needed. Thus, the quality and timeliness of communication become critical issues for making necessary adjustments or improvements in the future. Communication is necessary to ensure that the target audience fully understands the results achieved and how the results could either be enhanced in future meetings.

Communication Is Necessary to Explain Contributions

The contribution of the meeting, based on the seven types of measures, is confusing at best. The different target audiences will need a thorough explanation of the results. A communication strategy—including techniques, media, and the overall process—will determine the extent to which they understand the contribution. Communicating results, particularly with business impact and ROI, can appear complicated, even with the most sophisticated target audiences. Communication must be planned and implemented with the goal of ensuring that audiences understand the full contribution.

Communication Is a Politically Sensitive Issue

Communication is one of those issues that can cause major problems. Because the results of a meeting may be closely linked to political issues within an organization, communication can upset some individuals and, at the same time, please others. If certain individuals do not receive the information or it is delivered inconsistently from one group to another, problems can quickly surface. Not only is understanding the information an issue, but issues of fairness, quality, and political correctness make the task more difficult.

KEY PRINCIPLES OF COMMUNICATING RESULTS

The skills required to communicate results effectively are almost as delicate and sophisticated as those needed to obtain results. The style is as important as the substance. Regardless of the message, audience, or medium, a few general principles apply.

Communication Must be Timely

Usually, meeting results should be communicated as soon as they are known. From a practical standpoint, delaying the communication until a convenient time is sometimes best, such as the publication of the next newsletter or the next general management meeting. Several questions are relevant. Is the audience ready for the results in view of other issues that may have developed? Is the audience expecting results? When is the best time to have the maximum impact on the audience? Do circumstances dictate a change in the timing of the communication?

Communication Should be Targeted to Specific Audiences

Communication is usually more effective if it is designed for a specific group. The message should be specifically tailored to the interests, needs, and expectations of the target audience. The results of a meeting should reflect outcomes at all levels, including the seven types of data developed in this book. Some of the data are developed during the meeting and communicated early. Other data (impact data) are collected after application and communicated in a follow-up study. The results, in their broadest sense, may involve early feedback in qualitative terms all the way to ROI values in varying quantitative terms.

Media Should be Carefully Selected

Certain media may be more effective for a particular group than others. Face-to-face meetings may be better than special bulletins. A memo distributed exclusively to top executives may be more effective than the company newsletter. The proper method of communication can help improve the effectiveness of the process.

Communication Should be Unbiased and Modest

For communication to be effective, separating fact from fiction and accurate statements from opinions is important. Some audiences may accept communication with skepticism, anticipating biased opinions. Boastful statements sometimes turn off recipients, and most of the content is lost. Observable, credible facts carry far more weight than extreme or sensational claims. Although such claims may capture an audience's attention, they often detract from the importance of the results.

Communication Must be Consistent

The timing and content of the communication should be consistent with past practices. A special communication at an unusual time may provoke suspicion. Also, if a particular group, such as top management, regularly receives communication on outcomes, it should continue receiving communication even if the results are not positive. If unfavorable results are omitted, the impression that only positive results are reported may be given.

Testimonials are More Effective Coming from Respected Individuals

Opinions are strongly influenced by others, particularly those who are respected and trusted. Testimonials about results, when solicited from individuals respected by others within the organization, can influence the effectiveness of the message. This respect may be related to leadership ability, position, special skills, or knowledge. A testimonial from an individual who commands little respect can have a negative impact.

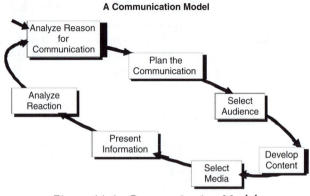

Figure 11-1. Communication Model.

The Audience's Opinion of the Meeting Will Influence the Communication Strategy

Opinions are difficult to change, and a negative opinion about a particular meeting may not change with the mere presentation of facts. However, the presentation of facts alone may strengthen the opinions held by those who already support the meeting. Presentation of results helps reinforce their position and provides a defense in discussions with others. A planning team with a high level of credibility and respect may have a relatively easy time communicating results. Low credibility can create problems when trying to be persuasive.

These general principles are important to the overall success of the communication effort. They should serve as a checklist for the planning team when disseminating results.

The Process Steps for Communicating Results

The process of communicating results must be systematic, timely, well-planned, and represent seven components that should occur in the sequence shown in Figure 11-1. These steps are briefly described in the next sections.

The Reasons for Communication

The reasons for communicating results depend on the specific meeting, the setting, and the unique needs. Some of the most common are:

- Securing approval for the meeting and allocating resources of time and money.
- Gaining support for the meeting and its objectives.
- Securing agreement on the issues, solutions, and resources.

- Building credibility for the meeting planning team.
- Reinforcing the need for the content in the meeting.
- Driving action for the improvement of the meeting.
- Preparing participants to provide data for the evaluation.
- Showing the complete results of the meeting.
- Underscoring the importance of measuring results.
- Explaining the techniques used to measure results.
- Motivating prospective participants to be involved in the meeting.
- Demonstrating accountability for expenditures.
- Marketing future meetings and events.

Because there may be other reasons for communicating results, the list should be tailored to each meeting.

Planning the Communications

Any successful activity must be carefully planned to produce the maximum results. This is a critical part of communicating the results. Communications planning is important to ensure that each audience receives the proper information at the right time and that appropriate actions are taken. Several issues are important when planning the communication of results:

- What will be communicated?
- When will the data be communicated?
- How will the information be communicated?
- Where will the information be communicated?
- Who will communicate the information?
- Who is the target audience?
- What are the specific actions required or desired?

When an evaluation plan is approved, the simple communication plan is usually developed. This should detail how specific information is developed and communicated to various groups and the expected actions. In addition, this plan details the timeframes for communication, and the appropriate groups to receive the information. The planner, key clients, and stakeholders need to agree on the extent of detail in the plan. To communicate appropriately with target audiences, four specific documents are usually produced when the evaluation is taken to the impact and ROI levels. The first report is an impact study showing the approach, assumptions, methodology, and results using all data categories. In addition, barriers and enablers are included in the study, along with conclusions and recommendations. The second report should be a five-to-eight page executive summary of the key points. The third report is a one-page overview of the results for those individuals who understand this method. The fourth report is a brief, two-page narrative of the process and results written as a story. These documents should be presented to the different groups based on their needs. A suggested approach is:

Audience	Document
Participants	Brief narrative
Managers of participants (optional)	Brief narrative
Senior executives	Complete study, executive summary, one page summary
Meeting and events staff	Complete study, one page summary
Client	Complete study, executive summary, one page summary
Key stakeholders who understand the methodology	One page summary
Prospective participants	Brief narrative

If this is the first ROI study conducted with a client, a face-to-face meeting should be administered with key executives. The purpose is to ensure that executives understand the methodology, the conservative assumptions, and each level of data. The barriers, enablers, conclusions, and recommendations are an important part of the meeting. Later, after two or three studies have been conducted, this group will receive only a one-page summary of key data items. A similar meeting should be conducted with the meetings and events staff, where the complete impact study is described and used as a learning tool.

THE AUDIENCE FOR COMMUNICATIONS

When approaching a particular audience, the following questions should be asked about each potential group:

- Are they interested in the meeting?
- Do they really want to receive the information?
- Has a commitment to include them in the communications been made?
- Is the timing right for this audience?
- Are they familiar with the meeting?
- How do they prefer to have results communicated?
- Do they know the meeting planner? The meetings and events staff?
- Are they likely to find the results threatening?
- Which medium will be most convincing to this group?

For each target audience, three actions are needed. To the greatest extent possible, the meeting planner should know and understand the target audience. Also, the planner should find out what information is needed, and why. Each group

Table 11-1
Common Target Audiences

Reason for Communication	Primary Target Audiences
To secure agreement with the results	Top executives, clients, sponsors, exhibitors
To gain support for the meeting	Client, sponsors, managers of participants
To build credibility for the meeting and events team	Top executives
To drive action for improvement	Meetings and events team, clients
To prepare participants for the meeting	Participants
To enhance results and quality of future feedback	Participants
To show the complete results of the meeting	All stakeholders, client
To underscore the importance of measuring results	Client, meetings and events team
To explain techniques used to measure results	Client, meetings and events team
To create desire for a participant to be involved	Prospective participants
To demonstrate accountability for expenditures	Top executives, clients
Top executives, clients	Prospective clients, executives, participants

may be different. Some want detailed information, while others prefer a brief report. Finally, the meeting planner should try to understand audience bias. Some audiences will quickly support the results, whereas others may not support them. Most will be neutral. The team should be empathetic and try to understand differing views.

The potential target audiences to receive information about meeting results are varied in terms of job levels and responsibilities. Determining which groups will receive a specific communication piece deserves careful thought, as problems can arise when one group receives inappropriate information or when another is omitted altogether. A sound basis for proper audience selection is to analyze the reason for the communication, as discussed earlier. Table 11-1 shows common target audiences and the basis for selecting each one.

CONTENT DEVELOPMENT

The type of evaluation report depends on the extent of detailed information presented to the various target audiences. Brief summaries of results with appropriate charts may be sufficient for some communication efforts.

In other situations, particularly with significant meetings requiring extensive funding, the amount of detail in the evaluation report is more crucial. A complete and comprehensive impact study report may be necessary. This report can then be used as the basis of more streamlined information for specific audiences and various media. The report may contain the sections detailed in Table 11-2.

Table 11-2
Format of an Impact Study Report

- General Information
  - Background
  - Objectives of study
- Methodology for Impact Study
  - Levels of evaluation
  - ROI Methodology
  - Collecting data
  - Isolating the effects of the meeting
  - Converting data to monetary values
- Data Analysis Issues
- Results: General Information
  - Response profile
  - Success with objectives
- Results: Reaction and Perceived Value
  - Data sources
  - Data summary
  - Key issues
- Results: Learning
  - Data sources
  - Data summary
  - Key issues
- Results: Application and Implementation
  - Data sources
  - Data summary
  - Key issues
- Results: Impact and consequences
  - General comments
  - Linkage with business measures
  - Key issues
- Cost of Meeting
- Results: ROI and Its Meaning
- Results: Intangible Measures
- Barriers and Enablers
  - Barriers
  - Enablers
- Conclusions and Recommendations
  - Conclusions
  - Recommendations
- Exhibits

While this report is an effective, professional way to present ROI data, several cautions need to be followed. Since this document reports the success of a meeting involving a group of participants, complete credit for the success must go to the participants (and sometimes their immediate leaders). Their performance generated the success. Another important caution is to avoid boasting about results. Huge claims of success can quickly turn off an audience and interfere with the delivery of the desired message.

The methodology should be clearly explained, along with assumptions made in the analysis. The audience should easily see how the values were developed and how the specific steps were followed to make the process more conservative, credible, and accurate. Detailed statistical analyses should be placed in the appendix.

COMMUNICATION MEDIA SELECTION

Many options are available to communicate meeting results. In addition to the impact study report, the most frequently used media are meetings, interim and progress reports, a variety of publications, and case studies. Table 11-3 shows the variety of options.

If used properly, meetings are fertile opportunities for communicating results. All organizations have a variety of meetings, and some may provide the proper context for reporting meeting results. Regular meetings with management groups are common. A discussion of a meeting and event and the subsequent results can be integrated into the regular meeting format. A few organizations have initiated periodic meetings for all key stakeholders, in which the meeting planner reviews progress and discusses the next steps. A few highlights of the meeting results can be helpful to build interest, commitment, and support for the continuation of the meeting.

To reach a wide audience, the meeting planner can use internal, routine publications. Whether a newsletter, magazine, newspaper, or electronic file, these types of media usually reach all employees or stakeholders. The information can

Table 11-3
Options for Communicating Results

Meetings (Audiences)	Detailed Reports	Brief Reports	Electronic Reporting	Mass Publications
Executives	Impact study	Executive summary	Web site	Announcements
Managers	Case study (internal)	Slide overview	E-mail	Bulletins
Stakeholders	Case study (external)	One-page summary	Blogs	Newsletters
Meeting and Events Team	Major articles	Brochure	Video	Brief articles

be effective if communicated appropriately. The scope should be limited to general interest articles, announcements, and interviews. For most meetings, results are achieved weeks or even months after the meeting is conducted. Participants need reinforcement from many sources. If results are communicated to a general audience, additional pressure may exist to continue the meeting or similar ones in the future. Internal and external Web pages on the Internet, company-wide intranets, and e-mail are excellent vehicles for releasing results, promoting ideas, and informing participants and other target groups. E-mail, in particular, provides a virtually instantaneous means with which to communicate and solicit responses from large numbers of people. For major meeting evaluation studies, some organizations create blogs to present results and secure reaction, feedback, and suggestions.

A brochure might be appropriate for meetings conducted on a continuing basis, where participants have produced excellent results. Also, a brochure may be appropriate when the audience is large and continuously changing. The brochure should be attractive and present a complete description of the meeting, with a major section devoted to the results obtained with previous participants, if available. Measurable results and reactions from participants, or even direct quotes from individuals, could add spice to an otherwise dull brochure.

Case studies represent an effective way to communicate the results of a meeting. A typical case study describes the situation, provides appropriate background information (including the events that led to the meeting), presents the techniques and strategies used to develop the study, and highlights the key issues in the evaluation. Case studies tell an interesting story of how the meeting was conducted and how the evaluation was developed, including the issues and concerns identified along the way.

Case studies have value for both internal and external use. As shown in Table 11-4, the internal use is to build understanding, capability and support. Case studies are impressive to hand to a potential client and convincing for others who are seeking data about the success of meetings and events. Externally, case studies can be used to bring exposure and recognition to the meetings and events team and help the organization brand its overall meetings and events function. Professionals in this industry are eager to read actual studies. A variety of publication outlets are available for case studies—not only in meetings and events publications, but also in general publications.

Table 11-4
Internal and External Use of Case Studies

Case Study: Internal Use	Case Study: External Publication
Communicate results	Provide recognition to participants
Teach others	Improve image of function
Build a history	Enhance brand of function
Serve as a template	Enhance image of organization
Make an impression	

Presenting Information

Routine Feedback

One of the most important reasons for collecting reaction and learning data is to provide feedback so that adjustments or changes can be made throughout the life of a meeting. For most meetings, reaction and learning data are routinely collected and quickly communicated to a variety of groups. Sometimes, application and impact data are routinely communicated using feedback designed to provide information to several audiences using a variety of media. This process becomes comprehensive and has to be managed in a very proactive way.

The following steps are recommended for providing feedback and managing the feedback process. Many of the steps and issues follow the recommendations of Peter Block in his successful consulting book, *Flawless Consulting* (Block, 2000).

- *Communicate quickly.* Whether good news or bad news, it is important to let individuals involved in the meeting have the information as soon as possible. The recommended time for providing feedback is usually a matter of days and certainly no longer than a week or two after the results are known.
- *Simplify the data.* Condense the data into a very understandable, concise presentation. This is not the situation for detailed explanations and analysis.
- *Examine the role of the meeting planning team and the client in the feedback situation.* Sometimes, the planner is the judge, jury, prosecutor, defendant, or witness. On the other hand, sometimes the client is the judge, jury, prosecutor, defendant, or witness. Examining the respective roles in terms of reactions to the data and the actions that need to be taken is important.
- *Use negative data in a constructive way.* Some of the data will show that things are not going so well, and the fault may rest with the participant, the planner, or the client. In either case, the story basically changes from "Let's look at the success we've made" to "Now we know which areas to change."
- *Use positive data in a cautious way.* Positive data can be misleading, and if they are communicated too enthusiastically, they may create expectations beyond what may materialize later. Positive data should be presented in a cautious way—almost in a discounting mode.
- *Choose the language of the meeting and communication carefully.* The language used should be descriptive, focused, specific, short, and simple. Language that is too judgmental, macro, stereotypical, lengthy, or complex should be avoided.
- *Ask the client for reactions to the data.* After all, the client is the number one customer, and the client's reaction is critical because it is most important that the client be pleased with the meeting.
- *Ask the client for recommendations.* The client may have some good recommendations of what needs to be changed to make the meeting more effective in the future.

- *Use support and confrontation carefully.* These two issues are not mutually exclusive. At times, support and confrontation are needed for the same group. The client may need support and yet be confronted for lack of improvement or sponsorship. The planning team may be confronted about problems, but may need support as well.
- *React and act on the data.* The different alternatives and possibilities should be weighed carefully to arrive at the adjustments and changes that will be necessary.
- *Secure agreement from all key stakeholders.* This is essential to ensure that everyone is willing to make adjustments and changes that may be necessary.
- *Keep the feedback process short.* Letting the process become bogged down in long, drawn-out meetings or lengthy documents is a bad idea. If this occurs, stakeholders will avoid the process instead of being willing participants.

Following these steps will help move the communication forward, often ensuring that adjustments are supported and made.

Presenting Results to Senior Management

Perhaps one of the most challenging and stressful communications is presenting an impact study to the senior management team, who funded the meeting and study. The challenge is convincing this highly skeptical and critical group that outstanding results have been achieved (assuming they have) in a reasonable timeframe, addressing the salient points, and making sure they understand the process. Two particular issues can create challenges. First, if the results are impressive, it may be difficult to convince the executives about the validity of the data. On the other extreme, if the data are negative, it may be challenging to ensure that executives do not overreact and look for someone to blame. Several guidelines can help ensure that this process is planned and executed properly.

Plan a face-to-face briefing with senior team members unfamiliar with the ROI Methodology for the first one or two major impact studies. The good news is they will probably attend the briefing because they have not seen ROI data developed for this type of meeting and may be skeptical. The bad news is that it takes a lot of time, usually one hour, for this presentation. After a group has had a couple of presentations, an executive one-page summary may suffice. At this point, they understand the process, so a shortened version may be appropriate. After the target audience is familiar with the process, a brief version may be necessary, which will involve a one- to two-page summary with charts and graphs showing the different types of measures.

When making the initial presentation, the results should not be distributed prior to, or even during, the presentation. It should be saved until the end of the session. This allows enough time to present the process and results and for the audience to react to them before they see the ROI calculation. Present the ROI Methodology step by step, showing how the data were collected, when they were collected, who provided the data, how the effect of the meeting was isolated from other influences, and how data were converted to monetary values. The various

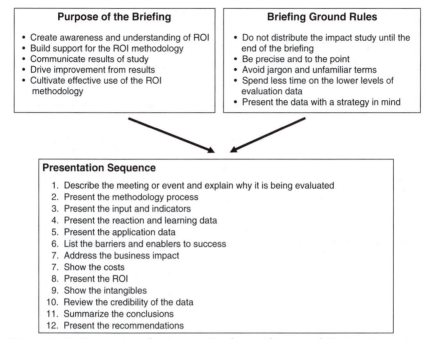

Purpose of the Briefing	**Briefing Ground Rules**
• Create awareness and understanding of ROI • Build support for the ROI methodology • Communicate results of study • Drive improvement from results • Cultivate effective use of the ROI methodology	• Do not distribute the impact study until the end of the briefing • Be precise and to the point • Avoid jargon and unfamiliar terms • Spend less time on the lower levels of evaluation data • Present the data with a strategy in mind

Presentation Sequence

1. Describe the meeting or event and explain why it is being evaluated
2. Present the methodology process
3. Present the input and indicators
4. Present the reaction and learning data
5. Present the application data
6. List the barriers and enablers to success
7. Address the business impact
7. Show the costs
8. Present the ROI
9. Show the intangibles
10. Review the credibility of the data
11. Summarize the conclusions
12. Present the recommendations

Figure 11-2. Presenting the Impact Study to Clients and Senior Executives.

assumptions, adjustments, and conservative approaches are presented along with the total cost of the meeting so that the target audience will begin to buy into the process of developing the ROI.

When the data are actually presented, the results are shown one level at a time, starting with Level 0, moving through Level 5, and ending with the intangibles. This allows the audience to see the inputs and indicators, reaction, learning, application and implementation, business impact, and ROI. After some discussion on the meaning of the ROI, the intangible measures are presented. Allocate time for each level as appropriate for the audience. This helps overcome the potentially emotional reactions to a particularly positive or negative ROI.

Collectively, these steps will help prepare for and present one of the most critical presentations in the ROI process. Figure 11-2 shows the approach to this important meeting with the client and senior executives. Improving communications with this group requires developing an overall strategy and a defined purpose.

Streamlining the Communication

Obviously, executives and management groups will not come to a face-to-face meeting for repeated evaluation studies, nor will they read a complete impact study. Therefore, an executive summary should be used. This represents about a six- to ten-page summary of the entire report. Still, the process can be further

ROI Impact Study

Meeting Title: Annual Franchise Meeting
Target Audience: All Franchise Owners and Managers (955)
Duration: 3 Days

RESULTS

Level 1: Reaction	Level 2: Learning	Level 3: Application	Level 4: Impact	Level 5: ROI	Intangible Benefits
Overall rating 4.23 out of 5 on the eight key items	74% increase post-test versus pre-test on new product	88% conducted briefings and completed briefing record	Sales increase: $2,942,900 (profits)	92%	Customer satisfaction
96% provided action items	Rating of 4.4 out of 5 for learning seven new objectives	4.1 out of 5 on follow-up action survey	Customer complaint reduction: $932,400		Brand awareness
		54% report all action items complete	Total improvement: $3,874,900		Market leadership
		83% report some action items complete			Improved recruiting

Technique to Isolate Effects of Meeting: Trend line analysis; participant estimation
Technique to Convert Data to Monetary Value: Standard values; internal experts
Fully Loaded Meeting Costs: $2,018,177
ROI Perspective: Company

Figure 11-3. An Example of a One-Page Summary of an ROI Study.

streamlined by considering a one-page summary, as shown in Figure 11-3. This summary, representing an annual franchise meeting, shows the key data collected. This is the ultimate in efficient communication, but is effective only when the managers understand the different types of data. The audiences must be educated on the methodology so they can understand the streamlined communications. This streamlined communication can be used on a progressive basis, gradually moving executives and managers to this more streamlined method.

Building Scorecards

Ultimately, the management team may need a scorecard showing the success of all meetings and events. This would show evaluation data that bridges all the meetings and uses all the different types of data outlined in this book. The concept of building a broader scorecard, called the macro scorecard, is explained in Figure 11-4. Essentially, when any meeting is evaluated at Level 0 or Level 1,

Micro-Level Scorecard   Macro-Level Scorecard

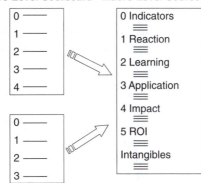

Figure 11-4. Micro-Level To Macro-Level Scorecard.

for example, this represents a scorecard of performance for that meeting. As the evaluation data are collected at higher levels including Levels 2, 3, and 4, each meeting essentially has a scorecard of performance. These are micro-level scorecards. The challenge is to take selective data sets out of the micro scorecard and use them in the overall macro-level scorecard. For example, the typical Level 1 evaluation form may contain 12–15 items. This is entirely too much data to include on the overall macro scorecard. Using the most critical 3–5 items on the macro-level scorecard would be appropriate. Figure 11-5 shows a simple and brief macro-level scorecard.

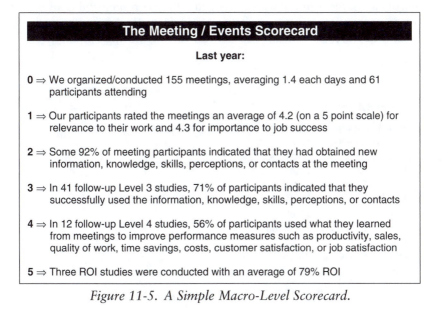

The Meeting / Events Scorecard

Last year:

0 ⟹ We organized/conducted 155 meetings, averaging 1.4 each days and 61 participants attending

1 ⟹ Our participants rated the meetings an average of 4.2 (on a 5 point scale) for relevance to their work and 4.3 for importance to job success

2 ⟹ Some 92% of meeting participants indicated that they had obtained new information, knowledge, skills, perceptions, or contacts at the meeting

3 ⟹ In 41 follow-up Level 3 studies, 71% of participants indicated that they successfully used the information, knowledge, skills, perceptions, or contacts

4 ⟹ In 12 follow-up Level 4 studies, 56% of participants used what they learned from meetings to improve performance measures such as productivity, sales, quality of work, time savings, costs, customer satisfaction, or job satisfaction

5 ⟹ Three ROI studies were conducted with an average of 79% ROI

Figure 11-5. A Simple Macro-Level Scorecard.

Reactions to Communication

The best indicator of how effectively the results of a meeting have been communicated is the level of commitment and support from clients, executives, and sponsors. The allocation of requested resources and strong commitment from top management are tangible evidence of management's positive perception of the meeting results. In addition to this reaction, a few techniques can measure the effectiveness of the communication efforts.

Whenever results are communicated, the reaction of the target audiences can be monitored. These reactions may include non-verbal gestures, oral remarks, written comments, or indirect actions that reveal how the communication was received. Usually, when results are presented in a meeting, the presenter will have some indication of how the results were received by the group. The interest and attitudes of the audience can usually be quickly evaluated. Comments about the results—formal or informal—should also be noted and tabulated.

Using Evaluation Data

One of the most important reasons for collecting evaluation data and communicating them to different audiences is to make improvements. After all, the principle premise for evaluation is to improve processes—not necessarily to evaluate the performance of a particular group. With process improvement in mind, Figure 11-6 shows some of the typical uses of evaluation data as they relate to the different levels. Many of the uses focus on making meetings and events better for the future. Others are involved in improving support and commitment for meetings and events.

Someone or some group must be charged with the responsibility of ensuring that these appropriate actions are taken. Sufficient effort is rarely focused on this area. Therefore, there is a lack of follow-through. If these ultimate changes

Use of Evaluation Data	Appropriate Level of Data				
	1	2	3	4	5
Adjust Meetings/Events Design	✓	✓			
Improve Meetings/Events Delivery	✓	✓			
Influence Application and Impact			✓	✓	
Improve Support for Meetings/Events			✓	✓	
Improve Stakeholder Satisfaction			✓	✓	✓
Recognize and Reward Participants		✓	✓	✓	
Justify or Enhance Budget				✓	✓
Develop Norms and Standards	✓	✓	✓		
Reduce Costs		✓	✓	✓	✓
Market Meetings and Events	✓	✓	✓	✓	✓
Expand Implementation to Other Areas				✓	✓

Figure 11-6. Using Evaluation Data.

or improvements are not made, much of the value of the evaluation is lost. For some meetings, particularly those of a comprehensive nature, the original project plan for the evaluation study includes all the steps throughout the process—communicating results, tracking the improvements that must be made, and making adjustments and changes to the meeting. This ensures that the appropriate use of data does not get left out or that the resources are not applied to it. This is a final piece of the puzzle.

FINAL THOUGHTS

Communication of results is the final process step in the evaluation of meetings and events. This is a crucial step in the overall evaluation process. If this step is not taken seriously, the full impact of the results will not be realized and the study may be a waste of time. The chapter began with general principles and steps for communicating results, which can serve as a guide for any significant communication effort. The various target audiences were discussed and, because of its importance, emphasis was placed on the executive group. A suggested format for a detailed evaluation report was also provided. Much of the chapter included a presentation of the most commonly used media for communicating results, including meetings, client publications, and electronic media.

REFERENCE

Block, P. *Flawless Consulting* 2nd edition. San Francisco, CA: Pfeiffer, 2000.

CHAPTER 12

Implementing and Sustaining the Evaluation System

Even the best-designed process, model, or technique is virtually worthless unless it is effectively and efficiently integrated into routine activities. Often, resistance to the additional evaluation arises. Some of this resistance is based on fear, misunderstanding, and lack of knowledge. Some is real, based on actual barriers and obstacles. Although the processes presented in this book is a step-by-step, methodical, and simplistic procedure, it can fail if it is not integrated properly, fully accepted, and supported by those who must make it work. This chapter focuses on some of the key issues needed to overcome resistance to implementing an evaluation process into the routine work of the meetings and events function.

WHY THE CONCERN?

With any new process or change, there is resistance. Resistance may be especially great when implementing a process as complex as ROI. To implement a comprehensive evaluation process and sustain it as an important accountability tool, the resistance must be minimized or removed. Successful implementation essentially equates to overcoming resistance. The four key reasons why a detailed plan should be in place to overcome resistance are explained below.

Resistance is Always Present

Resistance to change is a constant. Sometimes, good reasons for resistance are present, but it often exists for the wrong reasons. The important point is to sort out both kinds of resistance and try to dispel the myths. When legitimate barriers are the basis for resistance, minimizing or removing them altogether is the challenge.

Implementation is Key

As with any process, effective implementation is the key to its success. This occurs when the new technique, tool, or process is integrated into the routine framework. Without effective implementation, even the best process will fail. A process that is never removed from the shelf will never be understood, supported, or improved. Clearly defined steps must be in place for designing a comprehensive implementation process that will overcome resistance.

Consistency is Needed

As this process is implemented, consistency is an important consideration. With consistency comes accuracy and reliability. To ensure that consistency is achieved, a clearly defined process is needed with procedures to use each time an evaluation is conducted. Proper implementation will ensure that this occurs.

Efficiency is Necessary

Cost control and efficiency will always be issues in any major undertaking, and evaluation is no exception. During implementation, tasks must be completed efficiently and effectively. Doing this will help ensure that the process costs are kept to a minimum, time is used appropriately, and the process remains affordable.

IMPLEMENTING THE PROCESS: OVERCOMING RESISTANCE

Resistance appears in many ways, as comments, remarks, actions, or behaviors. Table 12-1 shows some comments from meeting professionals that indicate open resistance to the increased evaluation. Each of these represents an issue that needs

Table 12-1
Typical Objections to the Use of the ROI Methodology

Open Resistance

- It costs too much.
- It takes too much time.
- It is too complex.
- Who is asking for this?
- This is not in my job duties.
- I did not have input on this.
- I do not understand this.
- What happens when the results are negative?
- How can we be consistent with this?
- This looks too subjective.
- Our clients will not support this.
- ROI is too narrowly focused.
- This is not practical for our industry.

to be resolved or addressed in some way. A few of the comments are based on realistic barriers, while others are based on myths that must be dispelled. Sometimes, resistance to the process reflects underlying concerns. The individuals involved may have a fear of losing control of their processes, and others may feel that they are vulnerable to actions that may be taken if the process is not successful. Still others may be concerned about any process that brings change or requires additional learning efforts.

Meeting professionals may resist evaluation and ROI. Heavy persuasion and evidence of tangible benefits may be needed to convince planning team members that this is a process that must be used and is in their best interest to make successful. Although most clients would like to see the results of meetings, they may have concerns about the information they must provide and about whether their performance is being judged along with the evaluation of the meeting. In reality, they may express some of the same fears listed in the table.

The challenge is to implement evaluation systematically and consistently so that it becomes normal business behavior and a routine and standard process designed into meetings and events. The implementation necessary to overcome resistance covers a variety of areas. Figure 12-1 shows actions outlined in this chapter, presented as building blocks to overcoming resistance. They are all necessary to establish the proper framework to dispel myths and remove or minimize barriers. The remainder of this chapter presents specific strategies and techniques around each of the ten building blocks identified in Figure 12-1. They apply equally to the meeting planning staff and to the client organization, and no attempt is made to separate the two in this presentation. In some situations, a

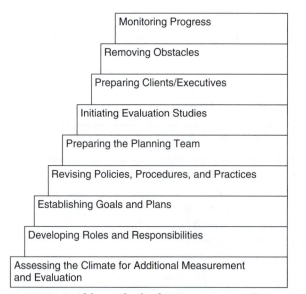

Figure 12-1. Building Blocks for Overcoming Resistance.

particular strategy would work best with the meeting planning team. In reality, all may be appropriate for both groups in certain cases.

ASSESSING THE CLIMATE FOR MEASUREMENT

As a first step toward implementation, some organizations assess the current climate for achieving results. One way to do this is to use a survey to determine current perspectives of the management team and other stakeholders in regard to results of meetings and events. An example is included in the Appendix another way is to conduct interviews with key stakeholders to determine their willingness to implement additional measurements and evaluation. With an awareness of the current status, the meeting planners can influence significant changes and pinpoint particular issues that need support as more evaluation.

DEVELOPING ROLES AND RESPONSIBILITIES

Defining and detailing specific roles and responsibilities for different groups and individuals addresses many of the resistance factors and helps pave a smooth path for implementing additional evaluation.

Identifying a Champion

As an early step in the process, one or more individual(s) should be designated as the internal leader for evaluation. As in most change efforts, someone must take responsibility for ensuring that evaluation is implemented successfully. This leader serves as a champion and is usually the one who understands measurement and evaluation best and sees vast potential for its contribution. More importantly, this leader is willing to teach others and will work to sustain sponsorship.

Developing the Evaluation Leader

The evaluation leader is usually a member of the meeting planning team who has the responsibility for evaluation. This person holds a full-time position in larger meeting planning teams or a part-time position in smaller teams. In a few situations, client organizations may also have an evaluation leader who pursues evaluation from the client's perspective. Some organizations assign this responsibility to a team and empower it to lead the evaluation effort.

In preparation for this assignment, individuals usually have special training that builds specific skills and knowledge. The role of the evaluation leader is quite broad and serves a variety of specialized duties. In some organizations, this leader can take on many roles, ranging from problem solver to communicator to cheerleader.

Leading the evaluation process is a difficult and challenging assignment that requires special skill building. Fortunately, programs are available that teach these skills. For example, one such program is designed to certify individuals who are assuming a leadership role in the implementation of the ROI evaluation (www.roiinstitute.net). This certification is built around ten specific skill sets linked to successful evaluation implementation, focusing on critical areas of data collection, isolating the effects of the meeting, converting data to money, presenting evaluation data, and building capability. This process is quite comprehensive but may be necessary to build the appropriate skills for taking on this challenging assignment.

Establishing a Task Force

Making evaluation work may require the use of a task force. A task force is usually a group of individuals from different parts of the meeting planning team or client team who are willing to develop a comprehensive measurement and evaluation process and implement it. The selection of the task force may involve volunteers, or participation may be mandatory, depending on specific job responsibilities. The task force should represent the necessary cross section for accomplishing stated goals. Task forces have the additional advantage of bringing more people into the process and developing more ownership and support for the evaluation. The task force must be large enough to cover the key areas, but not so large that it becomes cumbersome and difficult to function. Six to twelve members is a good size.

Assigning Responsibilities

Determining specific responsibilities is a critical issue because confusion can arise when individuals are unclear about their specific assignments in the evaluation process. Responsibilities apply to two areas. The first is the measurement responsibility of the entire meeting planning team. Everyone involved must have some responsibility for measurement and evaluation. These responsibilities include providing input on the design of instruments, planning specific evaluations, analyzing data, and interpreting the results. Typical responsibilities include:

- Ensuring that the initial analysis for the meeting includes specific business impact measures
- Developing specific application objectives and business impact objectives for the meeting
- Keeping participants focused on application and impact objectives
- Communicating rationale and reasons for evaluation
- Assisting in data collection activities
- Providing limited assistance for data analysis and reporting

While having each member of the planning team involved in all these activities may not be appropriate, each individual should have at least one or more responsibilities as part of his or her routine job duties. This assignment of responsibility keeps evaluation from being disjointed and separated during meetings. More importantly, it brings accountability to those directly involved in measurement and evaluation.

Another issue involves technical support. Depending on the size of the meetings and events function, establishing a group of technical experts to provide assistance with evaluation may be helpful. When this group is established, the remainder of the planning team must understand that the experts are not there to relieve them of evaluation responsibilities—only to supplement with technical expertise. These technical experts are typically the individuals who have participated in the certification process to build special skills. When this type of support is developed, responsibilities involve six key areas:

1. Designing data collection instruments;
2. Providing assistance for developing an evaluation strategy;
3. Analyzing data, including specialized statistical analyses;
4. Interpreting results and making specific recommendations;
5. Developing an evaluation report or case study to communicate overall results; and
6. Providing technical support in all phases of the measurement and evaluation.

The assignment of responsibilities for evaluation is also an issue that needs attention throughout the evaluation process. Although the planning team must have specific responsibilities during an evaluation, requiring others to be in support functions to help with data collection is not unusual. These responsibilities are defined when a particular evaluation strategy plan is developed and approved.

Establishing Goals and Plans

Establishing goals, targets, and objectives is critical to the implementation, particularly when several meetings are planned. This includes detailed planning documents for the overall process as well as individual evaluation studies. Several key issues relating to goals and plans are covered here.

Setting Evaluation Targets

Establishing specific targets for evaluation levels is an important way to make progress with measurement and evaluation. As discussed throughout this book, not all meetings should be evaluated to the ROI level. Knowing in advance to which level a meeting will be evaluated helps in planning which measures will be needed and how detailed evaluation must be at each level. Table 12-2 shows an example of the targets for evaluation at each level. Target-setting should be completed early in the process with the full support of the planning team. Also, if practical and feasible, the targets should have the approval of key executives—particularly the senior management team.

Table 12-2
Evaluation Targets in a Large Organization with over 200
Meetings and Events

Level	Target (%) (percent of meeting evaluation at this level)
Level 0, Inputs and Indicators	100
Level 1, Reaction and Perceived Value	100
Level 2, Learning and Confidence	80
Level 3, Application and Implementation	30
Level 4, Impact and Consequences	10
Level 5, ROI	5

Developing a Timetable for Implementation

An important part of implementing additional measurement and evaluation is establishing timetables for the complete implementation. This document becomes a master plan for the completion of the different elements presented earlier. Beginning with forming a team and concluding with meeting the targets previously described, this schedule is a plan for transitioning from the present situation

	J	F	M	A	M	J	J	A	S	O	N	D	J	F	M	A	M
Team Formed	■																
Responsibilities Defined	■																
Policy Developed			■	■													
Targets Set		■															
Workshops Developed				■	■	■											
ROI Study (A)					■			■									
ROI Study (B)							■					■					
ROI Study (C)									■	■				■			
Planning Teams Trained								■	■		■	■					
Managers Trained																■	■
Support Tools Developed					■	■											
Guidelines Developed			■	■	■												

Figure 12-2. Implementation Plan for a Large Organization.

to the desired future situation. The items on the schedule include developing specific ROI studies, building staff skills, developing policy, and teaching managers the ROI process. Figure 12-2 shows an example of this plan. The more detailed the document, the more useful it becomes. The plan is a living, long-range document that should be reviewed frequently and adjusted as necessary. More importantly, it should always be familiar to those who are working with evaluation.

Revising or Developing Policies and Guidelines

Another part of planning is revising or developing the organization's policy concerning measurement and evaluation. The policy statement contains information developed specifically for the measurement and evaluation process. It is developed with input from the planning team and key managers or stakeholders. Sometimes, policy issues are addressed during internal workshops designed to build skills for measurement and evaluation. The policy statement addresses critical issues that will influence the effectiveness of the measurement and evaluation process. Typical issues include: adopting the five-level framework presented in this book, requiring Level 3 and 4 objectives for some meetings, and defining responsibilities for the meetings and events team.

Policy statements are important because they provide guidance and direction for the staff and others who work closely with evaluation. These individuals keep the process clearly focused and enable the group to establish goals for evaluation. Policy statements also provide an opportunity to communicate basic requirements and fundamental issues regarding performance and accountability. More than anything else, they serve as learning tools to teach others, especially when they are developed in a collaborative and collective way. If policy statements are developed in isolation and do not enjoy ownership from the staff and management, they will not be effective or useful.

Guidelines for measurement and evaluation are important for showing how to use the tools and techniques, guide the design process, provide consistency in the ROI process, ensure that appropriate methods are used, and place the proper emphasis on each of the areas. The guidelines are more technical than policy statements and often contain detailed procedures showing how the process is undertaken and developed. They often include specific forms, instruments, and tools necessary to facilitate the process.

Preparing the Team

Team members may resist additional measurement and evaluation. They often see evaluation as an unnecessary intrusion into their responsibilities, absorbing precious time and stifling their freedom to be creative. The cartoon character Pogo perhaps characterized it best when he said, "We have met the enemy, and he is us." Several issues must be addressed when preparing the team for ROI implementation.

Involving the Team

For each key issue or major decision involving measurement and evaluation, the planning team should be involved in the process. As policy statements are prepared and evaluation guidelines developed, team input is essential. Resistance is minimized if the team helped design and develop it. Using meetings, brainstorming sessions, and task forces, the team should be involved in every phase of developing the framework and supporting documents for measurement and evaluation.

Using Measurement and Evaluation as a Learning Tool

One reason the meeting planning team may resist measurement and evaluation is that the effectiveness of meetings will be fully exposed, putting the team's reputations on the line. They may have a fear of failure. To overcome this, measurement and evaluation should be clearly positioned as a tool for learning and not a tool for evaluating planning team performance, at least during its early years of implementation. Team members will not be interested in developing a process that will reflect unfavorable on their performance.

Evaluators can learn as much from failures as from successes. If a meeting is not working, finding out quickly is best so that the issues are understood first-hand, not from others. If a meeting is ineffective and not producing the desired results, the failure will eventually be known to clients, if they are not aware of it already. A lack of results will cause some executives to become less supportive of the meeting or other meetings in the future. If the weaknesses of meetings are identified and adjustments are made quickly, not only will more effective meetings be developed, but the credibility and respect for measurement and evaluation will be enhanced.

Teaching the Planning Team

The planning team and evaluators usually have inadequate skills in measurement and evaluation and will need to develop some expertise. Measurement and evaluation are not always a formal part of their job preparation. Consequently, the evaluators must learn the comprehensive measurement and evaluation, including the ROI Methodology and its systematic steps. In addition, the evaluator must know how to develop an evaluation plan, collect and analyze data from the evaluation, and interpret results from data analysis. The evaluators must have special training, such as the ROI certification described earlier. (Go to www.roiinstitute.net for more information.) For the remainder of the planning team, a one- to two-day workshop is needed to build adequate skills and knowledge for understanding the process, appreciating what the process can do, seeing the necessity for it, and participating in a successful implementation.

Initiating Evaluation Studies

The first tangible evidence of using a comprehensive measurement and evaluation process may be the initiation of the first meeting for which an impact ROI or study is planned. Several key issues are involved in identifying the meetings and keeping them on track.

Selecting the Initial ROI Study

Selecting a meeting for impact/ROI analysis is an important and critical issue. Only specific types of meetings should be selected for comprehensive, detailed analysis. Typical criteria for identifying meetings for analysis are those that involve large groups of participants; are expected to have a long life cycle; when completed, are linked to major operational problems/opportunities; are important to strategic objectives; are expensive; are time-consuming; have high visibility; and have management's interest in evaluation. Using these or similar criteria, the planning team must select appropriate meetings to consider for an impact/ROI evaluation. Ideally, sponsors should agree with or approve the criteria.

Developing the Planning Documents

Perhaps the two most useful documents are the data collection plan and the ROI analysis plan. The data collection plan shows what data will be collected, the methods used, the sources, the timing, and responsibilities. The ROI analysis plan shows how specific analyses will be conducted, including isolating the effects of the meeting and converting data to monetary values. Each evaluator should know how to develop these plans. These documents were discussed in detail in Chapter Two. Figure 12-3 shows the data collection plan for an ROI study for an all-employee meeting on sexual harassment prevention. Figure 12-4 shows the ROI analysis plan for the same program (Phillips, Myhill and McDonough, 2007).

Reporting Progress

As the meetings are developed and implementation is under way, status meetings should be conducted to report progress and discuss critical issues with appropriate team members. This keeps the planning team focused on the critical issues, generates the best ideas for addressing particular problems and barriers, and builds a knowledge base for better evaluations of other meetings. Sometimes, this group is facilitated by an external consultant, perhaps an expert in the ROI process. In other cases, the evaluator may facilitate the group.

In essence, these meetings serve three major purposes: reporting progress, learning, and planning.

Evaluation Purpose: Show the Impact of Compliance issues

Meeting: Preventing Sexual Harassment **Responsibility:** Patti Phillips **Date:** _____

Level	Broad Meeting Objective(s)	Measures	Data-Collection Method/ Instruments	Data Sources	Timing	Responsibilities
1	**REACTION/SATISFACTION & PERCEIVED VALUE** • Obtain a positive reaction to meeting and materials • Obtain input for suggstions for improving meeting	• Average rating of at least 4.0 on 5.0 scale on quality, usefulness and achievement of objectives.	• Reaction feedback questionnaire	• Participant	• End of Meetings	• Meeting Planner
	• Identify planned actions (Managers Only)	• 90% submit planned actions (check off)	• Action plan	• Manager (Participants)	• End of Meetings	
2	**LEARNING** • Knowledge of policy on sexual harassment • Knowledge of inappropriate and illegal behavior	• Ability to identify 7 of 10 policy issues • From a list of actions, and lack of actions, be able to identify 7 of 10 that constitute sexual harassment	• Pre- and Post-Test	• Participant	• Beginning of Meetings • End of Meetings	• Meeting Planner
3	**APPLICATION/IMPLEMENTATION** • Administer policy appropriately • Ensure that workplace is free of sexual harassment	• At least 4 on 5 scale on appropriate application of policy and removal of SH activity	• Employee Survey (25% sample)	• Sample of Participants	• 6 months after meeting	• HR Staff
	• Complete action plan	• Actions taken to eliminate sexual harassment (checklist) • Isolation estimates	• Action plan	• Managers	• 6 months after meetings	• Meeting Planner
4	**IMPACT** • Reduce internal complaints • Reduce voluntary employee turnover	• Decrease formal internal complaints related to sexual harassment • Voluntary turnover	• Performance Records Monitoring	• Human Resources complaint records • Human Resources exit Records • Managers	• Monthly for one Year Before and after meetings • 6 Months after program	• Meeting Planner and HR staff
5	**ROI** Target ROI → 20%	Comments: *Managers attend separate session, same content.*				

Figure 12-3. Data-Collection Plan.

Meeting: Preventing Sexual Harassment   **Responsibility**: Patti Phillips   Date: _____

Data Items (Usually Level 4)	Methods for Isolating the Effects of the Meeting	Methods of Converting Data to Monetary Values	Cost Categories	Intangible Benefits	Communication Targets for Final Report	Other Influences/ Issues During Application	Comments
1. Formal Internal Complaints of Sexual Harassment	1. Trendline Analysis 2. Participant Estimation (for back up)	1. Historical Costs with Estimation from EEO/AA Staff (Standard values and expert input)	• Needs Assessment • Meeting Development • Coordination/ Speaker Time	• Job Satisfaction • Absenteeism • Stress Reduction	• All Employees (Condensed Info.) • Senior Executives (Summary of Report with Detailed Backup)	• Several initiatives to reduce turnover implemented during this time period	Complaints of sexual harassment is a significant issue with management
2. Voluntary Employee Turnover	2. Forecasting Using Percent of Turnover Related to Sexual Harassment	2. External Turnover Cost Studies within Industry	• Program Materials • Food/ Refreshments • Facilities/ Travel • Participant Salaries and Benefits (For the meeting time) • Evaluation (time and materials)	• Image of FH • Recruiting	• All Supervisors and Managers (Brief Report) • All HR Staff (Full Report) • All Meeting and Events Staff		

Figure 12-4. ROI Analysis Plan.

Establishing Discussion Groups

Because a comprehensive measurement and evaluation may be considered difficult to understand and apply, establishing discussion groups to teach the process may be helpful. These groups could supplement formal workshops and other learning activities and are often very flexible in their format. Groups are usually facilitated by an external ROI consultant or by the evaluation leader. In each session, a new topic is presented and discussed thoroughly. Concerns and issues about the topic are discussed, including how they apply to the organization. The process can be adjusted for different topics as the needs of the group drive the issues. Ideally, participants in group discussions should have an opportunity to apply, explore, or research the topics between sessions. Assignments such as reviewing a case study or reading an article are also appropriate between sessions to further the development of knowledge and skills associated with the process.

Preparing the Clients and Management Team

Perhaps no group is more important to the success of measurement and evaluation than the management team that must allocate resources for meetings and events and support measurement and evaluation implementation. In addition, the management team often provides input and assistance for the measurement and evaluation. Specific actions for preparing and training the management team should be carefully planned and executed.

One effective approach for preparing executives and managers for more measurement and evaluation is to conduct a briefing on ROI. Varying in duration from one hour to half a day, this practical briefing provides critical information and changes perceptions needed to enhance support for ROI use. Because managers and executives have a keen interest in ROI, they will usually come. Managers leave the briefing with an improved perception of the use of ROI, the potential impact of meetings, and a clearer understanding of their roles for implementing the ROI Methodology. More importantly, they often develop a renewed commitment to react to and use the data collected by the ROI Methodology.

Removing Obstacles

As additional measurement and evaluation is implemented, there will be obstacles to progress. Many of the concerns discussed in this chapter may be valid, while others may be based on unrealistic fears or misunderstandings.

Dispelling Myths

As part of the implementation, attempts should be made to dispel the myths and remove or minimize the barriers or obstacles. Much of the controversy regarding measurement, evaluation, and ROI stems from misunderstandings about what the process can and cannot do and how it can or should be implemented in an organization. After years of experience with comprehensive measurement and evaluation and ROI and observing reactions during hundreds of evaluation studies and workshops, many misunderstanding regarding measurement and evaluation and ROI have been recognized. These misunderstandings were described in Chapter 1 and are listed below as myths about the ROI Methodology:

- Measurement and evaluation is too complex for most users.
- Measurement and evaluation is too expensive, consuming too many critical resources.
- If senior management does not require ROI, there is no need to pursue it.
- ROI is a passing fad.
- ROI is only one type of data.
- ROI is not future-oriented; it only reflects past performance.
- ROI is rarely used by organizations.
- Measurement and evaluation cannot be easily replicated.
- Measurement and evaluation is not credible. It is too subjective.
- Isolating the influence of other factors is not always possible.
- ROI is appropriate only for large organizations.
- No standards exist for measurement and evaluation.

For more information on these myths and how to overcome them, see www.roiinstitute.net.

Delivering Bad News

Perhaps one of the most difficult obstacles is addressing inadequate, insufficient, or disappointing news. This is an issue for most meeting planners and other stakeholders involved in meetings—how to address a bad-news situation. These specific steps and issues are important to consider when addressing bad news:

- Never fail to recognize the power to learn and improve with a negative study.
- Look for red flags along the way.
- Lower outcome expectations with key stakeholders along the way.
- Look for data everywhere.
- Never alter the standards.
- Remain objective throughout the process.
- Prepare the team for the bad news.
- Consider different scenarios.
- Find out what went wrong.
- Adjust the story line to "Now we have data that show how to make this meeting more successful." In an odd sort of way, this becomes a positive spin on less-than-positive data.
- Drive improvement.

The time to think about bad news is early in the process, never losing sight of the value of bad news. In essence, bad news means that things can change and need to change and that things can get better. The team and others have to be convinced that good news can be found in a bad-news situation.

MONITORING PROGRESS

A final part of the implementation of a measurement and evaluation process is monitoring the overall progress made and communicating that progress. Although it is an often-overlooked part of the process, an effective implementation plan can help keep the measurement and evaluation on target and let others know what the process is accomplishing for the meetings and events staff and for the client.

The initial schedule for implementation provides a variety of key events or milestones. Routine progress reports should be developed to communicate the status and progress of these events or milestones. Reports are usually developed at six-month intervals. Two target audiences—the meeting planners and senior managers—are critical for progress reporting. All planning team members should be kept informed of the progress, and senior managers need to know the extent to which measurement and evaluation is being implemented and how it is working within the organization.

FINAL THOUGHTS

Even the best model or process will die if it is not used and sustained. This chapter explored the implementation of a measurement and evaluation process and the ways to sustain its use. If not approached in a systematic, logical, and planned way, measurement and evaluation will not become an integral part of the meetings cycle and, therefore, accountability will suffer. This chapter presented the different elements that must be considered and issues that must be addressed to ensure that measurement and evaluation implementation is smooth and uneventful. This is the most effective way to overcome resistance to additional measurement and evaluation. The result provides a complete integration of measurement and evaluation as a mainstream activity.

REFERENCE

Phillips, J.J., Myhill, M. and McDonough, J.B. *Proving the Value of Meetings and Events*. ROI Institute and MPI, Birmingham, AL, 2007.

How Results-Based Are Your Meetings and Events? Survey for Executives, Clients, and Managers

OVERVIEW

The amount of management support needed for meetings and events is very critical to their success. In most situations, support senior executives and managers are willing to provide is directly linked to their perception of the effectiveness of meetings and events. If the meetings and events are achieving results and helping the organization reach its goals, managers are often willing to support them, provide resources to make them successful, reinforce specific objectives, and become more actively involved in the process.

The following instrument provides an assessment of the extent to which senior executives and managers perceive that meetings and events are achieving results. It provides the organization with an assessment of the effectiveness of these meetings and events as perceived by the senior executives and managers. Although it is ideal for the corporate meeting context, most of the issues apply to all types of events, conferences, and exhibitions.

USE

The instrument can be used in the following ways:

- It can serve as a benchmark for specific efforts and activities aimed at enhancing the level of support.
- In efforts to increase the effectiveness of meetings and events, this instrument will serve as a periodic assessment of the progress made.
- It can serve as a useful discussion tool in workshops for senior executives and managers where the goal is to enhance their support for meetings and events.

- It is a helpful tool to compare one group of senior executives or managers in a division, region, or subsidiary company with others to determine where specific attention may be needed.

TARGET AUDIENCE

The target audience for the instrument is senior executives and middle and upper managers who request and provide support for meetings and events. These are the key individuals who can influence the success of those efforts.

ADMINISTRATION

The instrument should be administered without discussion. Participants should be instructed to provide very candid responses. The results should be quickly tabulated by the respondents and discussed and interpreted in a group discussion.

MEETING AND EVENTS ASSESSMENT: A SURVEY FOR EXECUTIVES, CLIENTS, AND MANAGERS

Instructions. For each of the following statements, please circle the response that best matches the meetings and events function at your organization. If none of the answers describe the situation, select the one that best fits. Please be candid with your responses.

1. The direction of the meeting and events function at your organization:
   (a) Shifts with requests, problems, and changes as they occur.
   (b) Is determined by marketing, sales, corporate communications, etc. and adjusted as needed.
   (c) Is based on a mission and a strategic plan for the function.
2. The primary mode of operation of the meetings and events function is:
   (a) To respond to requests by managers and other employees to deliver meetings and events.
   (b) To help management react to crisis situations and reach solutions through meetings and events.
   (c) To implement meetings and events in collaboration with management to prevent problems and crisis situations.
3. The goals of the meetings and events function are:
   (a) Set by the meetings staff based on perceived demand for meetings.
   (b) Developed consistent with marketing, sales, corporate communications, etc. plans and goals.
   (c) Developed to integrate with operating goals and strategic plans of the organization.

4. Most new meetings and events are initiated:
   (a) When a meeting or event appears to be successful in another organization.
   (b) By request of top management.
   (c) After a needs analysis has indicated that the meeting or event is needed.
5. To define meeting and event plans:
   (a) The senior executive, manager, or department sets the meeting needs and objectives and then the meetings department facilitates and plans the logistics only.
   (b) Management and senior executives are asked about their meeting needs and objectives, and then the meetings department helps them with the logistics and content.
   (c) Meeting needs are systematically derived from a thorough analysis of performance problems and/or business needs.
6. The responsibility for results from meetings and events:
   (a) Rests primarily with the senior executive, manager, and/or department that requests and pays for the meeting.
   (b) Is the joint responsibility of the meetings staff and the senior executive, manager, and/or department that requests and pays for the meeting.
   (c) Is a shared responsibility of the meetings staff, participants, and senior executive/manager/department all working together to ensure success.
7. Systematic, objective evaluation, designed to ensure that meeting attendees are performing appropriately on the job:
   (a) Is never accomplished. The only evaluations are during the meeting, and they focus on how much the participants enjoyed the meeting.
   (b) Is occasionally accomplished. Participants are asked if the meeting content was used in the workplace.
   (c) Is frequently and systematically pursued. Sometimes, performance is evaluated before the meeting and after the meeting.
8. New meetings and events are developed:
   (a) Internally, using a staff of meeting professionals, subject matter experts, and persons requesting the meeting.
   (b) By suppliers and vendors (such as outside independent planners, meeting planning companies, or event communication firms).
   (c) In the most economical and practical way to meet deadlines and cost objectives, using internal staff and vendors.
9. Costs for meetings and events are accumulated:
   (a) On a total aggregate basis only.
   (b) On a meeting-by-meeting basis.
   (c) By specific process components such as development and delivery, in addition to a specific meeting.
10. Management involvement in the meeting design and planning process is:
   (a) Very low with only occasional input.
   (b) Moderate, usually by request, or on an as needed basis.
   (c) Deliberately planned for all major meetings and events, to ensure a partnership arrangement.

11. To ensure that information, skills, knowledge, and messages are transferred into workplace performance, we:
    (a) Encourage only participants to apply what they have learned.
    (b) Ask managers to support and reinforce the meeting content.
    (c) Require participants to apply the content and report results for a few, select meetings.
12. The meetings and events staff's interaction with senior executives and management is:
    (a) Rare, we almost never discuss issues of content or logistics with them.
    (b) Occasional, during activities such as needs analysis or meeting coordination.
    (c) Regular, to build relationships, as well as to develop and deliver meetings.
13. The Meeting and Event staff's role in major change efforts is:
    (a) To logistically plan meetings to support the project, as required.
    (b) To provide logistical and content support for the meetings and events within the change effort.
    (c) To recommend, plan and coordinate change efforts through meetings and events.
14. Most managers view the meetings and events function as:
    (a) A questionable function that wastes too much time.
    (b) A necessary function that probably cannot be eliminated.
    (c) An important resource that can be used to improve people and organizations.
15. Meetings and events are:
    (a) Activity-oriented (All managers attend the annual management retreat).
    (b) Individual results-based (The participant will increase his or her sales in the coming year by at least 20%).
    (c) Organizational results-based (Compliance penalties will decrease by 25%).
16. The impact of meetings and events is measured primarily by:
    (a) Subjective opinions.
    (b) Observations by management and reactions from participants.
    (c) Monetary value through improved productivity, cost savings, time savings, or better quality—at least for a few meetings.
17. The meetings and events effort consists of:
    (a) Usually one-time meetings and events.
    (b) A full array of meetings and events to meet participant, senior executive, and management needs.
    (c) A variety of meetings and events implemented to bring about change within the organization.
18. New meetings and events, without some formal method of evaluation, are implemented at my organization:
    (a) Regularly
    (b) Seldom
    (c) Never

19. The results of meetings and events are communicated:
    (a) When requested, to those who have a need to know.
    (b) Occasionally, to the client and management only.
    (c) Routinely, to a variety of selected target audiences.
20. Management's involvement in meeting evaluation:
    (a) Is minor, with no specific responsibilities and few requests.
    (b) Consists of informal responsibilities for evaluation.
    (c) Very specific. Most managers have some responsibilities to help evaluate meetings.
21. During a business decline at my organization, the meetings and events function will:
    (a) Be the first to have its staff reduced.
    (b) Be retained at the same staffing level.
    (c) Go untouched in staff reductions and possibly increase the budget.
22. Budgeting for meetings and events is based on:
    (a) Last year's budget.
    (b) Whatever the meetings department can "sell."
    (c) A zero-based system, where each major event is justified.
23. The principal group(s) that must justify meetings and events is:
    (a) The meetings and events department.
    (b) The marketing, sales, or administrative function.
    (c) Management, participants, and clients.
24. Over the last two years, the meetings and events budget as a percent of operating expenses has:
    (a) Decreased
    (b) Remained stable
    (c) Increased
25. Senior executives' involvement in the implementation of meetings and events:
    (a) Is limited to placing their names on meeting invitations/marketing info, extending congratulations, etc.
    (b) Includes monitoring progress, opening/closing speeches, presentation on the outlook of the organization, etc.
    (c) Includes meeting participation to see what's covered, conducting major segments of the meeting, requiring key executives to be involved, etc.
26. In our organization, the most appropriate terms to describe the outcomes of meetings and events are:
    (a) Entertainment and enjoyment.
    (b) Learning and networking.
    (c) Change management and business improvement.
27. When a participant attends our most important meeting or event, upon return, he or she is:
    (a) Required to do nothing.
    (b) Encouraged to "Let us know how it turned out."
    (c) Required to provide data about application and impact—at least for a sample of participants.

INTERPRETING THE MEETINGS AND EVENTS ASSESSMENT

Score the assessment instrument as follows. Allow:

1 point for each (a) response
3 points for each (b) response
5 points for each (c) response

The total will be between 27 and 135 points.

The interpretation of the scoring is provided below.

Score Range	*Analysis of Score*
109–135	*Outstanding Environment* for achieving results with meetings and events. Great management support. A truly successful example of results-based meetings and events.
82–108	*Above Average* in achieving results with meetings and events. Good management support. A solid and methodical approach to results-based meetings and events.
55–81	*Needs Improvement* to achieving desired results with meetings and events. Management support is ineffective. Meetings and events do not usually focus on results.
27–54	*Serious Problems* with the success and status of meetings and events. Management support is non-existent. Meetings and events are not producing results.

Index

Special Offer from The ROI Institute

Case studies are available to download at www.roiinstiute.net under the meetings and events tab. The ROI Process Model, an indispensable tool for implementing and presenting ROI in your organization, is available to readers at no charge. This 11″× 25″ multicolor foldout shows the ROI Methodology flow model and the key issues surrounding the implementation of the ROI Methodology. This easy to understand overview of the ROI process has proven invaluable to countless professionals when implementing the ROI Methodology. Please return this page or email your information to the address below to receive your free foldout (a $6.00 value). Please check your areas of interest in ROI.

Please send me the ROI Process Model described in the book. I am interested in learning more about the following ROI materials and services:

☐ Workshops and briefings on ROI   ☐ Books and support materials on ROI

☐ Certification in the ROI Methodology   ☐ ROI software

☐ ROI consulting services   ☐ ROI Network information

☐ ROI benchmarking   ☐ ROI research

Name _____

Title _____

Organization _____

Address _____

_____

Phone _____

E-MailAddress _____

Functional area of interest:

☐ Corporate Meeting Professional   ☐ Government Meeting Professional   ☐ Meeting Management Professional

☐ Association/Non-Profit Meeting Professional   ☐ Supplier Meeting Professional   ☐ Other (Please specify)

Return this form to: The ROI Institute
P.O. Box 380637
Birmingham, AL 35238-0637
Or e-mail information to info@roiinstitute.net
Please allow four to six weeks for delivery.